History of the Present is published twice yearly by
Duke University Press, 905 W. Main St., Suite 18B, Durham, NC, 27701.

ISSN: 2159-9785

Direct correspondence to *History of the Present*, c/o Professor Joan Scott, School of Social Science Institute for Advanced Study, 1 Einstein Dr., Princeton, NJ 08540.

Direct all subscription orders to Duke University Press, Journals Customer Relations, 905 W. Main St., Suite 18B, Durham, NC 27701.

Annual subscription rates: print-plus-electronic institutions, $212; print-only institutions, $190; e-only institutions, $180; individuals, $40 (e-only, $30); students, $25. For information on subscriptions to the e-Duke Journals Scholarly Collections, contact libraryrelations@dukepress .edu. Print subscriptions: add $8 postage and applicable HST (including 5% GST) for Canada; add $10 postage outside the US and Canada. Back volumes (institutions): $190. Single issues: institutions, $95; individuals, $15. For more information, contact Duke University Press Journals at 888-651-0122 (toll-free in the US and Canada) or 919-688-5134; subscriptions@dukeupress.edu.

Direct inquiries about advertising to Journals Advertising Manager, journals_advertising@ dukeupress.edu.

For a list of sources in which *History of the Present* is indexed and abstracted, see dukeupress.edu /history-of-the-present.

Visit the editorial office website at historyofthepresent.org and Duke University Press at dukeupress.edu.

The editors invite submissions that approach history as a critical endeavor. We are particularly interested in essays that press the boundaries of history's disciplinary norms. In that spirit, we also welcome work from scholars thinking through the past in fields outside of history.

We want to publish articles that:

- examine the historical construction of categories of knowledge;

- analyze how relationships of power are established and maintained, and how history has served to legitimize or challenge them;

- are explicitly theorized without being restricted to the discipline's conventional categorizations of method and subject (i.e., social, cultural, intellectual, legal, or political theory).

Manuscripts should be about 9,000 words, including notes, and are accepted on a rolling basis. Further submission guidelines are available at historyofthepresent.org.

HISTORY *of*
the Present

A JOURNAL OF CRITICAL HISTORY

Psychoanalysis and History

BRIAN CONNOLLY AND JOAN WALLACH SCOTT, SPECIAL ISSUE EDITORS

1   **Introduction: Psychoanalysis and History**
      Brian Connolly

4   **Ante-Oedipus: Gender and Racial Capitalism
      in Plantation Modernity**
      Elizabeth Maddock Dillon

34   **The History of the Subject and the Subject of History**
      David L. Eng

60   **Just In Time: Managing Fear and Anxiety
      at the End of the World**
      Michelle Stephens

80   **In the Interest of History**
      Max Cavitch

103   **Paranoid Publics**
      Zahid R. Chaudhary

      INTERVENTION

127   **Left Freudians: The Psychoanalytic Politics
      of Disobedience**
      Alex Colston

143   **Vicissitudes and Their Inscriptions**
      Carolyn Shapiro

Volume 12 ▪ Number 1 ▪ April 2022

Brian Connolly

Introduction
Psychoanalysis and History

The relationship between psychoanalysis and history has long been a vexed
one. Indeed, in Freud's writings, history occupies an ambivalent place—the
analytic situation offered a radical revision of personal history, which had a
profound effect on larger, collective history.[1] Simultaneously, in his drawing
on archaeology and anthropology, Freud offered a civilizational history that
was deeply implicated in racial, national, and colonial formations that have
long structured dominant configurations of modernity. By the middle of the
twentieth century, historians and historically minded intellectuals took up
psychoanalysis as a new way of thinking historically. While radical outliers
such as Herbert Marcuse and Norman O. Brown offered liberationist historical projects grounded in revisionist readings of Freud (in conjunction with
Marx), the more common trajectory was evident in psychohistory, which
drew primarily on ego psychology. By the 1980s, psychohistory was on the
decline. While the work of Michel de Certeau might show up in various
courses and texts on historiography, Freud and the larger psychoanalytic
project seemed doomed. And yet, in recent years, one can discern a revival
of sorts at the conjuncture of psychoanalysis and history, at times more
indebted to the feminist psychoanalytic criticism that emerged out of an
engagement with the work of Jacques Lacan beginning in the 1970s. In
other works, the engagement between psychoanalysis "and the rest of the
world," to borrow Derrida's formulation, has been the impetus for new
and vital critical histories (El Shakry and Pursley; Khanna). For all the
fraught engagements, a specific turn toward psychoanalysis, which would
privilege the unhistoricizable conditions of the Real, the disruptive trajectories of desire, the (anti-)foundational foundation of sexual difference, and

HISTORY of the PRESENT ▪ A Journal of Critical History ▪ 12:1 ▪ April 2022
DOI 10.1215/21599785-9721050 © 2022 Duke University Press

the phantasmatic condition of historical knowledge and narrative seems more relevant, vital even, than ever.

Nonetheless, the dominant epistemological conditions of history, which, since the nineteenth century, have tended toward empiricism and positivism, work to exclude psychoanalysis. On the one hand, this stems from a misunderstanding of the psychoanalytic project, reducing it to the psychological and then claiming that there is no evidence to document the complex inner workings of the psyche. Yet this misunderstands the fact that psychoanalysis captures the interplay of inner and outer, interiority and sociality, so that the psyche is something like a hinge between the two. As Norman O. Brown put it in 1959, "the psychoanalytical approach to history is pressed upon the historian by one question: Why does man, alone of all animals, have a history? . . . the historical process is sustained by man's desire to become other than what he is. And man's desire to become something different is essentially an unconscious desire. . . . The riddle of history is not in Reason but in Desire; not in labor, but in love" (15–16).

On the other hand, we might turn to Theodor Adorno's oft-repeated aphorism from *Minima Moralia*: "In psychoanalysis nothing is true except the exaggerations" (54). While history as a discipline has excavated stories both mundane and spectacular, methodologically it may best be described as a discipline averse to exaggeration. This is true even of some of the most searching twentieth-century critics of conventional historical method. Michel Foucault described genealogy as essentially anathema to exaggeration. "Genealogy is gray, meticulous, and patiently documentary," Foucault wrote, "it operates on a field of entangled and confused parchments, on documents that have been scratched over and recopied many times" (139). If there is something in the second sentence here that resonates with psychoanalysis, there is nonetheless a more general sense that exaggeration is the province neither of history nor genealogy. While it would be wrong simply to deem Adorno's aphorism true—psychoanalysis is more than exaggeration and it has its own rigorous, documentary aspects—it does, nonetheless, capture that vexed meeting between psychoanalysis and history—psychoanalytically informed history has always struck many observers as exaggerated, without basis in the documentary record, wild speculation obscuring the real stuff of history.

The articles in this issue all rethink the complicated relationship between psychoanalysis and history and in doing so push well beyond the strictures of psychohistory and the trajectories laid out by the feminist critique of Lacan. Indeed, the authors collectively draw on a wide range of psychoanalytic thought in efforts to interrogate received historical narratives and, simultaneously, to interrogate psychoanalytic categories through a close attention to the tension between analysis and historical evidence. The issue as a whole demonstrates the uses of psychoanalysis for thinking about concrete historical materials and the importance of history for thinking psychoanalytically, whether it is the contrasting ways in which historians have represented the Holocaust and the bombings of Hiroshima and Nagasaki or the puzzling emergence of QAnon and new forms of paranoia as a political movement. The concern generated about the Anthropocene by climate historians turns out to contain traces of colonialist thinking embedded in it and there are previously unexplored links to be made between Freud and the US plantation economy. The political trajectories of psychoanalysis, particularly that of the Left Freudians of the mid-twentieth century, are revisited to offer fresh insights on the politics of history and psychoanalysis. And the vicissitudes of the instincts, about which Freud famously wrote, are here addressed for their intersection with history and inscription to generate more attentive, ambivalent critical readings. These original and incisive essays, though they are on disparate topics and historical periods, testify to the importance of taking the unconscious dimensions of our thinking into account when we try to understand the workings of politics and the ways in which we represent our pasts. ∎

Brian Connolly is an associate professor of history at the University of South Florida. He is the author of *Domestic Intimacies: Incest and the Liberal Subject in Nineteenth-Century America* (2014).

NOTE

1   The first two paragraphs appear, in a slightly different form, in Connolly 2021.

WORKS CITED

Adorno, Theodor. *Minima Moralia: Reflections from Damaged Life,* translated by E. F. N. Jephcott. New York: Verso, 2020.

Brown, Norman O. *Life against Death: The Psychoanalytical Meaning of History.* Middletown, CT: Wesleyan University Press, 1959.

Connolly, Brian. "Psychoanalysis." In *Routledge Companion to Historical Theory,* edited by Chiel van den Akker, 179–96. London: Routledge, 2021.

El Shakry, Omnia, and Sara Pursley, eds. "Psychoanalysis and the Middle East: Discourses and Encounters." Special issue, *Psychoanalysis and History* 20, no. 3 (2018).

Foucault, Michel. "Nietzsche, Genealogy, History." In *Language, Counter-Memory, Practice: Selected Essays and Interviews,* edited by Donald F. Bouchard, 139–64. Ithaca, NY: Cornell University Press, 1977.

Khanna, Ranjana. *Dark Continents: Psychoanalysis and Colonialism.* Durham, NC: Duke University Press, 2005.

Elizabeth Maddock Dillon

Ante-Oedipus
Gender and Racial Capitalism in Plantation Modernity

ABSTRACT This article argues that Freud's account of binary sexual difference, articulated in the Oedipus complex, is conditioned by a history of racial capitalism. Turning to the foundational work of Hortense Spillers on gender and Atlantic race slavery, this article proposes that dominant models of binary gender are ineluctably racialized, created by the property regimes and systemic sexual violence of colonial modernity that emerged in the Atlantic World of the eighteenth century—a space defined by the structures of labor, race, sexuality, and capital accumulation that developed in and around the first factories of the modern world, namely, the sugar plantations of the colonial Caribbean. The article links Freud's own economic and intellectual history to the production of capital and the theft of land and labor in the Caribbean by way of the central European trade in textiles and global cotton production. Examining a series of family portraits, the article locates the eclipsed yet central force of Black women's productive and socially reproductive work extracted for the creation of white, heteropatriarchal reproduction and property accumulation.

KEYWORDS racial capitalism, Oedipus complex, racialization, rape, Atlantic World

Perhaps we could argue that the "race" matrix was the fundamental interdiction within the enabling discourse of founding psychoanalytical theory and practice itself.

—Hortense Spillers, "'All the Things You Could Be by Now if Sigmund Freud's Wife Was Your Mother': Race and Psychoanalysis"

Ante-Oedipus

In the work of Sigmund Freud, binary sexual difference derives from the Oedipal complex. The fundamental concept of human difference—sex—is explicable through the myth of Oedipus, the man who (unwittingly) had sex with his mother and killed his father and thus broke the law and inaugurated it at once. Hortense Spillers proposes that in place of this myth, we might

HISTORY of the PRESENT ▪ A Journal of Critical History ▪ 12:1 ▪ April 2022
DOI 10.1215/21599785-9547212 © 2022 Duke University Press

turn to a historical event as the locus of the foundational psychic and cultural structuring difference of Western modernity, namely, the Atlantic slave trade. Spillers thus replaces the mythic event of Oedipal incest with the historical event of kinship annihilation: in doing so, she also names race, rather than sex, as the foundational difference that structures modern identity. For Spillers, race serves as the *ground* of the theory of psychoanalysis, invisibly underwriting Freud's theory of sexuality; race is an a priori that has been rendered invisible by its status as the vantage point from which psychoanalysis is articulated ("All the Things" 386).

Turning to the slave trade rather than the Oedipus myth to orient an account of contemporary sexual and psychic identity has two distinct results for Spillers: first, the resolution brought by the Oedipal myth (the internalization of the incest taboo that results in sexual identity as male or female) is "essentially cancelled by the Atlantic trade" for diasporic Blacks and their kin given that race slavery violently destroyed genealogical connection and kinship forms among the enslaved. Such a consequence might, at first glance, seem to point toward a narrative of failed Black subjectivity—naming an incapacity to resolve the Oedipal drama into normative, binary sexualized identity. But that would be a misreading of Spillers's argument: rather, Spillers suggests (and this is the second distinct result of reading historically rather than mythically) the unresolved "crisis" of the slave trade and its destruction of kinship reveals paternity itself as a "function" or a structure rather than a biological or genetic relation. For Africans in the Americas, this narrative is one of profound disruption but also one that orients a radically new relation and set of possibilities with respect to both language and law. "We might be able to see," writes Spillers, "in an apposite psychoanalytic protocol for the subjects of 'race,' broken away from the point of origin, which rupture has left a hole that speech can only point to and circle around, an entirely new repertoire of inquiry into human relations" ("All the Things" 426).

Building on Spillers's insights, I aim to locate gender—in its binary, Freudian-formulated incarnation—as an aspect of racial capitalism: if the ground on which Freud's account of sexuality is erected is historically conditioned by the Atlantic slave trade, then it is *not only* the case that Freud's account of gender and sexuality is inadequate to account for the lives and cultures of New World Africans but *also* the case—and this is the thrust of my argument in this article—that the white, binary concept of heteronormative gender and sexuality at the heart of Freudian theory is made possible (indeed, necessitated) by race slavery, settler colonialism, and racial capitalism. In short, the theory of sex and gender articulated by Freud is itself ineluctably racialized. Binary hetero-reproductive gender is always-already white: race *creates* gender as Freudianism knows it. More broadly, as I argue below, the desire for whiteness as property is intrinsic to the epochal shift to a new geography and economy of racial capitalism and conditions the emergence of (white) binary gender as the episteme of which Freud is the eminent theorist. In this sense, Freud is more symptom than cause of dominant accounts of a binary sex-gender system, and for this reason as well, it is worth attending to his work closely.[1] This is a historical story—one that begins before Freud, one that precedes the centering of the Oedipal myth as the origin of sexual difference. It is a story that begins in the Caribbean, the navel of plantation modernity and racial capitalism.[2]

Before Freud: Two Scenes

In the place of a mythical Oedipal scene, then, I begin with a history that juxtaposes two scenes of sexual violence, racialization, language, law, and geography. *Scene One*: On August 22, 1768, Sally, a fifteen-year-old Congo girl enslaved in Jamaica on an estate owned by Thomas Thistlewood was sent to Savannah la Mar to purchase bread and did not return that day.[3] Captured the next evening and returned to Thistlewood's estate, Vineyard, Sally was placed by Thistlewood in "bilboes"—U-shaped iron shackles that were forged to be placed on the ankles, with holes through which an iron bar passed, engineered to inflict both pain and shame on their wearer— overnight. In the morning, Thistlewood placed an iron collar and chain around her neck, and with a metal brand heated in the fire, seared his initials—"TT" contained within an upside-down triangle—into her right cheek. In his diaries, Thistlewood includes an additional comment about Sally on this day: "Note her private parts is tore in a terrible manner, which was discovered this morning by her having bled a great deal, while she was lay in yl: bilboes last night. being threatened a good deal she at last confest that a sailor had laid with her while away. Mr Say's Vine undertook to doctor her" (Hall 150). Elsewhere in his diary, Thistlewood reports raping Sally a total of thirty-seven times. After this event, he reports raping her again in October: "Thursday, 20th October: p.m. *Cum* Sally, *mea, Sup. Terr* at foot of cotton tree by New Ground side, West north west from the house (*sed non bene*)" (Hall 150). Sally subsequently ran away from Thistlewood's Vineyard dozens of times over the next sixteen years; Thistlewood sold her and another slave for forty pounds in 1784.

I use the term "rape" here to name the violence of the sexual acts that Thistlewood records in his diaries, with the reservation that the word speaks inadequately to the systemic nature of the sexual terrorism he inflicts and records. In the passage cited above, Thistlewood follows a standard Latin-encoded notation method he created in his diary for recording the sex acts he engaged in with enslaved women. He typically notes the name of the enslaved woman (in the case above, Sally), the name of her owner (*"mea"*—himself), the location of the sex act (*"Sup. Terr"*—on the ground), and on many occasions includes the additional notation found here—*"sed non bene"*—which translates roughly as "but not well," indicating that the sex was "not good" for him. Every sexual interaction between Thistlewood and Sally recorded in the *Diaries* is annotated with *"sed non bene."* Jenny Sharpe suggests that this is an indication of noncompliance on Sally's part and force on Thistlewood's, an assessment I would agree with (66). Yet the term "rape," while it seems to be the most adequate one available to characterize Thistlewood's treatment of Sally, remains insufficient insofar as it appeals to a logic of consent and its refusal—notions embedded in ideas of liberal subjectivity and agency—that were categorically unavailable to enslaved women. As Marisa Fuentes succinctly writes, "[Enslaved and free(d) women of color's] core experiences, shaped by sexual violence and impossible choices, are not fully elucidated by progressive notions of agency. . . . Agency cannot be examined outside the constraints of slavery's systematic mechanisms of domination" (69).

Recently, feminist scholars have taken to task historians of Thistlewood's sexual terrorism who have not used the word "rape" but instead have chosen terms such as "sexual athleticism," "voracious libido," and "sexual conquests," to describe the sex acts he engaged in with enslaved women—terms that seem aimed at "imaging [Thistlewood] as some sort of hyper-'heterosexual' person" rather than acknowledging the brutality of his acts (Vermeulen 19, 22).[4] The difficulty of finding the right language to tell this story, as this scholarship points out, is itself part of the story: that is, the violence of serial rape and systemic sexual terrorism is perpetuated in the violence of linguistic erasure and foreclosure of meaning with respect to sex and sexuality for enslaved women in the colony. The erasure is particularly acute with respect to articulating this scene from the perspective of Sally rather than Thistlewood. It is not just that her perspective is effaced in his record-keeping, but rather that there is no structural possibility of its enunciation within the language and law that brings Thistlewood's text into being. It seems impossible, for instance, that Sally would state that she had "laid" with a sailor who had so violently attacked her that she remained bleeding and in need of medical attention two days later. Our familiar (albeit fuzzy) taxonomies of forced sex, coerced sex, sex for pay, and consensual sex cease to have meaning in a world where consent has no legal or linguistic possibility.

The inadequacy of the archive to tell the stories of enslaved women, then, is not just a question of whose voices have been discovered, preserved, translated, and circulated but also a question of language itself—one that wraps us today within forms of complicity that are difficult to expose or disavow. As Jennifer Morgan reflects, "Archival lacunae lead to other interpretive errors: in the absence of written records, enslaved women's experiences get reduced to the sensate, all rape and blood and birth trauma and breasts. What becomes unthinkable is the possibility of critical, intelligent, strategic assessments of, and responses to, the violent structures of value and commerce in which they were embedded" ("Partus sequitur ventrem" 17). In Thistlewood's diaries, we find the slaveowner's Latinate tally of sexual conquest: against that language, we have only the critical, strategic record of Sally's feet, perpetually escaping from Thistlewood's property and perpetually returned to his calculating grasp. And as scholars we have a language to describe this history that implicitly attempts to parse Sally's degree of consent to being, in Saidiya Hartman's translation of Thistlewood's Latin, "fucked . . . on the ground" ("Venus in Two Acts" 1).

Scene Two: In London, England, on April 11, 1796, Sir Philip Francis, Esquire, introduced a bill for debate in Parliament "respecting the Regulation of Slaves in the West Indies." The aim of this bill was to increase reproduction rates among enslaved women in the West Indies. To do so, Francis argued, would require the radical changes proposed in his bill: enslaved individuals must be allowed to own property, they must be allowed to marry, they must only be subject to corporal punishment on the ruling of a jury of other enslaved individuals, and white men who rape enslaved women must be punished by death. In Parliament that day, Francis stated: "By the laws of some of the Grecian states, if a master violated the wife of his slave, the husband and the wife were instantly free. *Leges pudicitiae sunt juris naturalis.* Direct force or violent compulsion of any kind, employed against a Negress, should be punished with death. Corruption of the wife should make the husband free. It is shocking to human nature to think that personal protection, even to this amount, would constitute in itself a state of improvement" (46). Francis's proposed bill did not pass; significantly, the extended debate over the bill in Parliament focused primarily on the issue of whether requiring plantation owners to give property to enslaved people constituted a "tax" on English colonials and thus amounted to a violation of their right to self-government. Not a single person mentioned, even in passing, the question of white men's sexual violence wielded against enslaved women. And indeed, even historians have remained virtually mute on this subject; it is as if punishing white men for the rape of Black women is unspeakable.

The juxtaposition of Thistlewood's actions in Jamaica and Francis's language in Parliament is jarring; by placing them together, I ask us to see their intimate relation to each other despite the geographical distance separating them. Insisting that these two scenes are of a piece and should be viewed together enables us to map not only a profoundly important and formative metropolitan/colonial geography of violence, sex, and race but also one of speech, language, and knowledge-making. With respect to the writings cited in the two scenes above—the words of Thistlewood in his diary and those of Francis in the records of Parliament—we might note that both men lapse from English into Latin at key moments. Francis's Latin phrase translates, roughly, as "Laws of purity are natural laws." The phrase he uses is not a commonplace but is rather one of his own construction that seems rhetorically aimed, first, at bolstering the legal and ethical force of his argument that white men should not be allowed to rape Black women with impunity and, second, at deploying a degree of *legerdemain* with respect to naming the "violation" at issue—namely, rape. Francis's use of the word "pudicitiae"/purity obliquely names the sexually violable status of a woman/wife, but it is worth noting that this is a status to which enslaved women historically did not have legal, cultural, or practical access. Thistlewood, in the passage cited above, as we have seen, uses, "*sed non bene*" as a Latin circumlocution for rape. The Latin evasions that Thistlewood and Francis both employ to name (while not naming) rape are significant because they indicate more than just a dynamic of power enunciated in terms of education, literacy, and erasure; rather, they indicate the presence of catachresis—the naming of a thing which cannot be said because it does not exist within English logics/language.

The turn to Latin in lieu of English to speak of racialized sexual terror embedded at the roots of colonialism is not a coincidence but is, rather, a strategic move that is threaded through European discourses of racial domination and the erasure of the violent history of colonialism in the Americas. Jennifer Morgan, for instance, demonstrates that the crucial Latin phrase "*Partus sequitur ventrem*" ("offspring follows belly")—a term that mandated maternal descent for enslaved persons and fundamentally linked heritability of property and identity to whiteness—was a nineteenth-century emendation to the seventeenth-century Virginia law that codified this practice. As Morgan explains, "The Latin served to connect English slave law to Roman antecedents and thereby to a legal argument, rooted in eighteenth-century English abolitionist efforts, that it was only through Roman law that English slaveowners claimed the right to children born into slavery 'like cattle.' The phrase thus becomes a disavowal for English theorists intent on distancing the nation from the precedent of slaveownership" (4). The use of Latin in this decisive law—a law that codified a practice at the heart of the new racialized and gendered property regime that racial capitalism in the Atlantic world rested on—points to a fabricated historicity that seeks to impart the authority of classical law to the creation of new legal systems regarding Atlantic race slavery. Although the elision from English to Latin may seem slight, it is a rhetorical turn that occurs with revealing frequency in core texts of European history, law, and philosophy. It is also the rhetorical move that Freud uses to ground his theory of sexuality in the classical myth of Oedipal sexual violence rather than in the material history of racialized colonial violence. The strategic and familiar rhetorical turn to the timeless authority of classical language and law serves Freud, Thistlewood, Francis, and Virginia lawmakers in dissembling the historical role of racialized violence in creating the systems of meaning and authority they propound.

The failure of language marked with Latin grammar in the scenes described above is not, then, merely a lapse. Rather, it is itself a generative structure of meaning-making: indeed, as Spillers tells us, it is an American grammar. In an essay that we have yet to fully catch up with—the magisterial "Mama's Baby, Papa's Maybe,"—Spillers analyzes a dominant cultural narrative in which "the 'Negro Family' has no Father to speak of—his Name, his Law, his Symbolic function mark the impressive missing agencies in the essential life of the black community" (204).[5] This non-Oedipalized drama, Spillers shows us, is not a "pathology" of the Black family but is rather a grammar of American meaning—a dominant structure that is historical, geographical, and economic in its nature. The grammar of gender/ungendering originates in the middle passage, in the systemic horror of the Atlantic slave trade and plantation slavery in the Americas—all of which serve as a "vestibular" space, in Spillers's words, with respect to white European culture: a space that must be passed through, as a vestibule, to emerge into a whitened, hetero-patriarchal European culture. Importantly, the basis of non-Oedipality in the colony lies not in the fact that the Oedipal law did not apply to enslaved Africans (because both father- and mother-right were proscribed by slave codes) but in the fact that white men had unfettered sexual access to Black bodies without concern for the law—including laws against rape, incest, and murder. Furthermore, the exercise of unfettered sexual access on the part of white colonial men was not, as is too often suggested, an aberration but served as a structural feature of racial capital and plantation modernity (see, for example, Davis 175; Hine 912).

The failure of language around rape, race, and gender will not, then, be corrected by adding more words, uncovering more stories—because American grammar's meaning-making capacity is erected on the violence done to

Sally and its structural lack of place in our language. Christina Sharpe names this an "anagrammatical" Blackness: she states, "the birth canal of Black women is a space of the anagrammatical . . . the space of the womb of Black women and those who reproduce Blackness [is] another kind of domestic middle passage, the afterlife, the ongoing life of *partus sequitur ventrem* . . . the anagrammatical [names] the ways that mother falls apart, child falls apart: can you claim mother, can you claim child?" (Terrefe 120). Sharpe and Spillers thus pinpoint a structuring of language that precedes the grammar of gender as we know it. This anagrammatical language is literally unspeakable: our words cannot accurately name the relations of consent, pleasure, desire, and agency that inform these (non)relations. Spillers concludes, "Under these circumstances [i.e., slavery], the customary aspects of sexuality, including 'reproduction,' 'motherhood,' 'pleasure,' and 'desire,' are all thrown in crisis" ("Mama's Baby" 215). In short, our entire language of sex and gender is rendered mute and unstable when the structural relations of propertied white masculinity and enslaved Black femininity are at stake.

Origin Scenes: Rape and Incest

Freud's narrative of the foundation of sexual difference focuses, centrally, on incest, not on rape. In psychoanalytic accounts of gender and sexuality, including feminist revisions of Freud, sexual difference is inaugurated by imposing foundational laws of kinship and culture. Juliet Mitchell succinctly writes, "The laws are that there are some people with whom sex is forbidden, there are some people whom you must not murder. . . . [This] law is the law of the definition and prohibition of incest. An effect of this desire and its taboo institutes sexual difference" (86). But if the Atlantic slave trade is prior to the Oedipus complex (ante-Oedipus)—and if the colonial Caribbean forms the foundation of metropolitan modernity—then rape appears *prior* to incest as the structuring difference of the psyche and the subject. (See Beckert, especially 61; Acemoglu, Johnson, and Robinson; Draper.)

Indeed, Gayatri Spivak argues that the incest prohibition works to naturalize, through recourse to the language of biology, a prohibition that should more broadly be seen as a culturally fluid rape prohibition that serves to create the border between the humanized and the nonhumanized. Rape, for Spivak, names the entry point into the category of the human that is the ground of sexuality/gender: "We are—male and female—raped into humanity. . . . 'Rape' . . . indicate[s] a certain harsh unconditionality initiating all human beings before the altogether conditioned notion of consent and nature" (208).

Rape, then, can be understood as a term that marks the boundaries of a radical exogamy and endogamy—that is, the line between the humanized (among whom incest will be a crime, among whom consent and volition exist, among whom sexual difference will come to exist in culturally specific terms) and the nonhumanized. Furthermore, we could say that there is no such thing as exogamous rape; rape only becomes a crime (having sex with someone you are not supposed to because you are violating their consent/agency) when you are talking of people with agency, which is to say, humanized, nonradically-exogamous sex objects/partners. For Spivak, the cut of culture—the original mark of the subject—is thus not that of the incest taboo and binary sexual difference but that of rape and the humanized/nonhumanized. In this sense, we could say that there is no possibility of incest without rape as a prior demarcating taboo that defines those within and those without the circle of the human.

Indeed, following Spivak's language, the category of the human (insofar as it suggests a sort of biological identity) is less apt in this account of primal rape than that of the "humanized"—that is, the human who is accorded the prerogatives of humanity, what Judith Butler calls "grievable life." As Michel-Rolph Trouillot points out, Atlantic race slavery relied on an episteme that assigned degrees of humanness to differently situated/raced individuals (76). It is worth underscoring, then, that the category of the humanized is culturally pliable and rife with contradictions in any given time and place, particularly with respect to race slavery and its legacies. Binary gender/sexuality in its association with whiteness might be seen, in turn, as a fantasy structure aimed at managing these contradictions (Scott). In the ante-Oedipal colonial scene, the nontaboo on the rape of Black women by white enslavers (and hence the unspeakability of rape in this context) might thus also be understood as prior to and, indeed, productive of incest (unacknowledged, licit, and nontaboo) because rape, coupled with the denial of the patronym, serves to destroy the structure of knowledge and relations that define kinship and its basic rules. And in a final twist, this ante-Oedipal colonial scene must *also* be seen as productive of the coeval metropolitan scenario in which the incest taboo emerges into stark legibility and serves to structure/produce *white* families, white binary gender identities, and white genealogies of descent through which the patronym and, importantly, property are amassed and retained.[6]

If we turn from rape to incest at the origin site of racial capitalism—the plantation—we see that the two are closely linked in their appearance and disappearance in that location. Whereas rape was unspoken (Black women were understood to be nonrapeable), the horror of incest was widely associated with slavery in the Atlantic world, including in the eighteenth-century Caribbean and the nineteenth-century United States. Both the theoretical possibility as well as the documented reality of incestuous relations between (most particularly) white male enslavers and their Black daughters devolved from unacknowledged paternity coupled with the unlimited right of sexual access to enslaved Blacks on the part of white men. As numerous scholars have argued, incest was not an aberration from the logic of white supremacy and sexual terrorism that structured the institution of slavery but was rather intrinsic to it (see Abdur-Rahman; Connolly; Garraway; Sollors). However, what arose from the incestuous nature of racial/sexual structures of plantation slavery in the Atlantic world was not the incest taboo of Freudian theory—one that would psychically enjoin a male child to redirect sexual desire from his mother to another woman—but rather an association of disordered/unconstrained sexuality with enslaved people. As Brian Connolly states: "To put it simply, in the discourse of slavery, incest was aligned with blackness, and the incest prohibition was aligned with whiteness. . . . The sentimental family and liberal subject were . . . cordoned off from blackness and incest" (168).

The association of incest and slavery was strong for two reasons: first, as indicated above, the forms of social death and natal alienation (the destruction of genealogy and of recognized kinship forms and the erasure of access to the patronym) produced a lack of knowledge about biological descent that facilitated incest—one that was unwitting and/or unpunishable because it did not register as incest. The Oedipus myth also hinges on unwitting incest: the incest taboo arises ex post facto, at the point when Oedipus realizes that his unknown parentage has made it possible for him to unknowingly have sex with his mother and to kill his father; in short, his incestuous act only becomes visible when his parentage is revealed. Race slavery enforced unknowable/unaccountable/unspeakable paternity (paternity might be known but it was legally and socially unrecognizable and thus unenforceable as a form of relation) on enslaved Blacks—a legal system that required the status of the child to follow the mother and sustained the systemic denial of property rights to Blacks because these rights inhered in patrilineage (Morgan, "Partus Sequitur Ventrem").

A harrowing legal case that unfolded in the southern United States indicates the parallels and divergence between incest during race slavery and that described in Freudian Oedipal theory. Connolly describes the history of a white enslaver who was murdered in 1830 by two Black individuals he enslaved, one of whom was his daughter. Charged with murder, she submitted witness testimony that her father had chained her up and attempted to rape her. The incestuous act in this case is not that of a son having sex with his mother, as in the Oedipus myth, but that of a father having sex with his daughter. Furthermore, the result is not an internalized taboo on incest that leads to a psychic positioning of the self and structuring of desire in relation to a binary model of male/female parentage but rather a daughter killing a father and then being prosecuted for it as a murderer. Connolly notes that the public testimony regarding the daughter's officially unrecognized paternity points to the presence of "vernacular kinship"—that is, an understanding of kinship that remains off the books and is unactionable in legal and white cultural terms but remains deeply present in the lives of individuals, particularly among the Black community (186–87). This dual system of knowledge creates what a number of scholars refer to as a "shadow family"—the "family" engendered by a white enslaver and a Black woman, distinguished by the fact that it is explicitly not linked to legal visibility, property ownership, lineal descent, and the inheritance of patrimony, patronym, and property. In short, the shadow family is wholly extractive in that it enables the appropriation of the reproductive labor of Black kinship in the service of white property accumulation. This extractive relation—the appropriation of the labor of social reproduction as a form of white capital—is a crucial, and largely unrecognized, element of racial capitalism.

A second dimension of the association of slavery and incest involves the proslavery ideology of the plantation-as-family—a white supremacist model that conferred paternal status on white enslavers and prescribed child-like status to Blacks of all ages. This ideological structure undergirds what Doris Garraway identifies as the "incestuous family romance" of Atlantic world slavery. As Garraway explains, given the practices of sexual terror, rape, and concubinage that were routinely practiced and viewed as acceptable behavior on the plantation, the white father/enslaver in this model bears no resemblance to the law-defining father of Freudian theory: "Rather than remaining the repository and potential transmitter of the law against incest, the father becomes himself the primary instigator of its violation" (280).[7] In sum, the widespread nature of the fantasy of unlimited sexual access to Black women uncoupled from prohibition and, in turn, wed to a paternalistic ideology of slavery is inherently incestuous.

Family Portraits: Two Scenes of Reproduction

The well-known engraving—the "Voyage of the Sable Venus" (1794) (see fig. 1)—celebrates the sexual allure and availability of an iconic enslaved Black woman as illustrative of the glory of the British Empire and the institution of slavery.

FIGURE 1. Family portrait I: William Grainger, *The Voyage of the Sable Venus, from Angola to the West Indies* (1801). Courtesy of the John Carter Brown Library.

The engraving does not present itself as a family portrait—a genre that was also used to celebrate British imperialism at the time—but regarded carefully, the image in fact depicts an ensemble of father, mother, and son. This unfamiliar family (Black mother—Sable Venus, white father—Neptune, "saffron" child—Cupid) remains barely legible within the engraving but nonetheless provides us with the constellation of the shadow family that served to support the propertied white family portrayed, in far more familiar and legible terms, in Johann Zoffany's contemporaneous portrait, "The Family of Sir William Young" (1767–69) (see fig. 2).

FIGURE 2. Family portrait II: Johann Zoffany, *The Family of Sir William Young, Baronet, ca. 1770*. Source: Walker Art Gallery.

As with the scenes of Philip Francis in Parliament and Thomas Thistlewood in Jamaica, I juxtapose these two familial scenes to insist on their intimate relation to each other despite their apparent difference in subject, genre, geography, and intent.

The "Voyage of the Sable Venus" stages a scene that is at once mythical and historical, visually citing Sandro Botticelli's famous fifteenth-century painting, "The Birth of Venus," as a means of narrating the voyage of an enslaved African woman from Angola to the West Indies. "Sable Venus" thus overlays the historical reality of the notorious middle passage with the scene of the birth of the classical goddess of love, Venus. The 1801 engraving was rendered by William Grainger in imitation of a painting (no longer extant) by Thomas Stothard, which, in turn, was a portrayal of a scene conjured in a poem penned by Isaac Teale, tutor of the enslaver, plantation owner, and proslavery statesman, Bryan Edwards. Grainger's engraving first appeared in the second edition of Edwards's influential tome, *The History, Civil and Commercial, of the British Colonies in the West Indies*—a multivolume history that went through six editions in England between 1793 and 1819 and served as an authoritative account (in England) of the history of Jamaica and other sugar colonies well into the twentieth century. The engraving appears in the volume next to Teale's ode, "The Sable Venus," that consists of twenty-seven rhyming five-line stanzas that praise the beauty of the Black woman transported from Africa to the West Indies and the lust of white men awaiting her arrival on the shores of Jamaica. In the poem, Neptune disguises himself as a ship captain and takes Sable Venus as his "prize," raising a cloud around the two while his desire is consummated, and their offspring, a "saffron" Cupid, is created from this act. Sable Venus, in the poem, offers a "consenting" look to Neptune, which provides an alibi against the aura of rape that pervades the scene and the poem. However, the language of "prize" and the figure of the ship captain and the enslaved Black woman as the historical referents of the poem suggest that such "consent" is a scrim drawn across the knowledge that rape is part and parcel of the glorified white male sexual access to Black women. And indeed, in the remaining stanzas of the poem, Sable Venus arrives on the shores of Jamaica and is heralded with "rapture" by its white male inhabitants. In short, the poem and the engraving marshal the prestige of Renaissance art, classical mythology, and poetic meter to authorize and celebrate the rape of Black women by white enslavers.

Not only rape but also incest appears in this depiction of the foundations of Atlantic race slavery. To conjoin Venus's birth to the historical event of the middle passage, significant revisions to the classical narrative occur that foreground the incestuous dimensions of this new narrative. In Botticelli's painting, as in Roman myth, Neptune does not appear with Venus at her birth, nor does he ever have sex with her. Rather, in classical myth, Mars is the sexual partner of Venus and Cupid is their offspring. In the engraving, however, Neptune appears beside the Sable Venus, depicted with a long white beard in an elderly (albeit virile), paternal form that contrasts with the young and nubile Black Venus. The visual distinction in their ages suggests a father-daughter relation; the implication of incest is furthered by the fact that in classical mythology, Venus is born of the sea, whereas Neptune is the father of the sea. Turning Venus into a "sable" figure then requires, for Edwards (and Teale, Stothard, and Grainger), the insertion of a white male father figure into the picture, indicating that the sexual abundance of Sable Venus only exists in relation to white, male, paternal control and desire.

It is commonplace to see the licensed "libertinage" afforded to white men in the discourse of the Sable Venus as offering an escape from the constraints of the laws and norms of sexual engagement enjoined on such men in metropolitan climes in relation to white women—indeed, that is precisely the "boys will be boys" story that the Sable Venus poem narrates with a wink to its white male audience. But if we understand this narrative of rape, incest, and racial/sexual configuration to be foundational to racial capitalism—that is, structural rather than incidental—then we must also view the sanctity of the nuclear white family and its hetero-patriarchal norms as conditioned by race slavery, not exterior and/or prior to it. In short, the shadow family is not secondary to the white family but is essential to its production. The shadow family is structured by its lack of patronym and, consequently, lack of a taboo on rape and incest; the white family, in turn, is defined by the patronym, property ownership, and the incest taboo that serves to perpetuate the link between patronym and property (see Abdur Rahman 120; Harris).

The shadow family is the source of the production of capital and also *is* the capital itself that will constitute the property that the white family claims ownership of; racialization, then, functions as a scene of ongoing primitive accumulation within racial capitalism. The Atlantic plantation economy and its monocropping model depended on a form of settler colonialism that required transforming large amounts of stolen land and labor into resources for the production and retention of capital. One mechanism for doing so was the development of a racialized heterosexual marriage regime that accrued the force of social reproduction and capital retention to a white, European middle class whose wealth was extracted from the violently broken and abrogated genealogies of Indigenous Americans, indigenous ecosystems, and enslaved Africans. In short, heterosexual marriage and heterosexuality, as they are codified in new ways in the mid-eighteenth century, speak directly of the forces of racial capitalism and colonialism, most particularly with respect to property ownership and capital accumulation and retention.

Johann Zoffany's massive oil painting, "The Family of Sir William Young" (ca. 1770), displays the glory of white property accumulation and futurity founded on the theft of the land of the Caribs and enslaved African labor in the Caribbean.[8] The sprawling painting depicts the British baronet, William Young, surrounded by his large family, domestic animals, and an enslaved servant on the grounds of his newly purchased hundred-acre estate in England, the Manor of Delaford. In contrast to the barely discernible shadow family depicted in the "Voyage of the Sable Venus," the Young family appears in a full genealogical constellation, embedded in English landed glory and laden with silk. Despite the suggestion of the painting that Young is thoroughly at home in a British manorial setting, Young was in fact born in Antigua, the son of a Scottish doctor who became a plantation owner and enslaver in Antigua; at the age of fifteen, William inherited a plantation in Antigua on which 325 people were enslaved. He used his wealth to propel himself into a life of flamboyant European luxury and status. He astutely managed relations with patrons in England—in part through his lavish entertainment at locations such as Delaford—to secure a patronage spot as the Commissioner of Lands in the Ceded Islands following the assigning of ownership of four Caribbean islands to the British at the 1763 Peace Treaty of Paris. During his tenure in this position, Young prosecuted a genocidal war against the largest Indigenous community in the Caribbean, the Caribs of St. Vincent, to appropriate additional land for British plantations and to expand the slave economy. He also used this position for personal enrichment—namely, to acquire lands for himself with government funds—and ultimately was forced to resign from his position under a cloud of charges of mismanagement (Marshall 173–90).

Zoffany's portrait depicts Young at the summit of his triumphant Britwashing: no longer an upstart creole but a landed, titled baronet, his wealth in this image is laundered of Caribbean taint and fabricated into a purely white, British aristocratic lineage. Arrayed in finery at the center of his family and engaged in leisure at his manor, Young holds a violoncello with the branches of a stately tree spread behind him and the branches of his family tree spread around him. Young and his family bask in a glowing surround of classical architecture, rich land, fine clothing, and the civility of stringed instruments, purebred domesticated animals, cultivated blossoms, printed books and music—all symbols of civility, leisure, and high culture and all purchased with the wealth extracted from the labor of enslaved workers in the Caribbean on land taken from Indigenous people. On the left side of the painting, a young Black man whose name does not appear in the historical record supports the ascension of the youngest son to the top of a steed where he is positioned in the lap of his older brother; Black labor serves as the prop for the production of whiteness and white prowess.

While the white son ascends with the props of animals and enslaved labor on the left side of the painting, the right side of the painting effects an explosion of shining silk-clad white femininity. At the visual center of the painting sits William's wife, Elizabeth Young, toward whom William directs his adoring gaze. Indeed, Elizabeth's womb is the centrifugal center of the painting; William Young gazes benignly at the pear-shaped Neapolitan mandolin that Elizabeth cradles in her lap while her younger child reaches toward the uterine focal point as well. The reproductive force of white womanhood is on full display in this painting, configured as blossoming white futurity. Africans and Caribs have, in turn, disappeared into the temporal and geographical distance far from the display of shining white wealth, leisure, abundance, and futurity. And indeed, we know something of that future from the historical record that postdates this painting: William Young's oldest son, Sir William Young, second baronet, remained ascendant—he would become a member of Parliament, governor of Tobago, a member of the Royal Society, a fellow of the Society of Antiquaries, and secretary to the Association for

Promoting the Discovery of the Interior Parts of Africa; he served in Parliament for twenty-three years where he distinguished himself as the vocal leader of the opposition to William Wilberforce's efforts to abolish slavery (Young).

Placing the middle passage of Sable Venus and the womb of Elizabeth Young next to each other as two interdependent images—two sides of the same coin—gives substance to the claim that white femininity depends on the erasure of the Black female body. Drawing on the pivotal language of Spillers, which names the nongendered, undifferentiated enslaved Black body as "flesh," theorists of African American studies have demonstrated the ways in which Black flesh is the condition of possibility of white, gendered embodiment that emerges in full binary substance from the history of the plantation and racial capitalism. Thus, for instance, C. Riley Snorton speaks of the development of the medical field of gynecology in the nineteenth century and the embodiment of white womanhood that is the subject of the field's constitution, as the site of a "medical plantation" (23). In related terms, Kyla Schuller traces nineteenth-century US discourses of biopolitics and affect in which "the rhetoric of distinct sexes of male and female consolidated as a function of race . . . throws open the category of woman . . . as an instrument of racial thought" (17). It is in this era that Freud writes as well.

Freud and Atlantic Race Slavery

Freud's Oedipal theory, famously cited as the origin of psychoanalysis, emerged at the moment when Freud rejected his earlier "seduction theory"—a theory that held that hysteria among women was the result of childhood sexual abuse by their fathers or other adults. The Oedipal theory absolves the father of this crime by locating incest in fantasy rather than historical event and displacing it from the hands of the father to the mind of the child who directs incestuous desire toward the parent of the opposite sex—a desire that must then be repressed and redirected to achieve stable and normative gendered identity and heterosexual orientation. This crucial transposition—from reality of paternal abuse to fantasy of infantile incestuous desire—has been the subject of some debate, perhaps most prominently in the controversial work of Jeffrey Masson, who argued in 1984 that Freud was aware of evidence of real sexual abuse among his patients but revised his theory to make it more palatable to the medical community. Masson's account has been and remains roundly rejected by a number of prominent historians as well as the psychoanalytical community (Robinson; Herman). Without entering into the voluminous details of the Masson debate, we can nonetheless place Freud's Oedipal theory in the context of the historical reality of rape and incest in the plantation economy of racial capitalism. Viewed in this context, the narrative of the development of the Oedipal theory (from the sexual abuse of a daughter by a father, to an erasure of that abuse dressed in the robes of classical myth) recapitulates the history of gender and racial capitalism in which incestuous rape of the Black daughter by the white father disappears behind authorized colonial narratives of white gendered property ownership.

The eighteenth-century history of Caribbean colonialism may seem temporally and geographically remote from the life and thought of Freud who formulated the Oedipal theory in 1895. Indeed, scholars interested in Freud and colonialism have largely focused on Africa and psychic structures of alterity rather than the material history of racial capitalism and race slavery in the Atlantic world (see, for example, Khanna and Nast). A turn to material history, however, suggests that racial capitalism was not a matter of the distant past in Freud's life but remained substantively present in shaping his influential theory of sexuality. In what follows, I trace the interwoven material history of Freud's biography, Atlantic colonialism, and racial capitalism: I look to the details of Freud's family history not to analyze his psyche but to trace an economic and racial narrative that concerns the accumulation of property and whiteness—an amalgam of properties that remain embedded within Freudian accounts of sexuality.

The 1876 photographic portrait constellating the family of Sigmund Freud around his mother, Amalia Freud, is a good starting point for this history (see fig. 3). The photograph locates Freud's mother at the center of a family grouping including eight offspring of her womb, together with her husband, a cousin, and two unidentified children. Sigmund, her oldest child, stands directly behind Amalia facing the camera, with one hand resting on the back of her chair; Jacob, her husband, is seated to her left, off-center with respect to the group as a whole. Although the affect of this family portrait is quite distinct from the portrait of William Young and family, the staging of it bears a visual similarity in projecting the shape of a family tree spreading widely in comfortable surroundings, albeit, in the Freud case, less one of luxuriant civility than dignified (exhausted? defiant?) success, staged in a Viennese photography studio designed to produce just such images of middle-class arrival.

Unlike William Young, patriarch Jacob Freud did not make his fortune in the Caribbean, rather, he was a Jewish cloth merchant who hailed from Tysmenyzja, a shtetl in the central European region of Galicia (now Ukraine). Furthermore, his economic success was precarious at best; the photo is taken

FIGURE 3. Family portrait III: The Freud Family in 1876. Sigmund Freud is standing, third from left, behind his mother, Amalia Freud. Courtesy of the Wellcome Collection.

at a time when the Freud family lived in Vienna where they had moved, historians speculate, following the failure of Jacob's cloth trading business in Příbor (Freiberg), a town northeast of Vienna, located in what is now the Silesia-Moravia region of Czechoslovakia. Although Jacob Freud left behind his own childhood in the rural east-European Jewish shtetl and moved toward a goal of economic and religious assimilation into the urban bourgeoisie, his son Sigmund, by all accounts, bore the mantle of the ambition Jacob was not able to achieve. In the years after this photo was taken, Sigmund Freud chose a career of medicine—the first in four generations of men in his father's family to leave the business of cloth trading—but doing so required the assistance of his two much older half-brothers who lived in England; as he pursued his studies, Freud was forced to call on them to send funds to keep the family afloat. Significantly, his brothers remained associated with the cloth business; on departing Příbor at the time of Jacob's decampment, Emmanuel and Philip Freud resettled in Manchester, England, a city known as "Cottonopolis"—the industrial center of cotton cloth produced in England from cotton grown on the plantations in the US South by enslaved Blacks.

The association of the Atlantic slave trade and the textile trade in which Freud's family engaged reaches back far before the industrialized production of cotton in Manchester. Despite its landlocked location, the central European textile trade that launched the Freud family into economic upward mobility and entry into the European bourgeoisie was linked to Africa and the Atlantic slave trade. Recent research by Anka Steffen and Klaus Weber documents that a new orientation toward the Atlantic slave trade (beginning in the seventeenth century and accelerating over the course of the eighteenth century) fueled the proto-industrialization of linen production and trade in central Europe. As they demonstrate, a large amount of the linen cloth that was traded in Africa for slaves and sold in the Caribbean was manufactured (by serfs) in Silesia, so much so that in the late seventeenth century, "hardly any East India ship would set sail from Britain for Africa without a substantial quantity of Silesian linen in its holds, labelled 'sletias.'" In the eighteenth century, the pattern continued with a "significantly Atlantic bias of the exports from Silesia" (91). By the mid-eighteenth century, fully three quarters of linen produced in Silesia fed the Atlantic trade. Indeed, as Steffen demonstrates, palaces built in landlocked Silesia in the eighteenth century by newly wealthy merchants profiting off the Atlantic trade in slavery and cloth featured decorative medallions of ocean-going ships, thus commemorating the source of their wealth in the Atlantic trade (Steffen, "Slave Fabrics"; see also Steffen, "A Cloth That Binds").

Jacob Freud, however, was not a wealthy merchant and he traded in the nearby region of Moravia rather than Silesia: nonetheless, evidence points to links between his trade in linen and wool and markets connected to the Atlantic world. The town of Tysmenyzja, in Galicia, where he was born, had a population of fewer than ten thousand, roughly half of which was Jewish. As a persecuted and policed minority, Jews were restricted from traveling in much of central Europe without special license, but Jacob received such a license for his work as a cloth merchant in Galicia and the adjacent Prussian state of Moravia. Jacob's work in the textile trade enabled him to permanently relocate from Tysmenyzja to Příbor by 1852, following the 1848 revolution that eventually led to citizenship rights for Austrian Jews. A biographer of Freud and his father describes this move as integral to Jacob's "great step from the narrow life of the Orthodox Jew to that of the emancipated bourgeois" (Krüll 95). Sigmund Freud was born in Příbor in 1856, although he left at the age of three when his father relocated the family to Vienna. Nonetheless, Sigmund evidently retained strong memories and a sense of connection to his birthplace; he revisited Příbor at the age of sixteen, during which time he contracted an affection for the sister of a friend living there. Writing about his infatuation, he contemplates the path not taken in Příbor: "If only I had stopped at home and grown in the country and grown as strong as the young men in the house, the brothers of my love! And *if only I had followed my father's profession* and if I had finally married her" (*SE* III: 312; my emphasis). Three years later, however, he embarked on a much-anticipated visit to his older half-brothers in Manchester and at this point describes the dream of a very different imagined career. Now a medical student in Vienna, he imagines moving to England to gain wide recognition for groundbreaking medical work: "A respected man, supported by the press and rich patrons [in England], could do wonders in curing physical ills, if only he is enough of an explorer to enter new curative paths" (Freud cited in Krüll 174). The two conflicting, equally robust images of the possible paths in life he constructs as a teenager indicate an acute awareness of his decision to step out of the path of his forefathers and the textile trade to embark on a distinct and "new curative path."

During his visit to England, Freud would also have seen the workings of Manchester in 1875, a city that had emerged, at that time, as the global hub of the "empire of cotton" in the words of historian Sven Beckert. By 1860, Manchester was home to two-thirds of the cotton spindles in the world and massive factories employed tens of thousands of workers that produced cotton fabric shipped around the world. The city had been transformed into a center of global industrialization fueled by the cotton grown by enslaved Blacks in the US South—the commodity that Ed Baptist has described as the "petroleum" of the nineteenth century that drove the world economy. Earlier in the century, Alexis de Tocqueville shared his own impression of a visit to the industrializing city of Manchester (1835), describing it as a modern hellscape: a "damp, dark labyrinth," choked with smoke and the incessant cacophony of "the crunching wheels of machinery, the shriek of steam from boilers" in which "300,000 human beings are ceaselessly at work" (107). On his visit to Manchester, Freud does not remark on the scenes described by de Tocqueville; rather, he appears to begin formulating a lifelong vision of England as the land of freedom—the land in which his half-brother Emmanuel became successful in the cotton trade in Manchester, as his series of increasingly affluent addresses indicates. By 1890, Emmanuel had moved into a large residence, a portion of which he used as a cotton warehouse for his business (M. Freud 13). In material terms, then, the house in which Freud stayed when he dreamed of being a path-breaking doctor supported by wealthy patrons and a liberal press was itself supported by cotton grown by enslaved Blacks. Jacob and Sigmund's trajectory, then, is delayed but parallel to that of William Young and many other eighteenth-century Europeans whose fortunes were leavened, directly or indirectly, by colonialism in the Americas and the advent of racial capitalism.

Despite the fact that all of the men in Freud's family were involved in the textile trade, as were many of the successful Jews in his orbit whom he saw as patients ("Dora"'s father, Philip Bauer, owned a textile factory in Vienna), Freud's own work is remarkable for its close association of textile production—spinning, weaving, sewing—with women and femininity rather than with men (Weissberg). Indeed, weaving is directly associated by Freud with female genitalia: he describes women's invention of weaving as linked to the wish to use pubic hair to hide their absence of a penis. Freud writes, "It seems that women have made few contributions to the discoveries and inventions in the history of civilization: there is, however, one technique which they may have invented—that of plaiting and weaving" (*SE* XXII: 131). Freud thus rewrites a male-associated history of textile production into a feminized narrative—one that directly rewrites the lineage of masculinity and economics in his own family. In racial capitalism, cloth (sewing) and sugar (cooking) are culturally linked to the domestic activities of white women in European culture—that is, to scenes of social reproduction in the nuclear family—whereas they are the basis of a regime of social death in the colony among enslaved women forced to produce sugar at the expense of the lives of their own children. In his feminization of textile production, Freud domesticated textiles—removing them from a global and racialized economy of production to become symbols of a universal womanliness—one that we should see marked as white in its claim to universality.

As a member of a racialized and persecuted minority, Freud's own anxiety about holding on to property and status was acute. Furthermore, contending with his own racial and religious identity was evidently pivotal to his formulation of the Oedipal theory: specifically, Freud arrived at the Oedipal theory of sexuality when he abandoned the notion that his own father was guilty of seduction and accepted his father's mandate of assimilation to the dominant, white European bourgeoisie. Scholars continue to debate the degree of Freud's assimilation to gentile society and whether or not this involved repudiating his own Jewish identity, but it is certainly the case that Freud feared, with good reason, that a close association between Jewishness and psychoanalysis would be detrimental to the success of the field (Rice; Yerushalmi). Four of Freud's sisters—all of whom appear in the photo above—were murdered in Nazi death camps; anti-Semitism could not but be a pressing dimension of Freud's work given its life and death stakes for himself and his family. The universalizing language of the Oedipus theory, I would suggest, speaks to Freud's negotiation of this racial terrain: more broadly, it arose from the material ground of racial capitalism and has succeeded in dominating accounts of gender in part because it does the work of erasing that ground to link binary gender to whiteness and property ownership/inheritance and white-only patrilineal genealogies.

The association of whiteness masquerading as universalism in the Oedipal screen of historical sexual violence is further underscored in Freud's turn to classicism to narrate his influential theory of sexuality. As biographers point out, Freud had a complicated relation to Rome and classicism—one that was directly related to his attempts to reckon with his cloth-trading father and his Jewish heritage. Recasting his own narrative in classical terms—identifying himself with Hannibal—Freud was able to "change his culture without ever betraying the Jewish identity of his ancestors" according to Elizabeth Roudinesco. Classicism, it seems, was the magic elixir for evading the racial conflicts of his own biography: "By tracing out his destiny in this way, Freud reconnected with the story of the sons of the Jewish bourgeois tradesmen of the Austro-Hungarian Empire, obliged to de-Judaize themselves to become intellectuals or scholars. To exist as Jews, they had to adopt Greek, Latin, and German cultures" (18). Freud—like Thomas Thistlewood, Philip Francis, Bryan Edwards, Isaac Teale, Thomas Stothard, William Grainger, and William Young—makes the choice to turn to classicism, rather than to a violently racialized history of oppression, and the Oedipus Complex and psychoanalysis are born. The conditions of racial capitalism, which thoroughly informed the life of Freud, served as the grounds of his theory of sexual difference, and in the world in which white, binary sexual difference helped to secure property ownership and white futurity, Freud's theory flourished. In this sense, Freud, precariously standing on the cusp of exclusion from white universalism, is also its astute theorist.

Coda: All the Things You Could Be by Now If Sally Hemings Were Your Foremother

Hortense Spillers's essay "All the Things You could Be by Now if Sigmund Freud's Wife Were Your Mother"—in which she posits that the slave trade and the middle passage are the invisible grounds of Freudian theories of sex and gender—borrows its title from a song by the jazz musician, Charles Mingus. Mingus's improvisational tune of that name is recorded on his 1960 album, *Charles Mingus Presents Charles Mingus*, and includes his introductory comment at the live performance of the song: "This is a composition dedicated to all mothers. And it's titled 'All the Things You Could Be By Now If Sigmund Freud's Wife Was Your Mother.' Which means if Sigmund Freud's wife was your mother, all the things you could be by now. Which means

nothing, you got it? Thank you."[9] The circumlocution around Freud's paternity in this title maps a kinship that cuts out Freud as father, moving toward
a maternal genealogy in its stead—a genealogy that is not normative, that has
no standing in our world, that is "nothing." Spillers closes her own essay by
riffing on Mingus's improvisational move with respect to the unspeakable
maternal kinship structure dancing around Freud: "What [Mingus] proceeds to perform on the cut is certainly no thing we know. But that really
is the point—to expand the realm of possibility for what might be known"
("All the Things" 426). The "nothing" that is not the name of Freud, or the
language of Freud, is no thing, or "no thing we know" in Spillers's words, but
something we might reach after in new ways. This "nothing"/"no thing" remains the present unsaid and the present possible, which Spillers gestures
toward as the space of improvisation, of a possible repertoire of being.

The present unsaid of who we might be in a differently authorized and
articulated genealogy and kinship system has also been described by Spillers
in her recent work in relation to the shadow family.[10] Thomas Jefferson
and Sally Hemings, she remarks, are representative of the ubiquity of the
shadow family that exists beneath and across the sexual and intimate economies of official families—albeit a family that is hard to name as such because
of the way it is riven by violence, erasure, and expropriation: "Sexual contact
that does not breed intimacy or recognition. What do you call that and what
kind of world is that?" asks Spillers ("To the Bone"). The question of what to
call the repetition of sexual intercourse between Thomas Jefferson and Sally
Hemings returns us to the question of the unspoken and the unspeakable:
Jefferson, who was a master of record-keeping, did not record the nature of
his interactions with Hemings, or indeed, the existence of them. Rather,
their offspring accrued to his bottom line as newly enslaved beings.

Pushed to acknowledge the sexual relation between Hemings and Jefferson on the basis of genetic evidence, historians have, as Kimberly Juanita
Brown writes, employed a variety of circumlocutions to exculpate Jefferson
from the stain of rape: "Filled with denial, subjection, exploitation, and rhetorical possession, historians across two centuries reenslaved Hemings'
memory the moment pen hit paper and a circle of self-preservation began"
(109). The relation of Hemings and Jefferson, Brown asserts, insofar as it is
marked with violence and erasure, is the story of the founding of US nationhood: "This rarely acknowledged series of repetitive relationships, played
out on the bodies of black women . . . if unearthed and deconstructed,
would be the back-story to the construction of a new nation" (114). Reading
this history in the material world (given that it is effaced from written records and our language of relationality), Brown turns to the physical site of

Jefferson's home, Monticello, as the location at which we might see both the erasure of enslaved labor and enslaved kinship and their founding presence. Monticello—a neoclassical Palladian villa—was built by the labor of enslaved people and was a monument as well to the erasure of their labor and very being. As Brown reports, the housing of the enslaved was hidden from the sightlines of the main house at Monticello, and indeed, Jefferson *invented* the dumbwaiter as a means of keeping enslaved laborers out of his line of vision. In architectural terms, James Ackerman writes, the Palladian villa enacts a familiar ideological fantasy of pastoral ease "through which . . . persons whose position of privilege is rooted in urban commerce and industry have been able to expropriate rural land often requiring the care of a laboring class or of slaves for the realization of the myth" (12). Brown, in turn, asks us to see Monticello differently, in terms of its material nature, to "reinvest the field of vision with a totality of investment . . . that has the ocular ability to include Sally Hemings and her children in an envisioning of the property, and of Jefferson's patriarchy" (116).

Like Freud, Thistlewood, Francis, Edwards, Teale, Grainger, Stothard, and Young, Jefferson relied on reference to the classical world as a means of erasing the material history of enslaved labor and its work in amassing capital in the hands of white men and women—in founding such things as villas, families, and nations. Sally Hemings, it is worth noting, was the half-sister of Jefferson's wife, Martha Wayles. Martha and Sally shared the same father, John Wayles, although Sally did not carry his patronym as Martha did. Sally was roughly age fifteen (or younger) when Jefferson first began having sex with her—we know this because of the date of the birth of their first child. And she was also, as we know, enslaved by him: she did not have the legal right, as Spillers notes, to refuse his touch. In this light, we might call what occurred between Jefferson and Hemings rape, or incest, or child sexual abuse. But it has not largely been called any of these things; for much of the history of the United States, it has been called nothing. In more recent years, Hemings has been described as Jefferson's "lover," "mistress," "partner," "wife," and "concubine." Perhaps we should name Sally Hemings not with these terms that carry erasure within them but call her instead our anagrammatical founding foremother. ▪

Elizabeth Maddock Dillon is a distinguished professor of English at Northeastern University. She is author of *The Gender of Freedom: Fictions of Liberalism and the Literary Public Sphere* (2004) and *New World Drama: The Performative Commons in the Atlantic World 1649–1849* (2014). She is cofounder and codirector of the Early Caribbean Digital Archive, an open access collection of texts and images that explores modes of decolonizing the archive.

ACKNOWLEDGMENTS

I am grateful to Kimberly Juanita Brown, Sonia Di Loreto, Kathleen Donegan, Ren Heintz, Anka Steffen, and SJ Zhang as well as the editors of the journal for invaluable support, suggestions, and ideas that informed this article.

NOTES

1 The "ante-Oedipus" of my title refers to and participates in a long tradition of critique of Freud's Oedipal theory, including Deleuze and Guattari's *Anti-Oedipus* and Fanon's *White Skin, Black Masks* as well as feminist psychoanalytic theory by scholars such as Juliet Mitchell. For particular focus on rethinking Oedipality in relation to queer theory and race, see Eng and Musser as well as Heintz's brilliant reading of the queer possibilities opened by the nonresolution of the Oedipal crisis of ruptured kinship linked to the history of the Atlantic slave trade. My critique here is distinct from this work in reading Freud's Oedipus theory less as responsible for imposing a heteropatriarchal, racialized gender norm than as richly symptomatic of the social, legal, economic, and even linguistic aspects of racial capitalism that served as the ground of this work and its subsequent theoretical dominance of the field.

2 Kris Manjapra's important recent work on racialized plantation economies as the origin and enduring backbone of capitalist modernity locates the early Caribbean sugar plantation as the "aperture" of modernity (382).

3 Portions of Thistlewood's diary concerning Sally are reproduced in Hall (150, 198), and Burnard (218–21).

4 See also Polcha, who coins the useful term "sexual exploitation logs," to describe the reports of sexual depredation that constitute a good portion of Thistlewood's diaries. For additional recent treatments of Thistlewood in a feminist context, see Hartman, "Venus in Two Acts" and Morrison.

5 Note that Spillers here describes the argument of the Moynihan Report, an argument she takes issue with—not because of its account of the non-Oedipalized Black family but because of the false equation of this structure with matriarchy as well as the mythologization and pathologization of this structure/grammar of gender and kinship.

6 On the universality of the incest taboo *and* its cultural specificity, see Connolly. I do not suggest that the incest taboo only appears in relation to the Atlantic slave trade— rather, its particular enunciation in Oedipal terms and in relation to binary gender and patrilineal descent emerge with specificity in relation to the slave trade and the production of white property ownership in Western modernity.

7 In the psychoanalytic terms used by Simone Vauthier, "When refusing to acknowledge his slave son, the father fails to transmit with his surname what Jacques Lacan calls the Name-of-the-Father, i.e. the universal Law that prohibits incest" (350; cited by Garraway 279).

8 In contrast to the curators of the Walker Gallery, Tobin dates the painting to 1773 or later in her valuable discussion of the laundering of the profits of slavery in British paintings such as this one (39–43).

9 In Mingus's autobiography, he uses the name "Freud" for an institutionalized, normative, white voice in contrast to a competing subversive Black voice. See McNeilly 45–70.

10 There is a rich array of important new scholarship by Black scholars engaged in precisely the work of bringing forward this differently authorized and articulated gender, sexuality, and history outside of the constraints of white property-ownership and binary heterosexuality: to name but a few see Finch; Fuentes; Hartman, *Wayward Lives*; Johnson; Morgan, *Reckoning with Slavery*; Snorton; and Turner.

WORKS CITED

Abdur-Rahman, Aliyyah I. *Against the Closet: Black Political Longing and the Erotics of Race.* Durham, NC: Duke University Press, 2012.

Acemoglu, Daron, Simon Johnson, and James Robinson. "The Rise of Europe: Atlantic Trade, Institutional Change, and Economic Growth." *American Economic Review* 95, no. 3 (2005): 546–79.

Ackerman, James. "The Villa as Paradigm." *Perspecta* 22 (1986): 10–31.

Beckert, Sven. *Empire of Cotton: A Global History.* New York: Alfred A. Knopf, 2014.

Breger, Louis. *Freud: Darkness in the Midst of Vision.* New York: Wiley, 2001.

Brown, Kimberly Juanita. "Saving Mr. Jefferson: Slavery and Denial at Monticello." In *On Marronage: Ethical Confrontations with Antiblackness,* edited by Tryon P. Woods and Paul Khalil Saucier, 109–30. Trenton, NJ: Africa World Press, 2015.

Burnard, Trevor. *Mastery, Tyranny, and Desire: Thomas Thistlewood and His Slaves in the Anglo-Jamaican World.* Kingston, Jamaica: University of the West Indies Press, 2005.

Connolly, Brian. *Domestic Intimacies: Incest and the Liberal Subject in Nineteenth-Century America.* Philadelphia: University of Pennsylvania Press, 2014.

Davis, Angela Y. *Women, Race, and Class.* New York: Vintage Books, 1983.

de Tocqueville, Alexis. *Journeys to England and Ireland,* edited by J. P. Mayer and translated by George Lawrence and J. P. Mayer. New Haven, CT: Yale University Press, 1988.

Deleuze, Gilles, and Félix Guattari. *Anti-Oedipus: Capitalism and Schizophrenia,* translated by Robert Hurley, Mark Seem, and Helen R. Lane. New York: Viking, 1977.

Draper, Nicholas. *The Price of Emancipation: Slave-Ownership, Compensation, and British Society at the End of Slavery.* Cambridge: Cambridge University Press, 2010.

Edwards, Bryan. *Poems Written Chiefly in the West Indies.* Kingston, Jamaica: Alexander Aikman, 1792.

Eng, David L. *The Feeling of Kinship: Queer Liberalism and the Racialization of Intimacy.* Durham, NC: Duke University Press, 2010.

Fanon, Frantz. *Black Skin, White Masks.* New York: Grove Press, 1967.

Finch, Aisha K. *Rethinking Slave Rebellion in Cuba: La Escalera and the Insurgencies of 1841–1844.* Chapel Hill, NC: University of North Carolina Press, 2015.

Francis, Philip. *Proceedings in the House of Commons on the Slave Trade, and State of the Negroes in the West India Islands. With an Appendix. By Philip Francis, Esq.* 2008. name.umdl .umich.edu/004899520.0001.000.

Freud, Martin. *Glory Reflected: Sigmund Freud—Man and Father.* London: Angus and Robertson, 1957.

Freud, Sigmund, James Strachey, Anna Freud, and Carrie Lee Rothgeb. "Screen Memories." In vol. 3 of *The Standard Edition of the Complete Psychological Works of Sigmund Freud,* 299–322.

Freudenberger, Herman. "Industrialization in Bohemia and Moravia in the Eighteenth Century." *Journal of Central European Affairs* 19, no. 4 (1960): 349–56.

Fuentes, Marisa J. *Dispossessed Lives: Enslaved Women, Violence, and the Archive.* Philadelphia: University of Pennsylvania Press, 2016.

Garraway, Doris Lorraine. *The Libertine Colony: Creolization in the Early French Caribbean.* Durham, NC: Duke University Press, 2005.

Gicklhorn, Renée. "The Freiberg Period of the Freud Family." *Journal of the History of Medicine and Allied Sciences* 24, no. 1 (1969): 37–43.

Hall, Douglas. *In Miserable Slavery: Thomas Thistlewood in Jamaica, 1750–86.* London: Macmillan, 1989.

Harris, Cheryl I. "Whiteness as Property." *Harvard Law Review* 106, no. 8 (1993): 1707–91.

Hartman, Saidiya. "Venus in Two Acts." *Small Axe* 12, no. 2 (2008): 1–14.

Hartman, Saidiya. *Wayward Lives, Beautiful Experiments: Intimate Histories of Social Upheaval.* New York: W. W. Norton, 2019.

Heintz, Lauren. "The Crisis of Kinship: Queer Affiliations in the Sexual Economy of Slavery." *GLQ: A Journal of Lesbian and Gay Studies* 23, no. 2 (2017): 221–46.

Herman, Judith L. "The Analyst Analyzed." *Nation*, March 10, 1984, 293–96.

Hine, Darlene Clark. "Rape and the Inner Lives of Black Women in the Middle West." *Signs: Journal of Women in Culture and Society* 14, no. 4 (1989): 912–20.

Johnson, Jessica Marie. *Wicked Flesh: Black Women, Intimacy, and Freedom in the Atlantic World.* Philadelphia: University of Pennsylvania Press, 2020.

Khanna, Ranjana. *Dark Continents: Psychoanalysis and Colonialism.* Durham, NC: Duke University Press, 2003.

Krüll, Marianne. *Freud and His Father.* New York: W. W. Norton, 1986.

Manjapra, Kris. "Plantation Dispossessions: The Global Travel of Agricultural Racial Capitalism." In *American Capitalism: New Histories,* edited by Sven Beckert and Christine Desan, 361–88. New York: Columbia University Press, 2018.

Marshall, P. J. "A Polite and Commercial People in the Caribbean: The British in St Vincent." In *Revisiting the Polite and Commercial People,* edited by Elaine Chalus and Perry Gauci, 173–90. Oxford: Oxford University Press, 2019.

Masson, Jeffrey Moussaieff. *Assault on Truth: Freud's Suppression of the Seduction Theory.* London: Faber and Faber, 1984.

McNeilly, Kevin. "Charles Mingus Splits, or, All the Things You Could Be by Now If Sigmund Freud's Wife Was Your Mother." *Canadian Review of American Studies* 27, no. 2 (1997): 45–70.

Mitchell, Juliet. "Debating Sexual Difference, Politics, and the Unconscious: With Discussant Section by Jacqueline Rose." In *Juliet Mitchell and the Lateral Axis: Twenty-First-Century Psychoanalysis and Feminism,* edited by Robbie Duschinsky and Susan Walker, 77–99. New York: Palgrave Macmillan, 2015.

Morgan, Jennifer L. *Laboring Women: Reproduction and Gender in New World Slavery.* Philadelphia: University of Pennsylvania Press, 2004.

Morgan, Jennifer L. "Partus Sequitur Ventrem: Law, Race, and Reproduction in Colonial Slavery." *Small Axe* 22, no. 1 (2018): 1–17.

Morgan, Jennifer L. *Reckoning with Slavery: Gender, Kinship, and Capitalism in the Early Black Atlantic.* Durham, NC: Duke University Press, 2021.

Morrison, Toni. *The Origin of Others*. Cambridge, MA: Harvard University Press, 2017.

Musser, Amber Jamilla. "Anti-Oedipus, Kinship, and the Subject of Affect." *Social Text* 30, no. 3 (2012): 77–95.

Nast, Heidi J. "Mapping the 'Unconscious': Racism and the Oedipal Family." *Annals of the Association of American Geographers* 90, no. 2 (2000): 215–55.

Phillips, Adam. *Becoming Freud: The Making of a Psychoanalyst*. New Haven, CT: Yale University Press, 2016.

Polcha, Elizabeth. "Redacting Desire: The Sexual Politics of Colonial Science in the Eighteenth-Century Atlantic World." PhD diss., Northeastern University, 2019.

Rice, Emanuel. *Freud and Moses: The Long Journey Home*. Albany: State University of New York Press, 1990.

Robinson, Paul. *Freud and His Critics*. Berkeley: University of California Press, 1993.

Roudinesco, Élisabeth. *Freud: In His Time and Ours*, translated by Catherine Porter. Cambridge, MA: Harvard University Press, 2017.

Schuller, Kyla. *The Biopolitics of Feeling: Race, Sex, and Science in the Nineteenth Century*. Durham, NC: Duke University Press, 2018.

Scott, Joan Wallach. *The Fantasy of Feminist History*. Durham, NC: Duke University Press, 2012.

Sharpe, Jenny. *Ghosts of Slavery: A Literary Archaeology of Black Women's Lives*. Minneapolis: University of Minnesota Press, 2003.

Snorton, C. Riley. *Black on Both Sides: A Racial History of Trans Identity*. Minneapolis: University of Minnesota Press, 2017.

Sollors, Werner. *Neither Black nor White Yet Both: Thematic Explorations of Interracial Literature*. New York: Oxford University Press, 1997.

Spillers, Hortense J. "'All the Things You Could Be by Now if Sigmund Freud's Wife Was Your Mother': Psychoanalysis and Race." In *Black, White, and in Color: Essays on American Literature and Culture*, 376–427. Chicago: University of Chicago Press, 2003.

Spillers, Hortense J. "Mama's Baby, Papa's Maybe: An American Grammar Book." In *Black, White, and in Color: Essays on American Literature and Culture*, 203–29. Chicago: University of Chicago Press, 2003.

Spillers, Hortense J. "To the Bone: Some Speculations on the Question of Touch." Paper presented at the Futures of American Studies Institute, Hanover, NH, June 2018.

Spivak, Gayatri Chakravorty. "Crimes of Identity." In *Juliet Mitchell and the Lateral Axis: Twenty-First-Century Psychoanalysis and Feminism*, edited by Robbie Duschinsky and Susan Walker, 207–27. New York: Palgrave Macmillan, 2015.

Steffen, Anka. "A Cloth That Binds: New Perspectives on the Eighteenth-Century Prussian Economy." *Slavery and Abolition* 42, no. 1 (2021): 105–29.

Steffen, Anka. "Slave Fabrics and Fabrics That Enslaved: Textiles within the Eighteenth-Century Atlantic Slave Trade." Paper presented at the conference "Clothing the Enslaved in the Eighteenth-Century Atlantic World," National Museum of Wales, Cardiff, Wales, July 8–10, 2019.

Steffen, Anka, and Klaus Weber. "Spinning and Weaving for the Slave Trade: Proto-Industry in Eighteenth-Century Silesia." In *Slavery Hinterland: Transatlantic Slavery and Continental Europe, 1680–1850*, edited by Felix Brahm and Eve Rosenhaft. Suffolk, UK: Boydell and Brewer, 2016.

Stevenson, Brenda E. "What's Love Got to Do with It? Concubinage and Enslaved Women and Girls in the Antebellum South." In *Sexuality and Slavery*, edited by Daina Ramey Berry and Leslie M Harris, 159–88. Athens: University of Georgia Press, 2018.

Terrefe, Selamawit. "What Exceeds the Hold? An Interview with Christina Sharpe." *Rhizomes*, no. 29 (2016). doi.org/10.20415/rhiz/029.e06.

Tobin, Beth Fowkes. *Picturing Imperial Power: Colonial Subjects in Eighteenth-Century British Painting*. Durham, NC: Duke University Press, 1999.

Trouillot, Michel-Rolph. *Silencing the Past: Power and the Production of History*. Boston: Beacon Press, 1995.

Turner, Sasha. *Contested Bodies: Pregnancy, Childrearing, and Slavery in Jamaica*. Philadelphia: University of Pennsylvania Press, 2017.

Vauthier, Simone. "Of African Queens and Afro-American Princes and Princesses: Miscegenation in Old Hepsy." In *Interracialism: Black-White Intermarriage in American History, Literature, and Law*, edited by Werner Sollors, 330–55. Oxford: Oxford University Press, 2000.

Vermeulen, Heather V. "Thomas Thistlewood's Libidinal Linnaean Project: Slavery, Ecology, and Knowledge Production." *Small Axe* 22, no. 1 (2018): 18–38.

Weissberg, Liliane. "Ariadne's Thread." *MLN* 125, no. 3 (2010): 661–81.

Yerushalmi, Yosef Hayim. *Freud's Moses: Judaism Terminable and Interminable*. New Haven, CT: Yale University Press, 2011.

"Young, Sir William, 2nd Bt. (1749–1815), of Delaford Park, Bucks." History of Parliament Online. www.historyofparliamentonline.org/volume/1790-1820/member/young-sir-william-1749-1815 (accessed July 18, 2021).

David L. Eng

The History of the Subject and the Subject of History

ABSTRACT This article explores unexamined links between psychic and political theories of trauma to investigate the constitution of victims deserving and undeserving of reparation as they emerge in the context of the Holocaust, Hiroshima, and the Nuremberg and Tokyo War Tribunals. While genocide and nuclear catastrophe oriented the world imagination toward the specter of planetary annihilation, the "final solution" and the atomic bombings also cleave from one another in significant ways. In the space of postwar Europe, the history of the Holocaust is settled: Nazis were perpetrators and Jews were victims. In contrast, in the space of postwar Asia, there was and continues to be little historical consensus as to who were the victims and who were the perpetrators. As such, this article investigates how the uneven distribution of trauma across different geopolitical spaces and times carves out a privileged zone of exhausted and victimized humanity, with significant implications for addressing the injuries of violated human beings in Europe and elsewhere. Throughout, this article examines how psychoanalytic approaches to the history of the traumatized subject supplement the subject of Cold War history in search of an impossible historical consensus.

KEYWORDS trauma, reparations, human rights, Holocaust, Hiroshima

But with Hiroshima, where the continuity of life was, for the first time, put into question, and by man, the existence of any survivors is an irrelevancy, and the interview with the survivors is an insipid falsification of the truth of atomic warfare. To have done the atom bomb justice, Mr. Hersey would have had to interview the dead.

—Mary McCarthy, "The Hiroshima *New Yorker*"

Let all the souls here rest in peace; For we shall not repeat the evil.

—Memorial Cenotaph
—Hiroshima Peace Memorial Park

HISTORY of the PRESENT ▪ A Journal of Critical History ▪ 12:1 ▪ April 2022
DOI 10.1215/21599785-9547221 © 2022 Duke University Press

Two signal events in the twentieth century marked a radical shift in our conception of the human being and, more specifically, of human precarity. The Holocaust and the atomic bombings of Hiroshima and Nagasaki invoked in graphic terms the specter of total human destruction whereby, in Mary McCarthy's sober assessment of the latter events, "the continuity of life was, for the first time, put into question, and by man" (367). In response, a new international order of human rights with attendant notions of reparations arose from the ruins of World War II. This new legal regime sought to subrogate the sovereignty of the nation-state in the hopes of defending the sovereignty of the individual. Traditionally, reparations could be claimed by one state from another as compensation for the costs of war. For the first time in history, reparations were extended to encompass individual and group claims against state-sponsored violence in the name of human rights. Together, reparations and human rights aspired to protect "the abstract nakedness of being human," to borrow a laden phrase from Hannah Arendt, beyond the striking failures of the modern nation-state to ensure the sanctity, indeed the very continuity, of human existence (299).

While genocide and nuclear holocaust oriented the world imagination toward the specter of planetary annihilation—a prospect accelerated by the advent of Cold War hostilities between East and West under the threat of mutual assured destruction—the "final solution" and the atomic bombings also cleave from one another in significant ways. In the space of postwar Europe, the history of the Holocaust is settled: Nazis were perpetrators and Jews were victims. In contrast, in the space of postwar Asia, there was and continues to be little historical consensus as to who were the victims and who were the perpetrators. Although the United States deployed two atomic weapons on Japan, the status of those responsible for the bombings as well as those who perished remains indeterminate, and nuclear arms to this day are considered legal instruments of warfare. Thus, unlike the Holocaust, whereby West Germany paid significant reparations to Jews as well as to the state of Israel, and whereby the Holocaust is excoriated as the epitome of "evil," the possibility of reparations for the atomic bombings remains unthinkable.

Consider one illustrative example of this important but largely unremarked cleaving of accountability for state-sponsored mass murder—the cryptic inscription on the Memorial Cenotaph in the Hiroshima Peace Memorial Park: "Let all the souls here rest in peace; For we shall not repeat the evil."[1] Who is the "we," and what exactly is "the evil" that shall not be repeated? Does the first-person plural pronoun refer to Japan, the United States, or to humanity in general? And does "the evil" encompass the singular event of the obliteration of Hiroshima by a US atomic weapon, a wider history of Japanese colonization and aggression in its so-called "Greater East Asia Co-Prosperity Zone," a longer legacy of Western imperialism in the region, or perhaps war and violence in general? If the Memorial Cenotaph seeks to commemorate the many souls who died in Hiroshima, accountability for these losses dim in the face of such regnant indeterminacies. In short, we have numerous victims, but there are no clear perpetrators. How did this come to be? This article, drawn from my forthcoming book on reparations and human rights in Cold War Asia, focuses on how psychoanalysis might offer some critical insights to address this significant historical divide.

Reparation is a key term in political theory, but it is also a central concept in psychoanalysis, most notably object relations, although the two are rarely discussed in relation to one another. I have published on this crossing in other venues (Eng). This article considers more specifically unexamined links between psychic and political theories of trauma to investigate the constitution of victims deserving and undeserving of repair, in the face as well as in the absence of identifiable perpetrators, from the Holocaust to Hiroshima, and from Nuremberg to the Tokyo War Tribunals. I argue that the uneven distribution of trauma across different geopolitical spaces and times comes to carve out a privileged zone of exhausted and victimized humanity, with significant implications for addressing the injuries of violated human beings in Europe and elsewhere.

Section one, "The History of the Subject," begins with an analysis of debates between psychoanalytic accounts of trauma and legal designations of victims and perpetrators as they emerge in the context of European genocide, the International Military Tribunals at Nuremberg (IMT), and what Joan Wallach Scott describes as "the judgment of history" arising from those formative events. Here, I examine Ruth Ley's critique of Cathy Caruth's concept of "unclaimed experience," which helped to establish the interdisciplinary field of trauma studies and the problem of witnessing. Section two, "The Subject of History," proceeds with a discussion of John Hersey's August 1946 *New Yorker* essay "Hiroshima," which detailed the aftermath of the atomic bombing through the eyes of six surviving inhabitants of the devastated city. In the wake of that catastrophe, as well as the corresponding International Military Tribunals of the Far East (IMTFE) based on legal precedents established earlier at Nuremberg, I consider how psychoanalytic approaches to the history of the traumatized subject supplement the subject of Cold War history in search of an impossible historical consensus.

The History of the Subject

I begin my investigation of the history of the subject by turning to the topic of this special issue—psychoanalysis and history—to remind us that psychoanalysis itself has a history, one embedded in colonial modernity. In recent years, various scholars in postcolonial studies and new European history have examined psychoanalysis from this perspective: in relation to the "anthropological" Freud; as a developmental discourse of European civilization versus its primitive others; in regard to the circulation of psychoanalytic theories, methods, practices, and practitioners between metropole and colony; and in terms of the rise of authoritarianism and fascism. Concomitantly, on this side of the Atlantic, a growing number of race scholars have considered how psychoanalysis provides a vocabulary for analyzing not only sexual but also racial desires and prohibitions constituted by legacies of dispossession, slavery, and exclusion haunting the foundations of US law and society. In this section, I focus on the history of the *traumatized* subject—on how psychoanalytic and legal accounts of traumatized subjects converge and diverge to affirm particular victims and perpetrators, while forgetting others who perished, in the face of total war and violence.

Writing about patterns of unremitting trauma exhibited by military combatants returning from the World War I battlefront, Sigmund Freud first outlined his theory of the death drive in *Beyond the Pleasure Principle*. "There exists in the mind a strong *tendency* toward the pleasure principle," he observes, "but that tendency is opposed by certain forces or circumstances, so that the final outcome cannot always be in harmony with the tendency toward pleasure" (*SE* XVIII: 9–10; emphasis in original).[2] Similar to hysterics, the soldiers Freud treated suffered from "reminiscences." Unlike these civilian patients, however, their reminiscences could be traced not to a primordial or pleasurable object of desire but, unexpectedly, to their recent participation in grisly violence on the battlefield. Witnessing the involuntary reliving of their painful experiences—what he came to diagnose clinically as "shell shock" and what later would evolve into contemporary paradigms of "post-traumatic stress disorder" (PTSD)—Freud wrote *Beyond the Pleasure Principle* to understand better the human drive toward death. A decisive turning point in his metapsychology, Freud's slim volume raised disturbing questions about a repetition compulsion outside of conscious control, one overriding, irreconcilable to, and indeed *beyond* the pleasure principle: compulsive and unacknowledged behavior that oriented its subjects not toward life but toward death.

Freud offers a series of contemporary examples drawn from daily life to illustrate this inexplicable compulsion toward a scene of pain—of the traumatized subject's *reliving* of an agonizing incident rather than *"remembering it as something belonging to the past"* (18; emphasis in original). These cases range from veterans returning from the WWI battlefront to survivors of industrial and railway accidents and even to his infant grandson's quotidian distress at the unanticipated departures of his beloved mother from the domestic space of the nursery—the much-discussed "fort-da" episode of the volume. In chapter 3, Freud unexpectedly withdraws from the war-torn landscape around him to develop yet another aspect of the death drive drawn from the battlefields of historical fiction. Here, he analyzes Torquato Tasso's *La Gerusalemme Liberata* (1581), an early modern epic poem recounting the story of Tancred and Clorinda, ill-fated lovers on opposing sides of the First Crusade.

For Freud, Tancred's accidental slaying of Clorinda during the liberation of Jerusalem (1099) flies in the face of the pleasure principle because of the soldier's inadvertent repetition of its tragic violence. He explains:

> Its hero, Tancred, unwittingly kills his beloved Clorinda in a duel while she is disguised in the armour of an enemy knight. After her burial he makes his way into a strange magic forest which strikes the Crusaders' army with terror. He slashes with his sword at a tall tree; but blood streams from the cut and the voice of Clorinda, whose soul is imprisoned in the tree, is heard complaining that he has wounded his beloved once again. (22)

Clorinda's demise is exemplary—especially painful and moving for Freud—insofar as the repetition of its violent ends seems initiated not by Tancred's active cultivation of the death drive but rather by his passive subjection to it. That is, it seems impelled by some sort of unfathomable fate to which the crusader is subjected beyond *any* conscious will or control: "We are much more impressed by cases where the subject appears to have a *passive* experience," Freud observes, "over which he has no influence, but in which he meets with a repetition of the same fatality" (22; emphasis in original).

In *Unclaimed Experience,* the literary theorist Cathy Caruth famously analyzes this passage in Freud's book as precipitating a crisis of historical reckoning that troubles our understanding of the traumatized subject. Caruth's analysis of "unclaimed experience"—experience not subjectively motivated yet subjectively felt—addresses both the historical and ethical implications of a repetition compulsion that, as she observes, "exceeds, perhaps, the limits of Freud's conceptual or conscious theory of trauma" (2). While Freud highlights Tancred's unwitting repetition of violence against his beloved—his repeated wounding of Clorinda outside of conscious control—Caruth emphasizes instead the enigmatic and sorrowful voice of the departed who cries out from the wounded tree. She thereby focuses our attention on the involuted relationship between psychoanalysis and history, on the problem of a traumatic history that arises precisely "where *immediate understanding* may not" (11; emphasis in original).

The mystery of Clorinda's unanticipated cry marks a history of trauma that, according to Caruth, is "referential precisely to the extent that it is not fully perceived as it occurs; or to put it somewhat differently, that history can be grasped only in the very inaccessibility of its occurrence" (18). Tancred does not just inadvertently repeat his act of violence, she asserts, "but, in repeating it, he for the first time hears a voice that cries out to him to see what he has done" (2–3). If Clorinda's recurrent demise and incessant protests situate Tancred's death drive in a repetition compulsion decidedly beyond the pleasure principle and in excess of any semblance of conscious control, it also insists on an understanding of this tragedy as an unresolved quandary between the history of the traumatized subject and the subject of traumatic history. This predicament exceeds its hero in both comprehension and scope.

For Caruth, the story of Tancred is also the story of Clorinda: trauma marks "the enigma of the otherness of a human voice that cries out from the wound, a voice that witnesses a truth that Tancred himself cannot fully know" (3). Even more, as Matthew Aiello points out, it is at this precise moment of their heated exchange that the voice of Clorinda expands to encompass both Christian and Pagan alike, moving from the individual woman warrior to a much larger collective: "I was Clorinda," she tells the hero, "now imprisoned here/Yet not alone within this plant I dwell/For every Pagan lord and Christian peer/ . . . But here they are confined by magic's spell" (162).[3] In the final analysis, history is never simply one's own but rather, as Caruth concludes, "precisely the way we are implicated in each other's traumas" (24).

Put otherwise, Clorinda's cry links a history of war and violence that belongs as much to the surviving Tancred as to the departed Clorinda and, equally important, to the numerous others who perished in the religious battle and whose collective traces remain condensed in a haunting and imprisoned voice emanating from the dark forest. The agent of her destruction, Tancred thus simultaneously bears witness to Clorinda's survival—more precisely, to her living on in history as an enigmatic voice that remains stubbornly opaque to him. From this perspective, we might describe Clorinda's cry as a kind of ethical call concerning dead and injured subjects outside circuits of repair but who nonetheless demand response. Her cry implores the anguished hero to see and, even more, to take responsibility for what he has done. Moreover, it insists that we, in turn, devise a more complex accounting of the slaughtered enemy—indeed, those deprived of any remembrance. It requires, that is, a better understanding of historical response and responsibility engendered by the nomination of victims and perpetrators in the aftermath of violence, one produced across both psychic and political registers. Put simply, who is the victim in this scenario between the ill-fated lovers? And who is the perpetrator?

Caruth's influential approach to the inverted relations between trauma and history helped to establish the contemporary field of trauma studies. In the process, her theories have garnered both considerable approbation and resistance. The historian Ruth Leys has been an especially vocal critic of Caruth. Leys contends that, by positing a nonreferential theory of history, a history that escapes understanding at the moment of its occurrence, Caruth traffics in both historical and political relativism. In particular, Leys takes issue with Caruth's implication of Tancred as the privileged "traumatized victim" of this violent encounter. She insists that, if Tancred is a traumatized survivor of this battle, he should not in turn be allowed to claim the status of victim insofar as it is Clorinda who is the unfortunate object of his repeated and fatal aggressions. According to Leys, it is the murdered Clorinda who is decidedly the victim; the surviving Tancred is necessarily the perpetrator.

Leys interprets Caruth's case of mistaken identity as the effect of a wayward poststructuralist literary critic who, on the one hand, is committed to installing the Holocaust as the paradigmatic trauma of modernity but, on the other hand, wrongly associates the event with precipitating "an epistemological-ontological crisis of witnessing, a crisis manifested at the level of language itself" (268). For Leys, the political implications of Caruth's deconstructive project are dangerous if not execrable. By prioritizing the breakdown of language and communicability in her theory about trauma over the *Realpolitik* of European genocide, Leys argues, Caruth excuses Tancred's gendered violence against Clorinda and, by extension, muddles victim and perpetrator in the historical context of Nazi and Jew. If "the murderer Tancred can become the victim of the trauma and the voice of Clorinda testimony to *his* wound," Leys concludes, "then Caruth's logic would turn other perpetrators into victims too—for example, it would turn the executioners of the Jews into victims and the 'cries' of the Jews into testimony to the trauma suffered by the Nazis" (297).

There is much to unpack in Ley's critique of unclaimed experience—the blurring of victim and perpetrator, friend and enemy—including Ley's will to moral certitude and judgment. Let me begin by returning to Tasso's poem—to the fact that Clorinda is a Muslim and not a Jew and that the violent historical encounter narrated by the poet concerns a religious holy war between a Christian crusader (Tancred) and an infidel Muslim (Clorinda).[4] In the transposed context of the Crusades, Christians are insistently configured in Western history as victims of unwarranted Islamic aggression. This tradition of a defensive Western civilization engaged in holy war binds the medieval to early modern to modern periods, emerging from the Crusades, continuing through the Golden Horde, Ottoman Empire, and Reconquista, and transforming under Enlightenment into what political theorist Carl Schmitt has described as a "political theology" of secularized Christian ethics. In our contemporary context, it appears as an interminable "war on terror" fixing a secular (Christian) West in opposition to a fundamentalist (Muslim) East—an abiding feature of Orientalism explored by Edward Said in his eponymous treatise inaugurating the field of postcolonial studies. Seen from this religious-racial divide, one embedded in a long history of European colonialism and conquest, describing Tancred as perpetrator rather than victim, or as enemy instead of friend, may be neither as historically viable nor as clear cut as Leys would desire.

In other words, to interpret Tancred's gendered aggression toward Clorinda solely as prefiguring the culminating violence of the "final solution," of the destruction of European Enlightenment under total war, would thus require an inquiry into how an extended history of Orientalism and religious-racial conflict becomes subsumed into an exclusive narrative about the dissolution of Western civilization and its storied history of consciousness through the Nazi extermination of Jews. From this perspective, Tancred's gendered violence can be examined from an additional angle. To the extent that Tancred is traumatized, his psychic distress may not be the result of killing per se but rather the killing of a *wrong* object. In other words, Tancred's trauma may be the result of a case of mistaken identity. The "Christian peer" believes that he has killed a "Pagan lord" when, in fact, he has killed his beloved Clorinda disguised as such.

Tasso's recounting of their tragic love story in *La Gerusalemme Liberata* underscores the unthinkable and repeated violation of this human intimacy, of kith and kin. Clorinda's enigmatic voice thus draws immediate attention to the problem of a divided collective, to our uneven responses to the cries of *different* objects—indeed, to the cries of dead and injured subjects that go often unheeded and remain unheard. In the final analysis, the enigma of Clorinda's voice raises the urgent *ethical* problem of whose cries deserve recognition and whose cries remain outside consideration.

As they blur the divide between victims and perpetrators, Clorinda's exhortations simultaneously trouble the boundaries between friend and enemy, intimate and stranger, that define the dichotomized politics of war.

Equally urgently, they force us to consider how the socialization of Tancred's psychic predicaments and the politicization of his death drive facilitate the legal arrogation of trauma and victimhood—indeed, the legal nomination of traumatized *human beings* deserving of repair and to what political ends. Put in slightly different terms, we do not necessarily repair injured human beings. Rather, it is those to whom we offer repair who *become* the very sign of the human, personified by those who merit this concern as well as by those who render it—a closed circuit of the self-same. It is this wider legal and ethical territory, I suggest, that Caruth's reading of Freud and the crises of witnessing opens up for renewed investigation across the political and psychic domains.

Without endorsing Leys's hyperbolic conclusions regarding Caruth's mis-recognition of Nazi for Jew, and victim for perpetrator, what I would like to highlight in this exchange between the historian and the literary critic is precisely the slippage between psychoanalytic and legal accounts of trauma and the boundaries between victims and perpetrators that are established through their cleaving. On the one hand, trauma in psychoanalysis is catholic: in the face of unremitting war and violence anyone can potentially be traumatized. Unlike law, psychoanalytic theory makes no categorical distinction between victims and perpetrators. Victims and perpetrators alike can suffer from trauma's debilitating effects. Put otherwise, as Michael Rothberg writes, the "categories of victim and perpetrator derive from either a legal or moral discourse, but the concept of trauma emerges from a diagnostic realm that lies beyond guilt and innocence or good and evil" (90). Remember that Freud's paradigmatic victim of trauma in *Beyond the Pleasure Principle* is, in fact, the shell-shocked *German* soldier.

On the other hand, trauma in law is highly restricted: it is the property of victims. If trauma in psychoanalysis has a universalizing impulse and therapeutic demand, trauma in law is concerned precisely with its limited distribution. Indeed, we might say that through trauma's uneven allocations law attempts to fix cause and effect, guilt and innocence, seeking ultimately to contain the violence it both engenders and monopolizes as its sovereign right through a discourse of moral culpability. As such, the arrogation of trauma in law functions to nominate victims and, in turn, to designate perpetrators. In short, it creates and sustains a boundary between these opposing subject-positions through trauma's pointed distribution in a politics of liberal rights and recognition. I will return to these fraught issues in the following section.

From this perspective, Leys desire to fix Jew and Nazi as "victim" and "perpetrator" in the aftermath of genocide represents an effort to ensure what Scott has described as the "judgment of history." There is a "popular belief," Scott observes in the context of the Holocaust, "that there is a certain moral impeccability about history's judgment. It is a secular version of the biblical day of reckoning at the End of Times, serving the same phantasmatic function, providing transcendent reassurance for one's moral positions" (xi). In the face of unthinkable violence, the moral force of history—a moral force for which law purports to speak and by which law seeks to punish the evil deeds of mortals through a detailed historical accounting of their unspeakable crimes—is something we "cannot not want," to borrow a concept from Gayatri Spivak's critique of human rights (279).

Yet, as Scott points out, history is not only made by humans, albeit under circumstances often beyond our own making, but also resists any final closure. Conceiving of history as an autonomous moral force bending toward the arc of justice underwrites an impossible narrative of universal human progress and reason. In the same breath, it reinscribes the modern nation-state—the *victorious* nation-state that seeks to adjudicate crimes against humanity—as the privileged agent and site of that redemptive history. The conflation of the modern state with the foundations of law and history, Judith Butler asserts, is "the temporal framework that uncritically supports state power, its legitimating effect, and its coercive instrumentalities" (*Frames* 134–35). And that modern state, as numerous postcolonial and critical race theorists have emphasized, and as the catastrophe of the Holocaust starkly underscores, is a racial state.

Scott observes that, in our contemporary context, the Holocaust serves as the urtext for the judgment of history, stubbornly resistant either to extending its moral force or, as some critics engaged in postcolonial and psychoanalytic theory have argued, to sharing its monopolization of trauma studies with other catastrophic events outside of non-Western contexts.[5] The International Military Tribunal at Nuremberg, Scott writes, was defined by the chief prosecutor at the trial, US Associate Supreme Court Justice Robert Jackson, as "a literal enactment of a judgment of history that had come with victory in war; the war had delivered the verdict, the role of the Tribunal was to put it into effect" (1). Both historians and political theorists have identified the Holocaust and the war tribunals at Nuremberg as the origin for contemporary theories in international law concerning human rights, crimes against humanity, and illegal war.

In the process, the Holocaust has accrued such a singular status that every other modern historical trauma is insistently analogized to this master signifier of European disaster. "Trauma theory's failure to give the sufferings of those belonging to non-Western or minority groups due recognition," writes Stef Craps, "sits uneasily with the field's ethical aspirations" (3). I would like to focus on the ways in which psychoanalysis might be redeployed not only for interrogating the leaps of bad faith that configure the victorious nation-state as the final arbiter of the judgment of history but also for dislodging any one group's privileged hold on traumatized victimhood in a wider history of globalized violence and genocide in colonial modernity.

Given this argument, it is crucial to emphasize the different work that law and psychoanalysis perform—both in tandem as well as at odds with one another—to align trauma and victimhood with the figure of the injured human being deserving of recognition and repair. On the one hand, insofar as trauma is dispositive of injury and harm in contemporary discourses of human rights, crimes against humanity, and demands for reparation—and insofar as psychoanalysis is the privileged vocabulary of trauma—law and psychoanalysis work together to produce this privileged figure for rights and representation: the Holocaust survivor. On the other hand, insofar as trauma in psychoanalysis often levels distinctions between victims and perpetrators—and insofar as law and the judgment of history is dependent precisely on the nomination of one victim and one perpetrator—psychoanalysis and law are at odds with one another.

This cleaving should not be bemoaned. To be clear, I offer this observation not to disavow the moral clarity of the Holocaust. Indeed, in the face of resurgent right-wing nationalism across the globe today, moral certitude is something we cannot not want. Rather, I offer this insight as a way to understand more clearly how legal boundaries between victim and perpetrators are secured precisely through the arrogation of trauma, and how these legal boundaries might become displaced, to bring justice to those murdered who remain unacknowledged by historical judgment and intent.[6] If trauma functions across psychoanalytic and legal registers to designate particular victims and perpetrators, to produce narratives of cause and effect, to create acts of illegal aggression and legitimate defense, to justify the redistribution of property and human life after violent conflict, and to render the judgment of history precisely *under the sign of justice*, then their coming apart keeps open a space, in Jacques Derrida's words, for "a justice to come" (27). It maintains a space for those left outside the judgment of history to stake a claim—and for those survivors and witnesses such as Tancred to be reattuned to the cries of women, Muslims, Jews, and Christians alike. Indeed, it creates a space to heed their calls.

In shifting from the Holocaust to Hiroshima, from Nuremberg to the Tokyo War Tribunals, and from the space of the Transatlantic to the space of the Transpacific, the judgment of history recedes. There is no historical consensus on the confounded relationship between victim and perpetrator in the aftermath of nuclear genocide. How, then, might heightened attention to the history of the traumatized subject illuminate the subject of Cold War history in the Transpacific? Equally so, how does attention to atomic warfare and its Cold War effects in this region work to contest the political and psychic constitution of the Holocaust as universal history?

The Subject of History

On August 6, 1945, the United States military detonated "Little Boy" over Hiroshima. Three days later, it detonated "Fat Man" over Nagasaki. These two atomic bombs are the only nuclear weapons ever used on a human population. On August 15, 1945, Japan announced its unconditional surrender to the Allied forces. Government representatives from Allied and Axis powers signed the Japanese Instrument of Surrender aboard the battleship USS *Missouri* docked in Tokyo Bay on September 2, 1945, thus terminating hostilities in the Transpacific and officially ending World War II. General Douglas MacArthur concluded the event with these solemn words: "Let us pray that peace be now restored to the world, and that God will preserve it always. These proceedings are closed!"[7] MacArthur's wish for peace would hardly come to pass, especially in the embattled space of Asia throughout the ensuing Cold War.

The deployment of Little Boy and Fat Man marked the advent of the atomic age in world history, but it also connected the specter of nuclear annihilation indelibly to Asia. Though we imagine atomic destruction today in the language of nuclear universalism—one threatening the existence of every living creature and thing on planet earth—the Asian origins of "ground zero" should not be forgotten.

A little more than one year after the destruction of Hiroshima and Nagasaki, the *New Yorker* provoked a widespread debate on these tangled issues, publishing its most famous volume in the magazine's storied history. The August 31, 1946, issue bore a seemingly innocuous, light-hearted pink and green cover depicting various summer frolics in a bustling and verdant park (see fig. 1).[8]

There was little hint of the disturbing essay that lay inside. That essay was written by John Hersey (1914–1993), a WWII correspondent for *Time* and *Life* magazines and a Pulitzer Prize–winning novelist born in Tianjin, China to US missionaries. It took up the entire editorial space of the magazine, an unprecedented publishing act the *New Yorker* had never done before and has yet to repeat.

Narrated in restrained and understated prose, "Hiroshima" chronicled the immediate aftermath of the first atomic bombing from the intertwined

FIGURE 1. *New Yorker* cover.

perspectives of six surviving inhabitants of the decimated Japanese city: a Japanese Methodist minister who was trained in the United States (Reverend Mr. Kiyoshi Tanimoto), a white Jesuit missionary from Germany (Father Wilhelm Kleinsorge), a young surgeon working in the city hospital (Dr. Terufumi Sasaki), a retired physician (Dr. Masakazu Fujii), a widowed seamstress with three small children (Mrs. Hatsuyo Nakamura), and a young woman employed as a personnel clerk in a local factory office (Miss Toshiko Sasaki). Hersey had spent three weeks in May 1946 interviewing numerous survivors of the event, eventually settling on these six civilian witnesses. He asked each of his informants to describe what they had experienced in Hiroshima and to try to make sense of the destruction of what had once been a thriving port city as well as an enormous military-industrial complex of 380,000 inhabitants.[9] Each person, Hersey reports, wondered "why they lived when so many others died" (15).

The essay "Hiroshima" started where the "Talk of the Town" column usually begins, and it was accompanied by this concise editorial directive:

The *New Yorker* this week devotes its entire editorial space to an article on the almost complete obliteration of a city by one atomic bomb, and what happened to the people of that city. It does so in the conviction that few of us have yet comprehended the all but incredible destructive power of this weapon, and that everyone might well take time to consider the terrible implications of its use. (15)

William Shawn, the managing editor of the *New Yorker* at the time, believed that despite numerous public debates about, as well as political justifications for, the use of nuclear weapons, insufficient attention had been paid to the "human dimensions" of the atomic bombings. Shawn hoped to bring Japanese voices absent in US accounts of the catastrophe to the American public. Harold Ross, the founder and editor-in-chief of the magazine, supported Shawn's aspirations, noting in a letter to staff writer E. B. White that his managing editor felt the *New Yorker* had a special obligation "to wake people up [to the implications of nuclear warfare], and says we are the people with a chance to do it, and probably the only people that will do it, if it is to be done." (Ross)

In scaling up its focus from the "almost complete obliteration" of a Japanese city to the more expansive goal of awakening "everyone" to the "terrible implications" and "the all but incredible destructive power" of nuclear weapons, the editorial directive attempts to confront the existential threat to human survival itself initiated by atomic warfare, returning us to my citation of McCarthy in this article's opening epigraph. In so doing, the statement exemplifies how nuclear destruction was transformed into a universal predicament, a nuclear universalism affecting everybody and everything. It simultaneously indexes a psychoanalytic structure of trauma with significant political and ethical implications regarding whose suffering deserves recognition and whose must remain outside consideration. To borrow a formulation from Caruth on the problem of witnessing, Hiroshima is an unclaimed experience that we—the human race—have not "yet comprehended," a violence that has passed us by and one whose significance is yet to be determined. From another angle, Hersey's reportage draws attention to the problem of how we are implicated in one another's traumas as well as how psychic and legal deployments of traumatized victimhood will come to overdetermine the historical meaning of the disaster.

The August 31 issue of the *New Yorker* was a historic event in and of itself. Hersey's article was an instant sensation. In the social media lingo of today, it went "viral." The magazine rocketed off the newsstands, with scalpers demanding fifteen or twenty dollars for a publication whose normal cover price was fifteen cents. Fewer than two weeks later, beginning on September

9, 1946, the full text of "Hiroshima" was read nationally over four consecutive days on ABC radio, and it was subsequently broadcast in England, Canada, and Australia.

Harry Scherman, the director of the Book of the Month Club, sent a free copy of "Hiroshima" to his entire membership, remarking that "we find it hard to conceive of anything being written that could be of more importance at this moment to the human race" (Rothman). Hersey's publisher Alfred A. Knopf reprinted the 31,000-word article as a short book in October 1946, and it has remained in print ever since, with a circulation of more than three million copies as well as translations into numerous languages. Variously described as the most celebrated piece of journalism to emerge from WWII and as the most significant piece of American reportage in the twentieth century, Hersey's account, as Priscilla Wald observes, "documented the experience not only of the bombing of Hiroshima, but of the bombing as an event that produced a remarkable transformation. Hersey's article retroactively documents the metamorphosis of human beings and of humanity in the wake of Hiroshima" (4).

In part III of "Hiroshima," at the dead center of Hersey's four-part essay, the Reverend Mr. Kiyoshi Tanimoto, pastor of the Hiroshima Methodist Church, comes upon a sandspit in Asano Park—one perhaps not so dissimilar from that depicted on the frolicking cover of the magazine—a designated evacuation zone where numerous, shell-shocked survivors have gathered on the evening of August 6. There, Reverend Tanimoto encounters approximately twenty exhausted men and women, and he beckons them to board the small boat he is piloting. They do not—they cannot—move, and he realizes with sudden alarm that they are too weak to lift themselves away from the rising tide. A modern-day Charon navigating the blazing deltas of the devastated city, Reverend Tanimoto, Hersey writes

> reached down and took a woman by the hands, but her skin slipped off in huge, glove-like pieces. He was so sickened by this that he had to sit down for a moment. Then he got out into the water and, though a small man, lifted several of the men and women, who were naked, into his boat. Their back and breasts were clammy, and he remembered uneasily what the great burns he had seen during the day had been like: yellow at first, then red and swollen, with the skin sloughed off, and finally, in the evening, suppurated and smelly. With the tide risen, his bamboo pole was now too short and he had to paddle most of the way across with it. On the other side, at a higher spit, he lifted the slimy bodies out and carried them up the slope away from the tide. He had to keep consciously repeating to himself, "These are human beings." (28)

These entwined emphases on Hersey's "human beings," on Scherman's "human race," and on Ross's "human dimensions" of the atomic bombing collectively produced, departing from Wald's compelling insight, a very specific image and transformation of humanity in the irradiated space of postwar Japan.

Remarkably, the figure of the human emerges in Hiroshima *only in the wake of nuclear holocaust,* only in the wake of total war and destruction. That is, only after the inhabitants of the devastated city are incinerated and destroyed, only after they become "slimy," "swollen," and "suppurated" creatures, only after they are reduced to nothing more than a repugnant state of blood and viscera, do they appear to be human at all. What are the psychic and legal implications of this emergence of the human in ruins—this metamorphosis of traumatized Japanese humanity from the ashes and bones of Hiroshima? How do psychic and legal conceptions of victim and perpetrator come together, and how do they fall apart, in these redolent images of suffering and to what social and political effects?

Psychically, to return to a key point from section one, this emergence of the human depends precisely on the redistribution of trauma. Hersey's shocking portrayal of the violated civilians of Hiroshima transforms them in "a noiseless flash" from perpetrators of aggressive war into traumatized victims of atomic devastation. Indeed, by drawing attention to the physical ministrations of Reverend Tanimoto and the wretched strangers to whom he selflessly attends, "Hiroshima" raises the question of how attention and care are unevenly distributed in the aftermath of catastrophe, creating in their wake those subjects deserving and undeserving of repair. Even more, I argue, by focusing his essay on two Christian clerics—a Japanese minister trained at Emory University and a white Jesuit missionary from Germany—as well as two Japanese doctors who tend to the sick and wounded, Hersey's article creates a circuit of identification between the violated civilians of Hiroshima and the liberal white readership of the *New Yorker.* It lays the psychic foundation for the emergence of a nuclear universalism precisely through this reallocation of traumatized humanity between the West and war-torn Japan.

Legally, this postwar redistribution of trauma and remarkable transformation of an exhausted and eviscerated Japanese humanity into atomic victimhood is notable given unrelenting Allied depictions throughout WWII of the Japanese enemy as precisely anything but human. Seen as treacherous and fanatic kamikazes all-too-ready to sacrifice their collective lives in an irrational drive to victory for their emperor, the Japanese, as John Dower notes, were "subhuman, inhuman, lesser human, superhuman—all that was lacking in the perception of the Japanese enemy was a human like oneself" (*War* 9). It was precisely such dehumanization, Dower observes, that "facilitated the decisions to make civilian populations the targets of concentrated attack, whether by conventional or nuclear weapons" (*War* 11). While "Hiroshima" begins to enact this metamorphosis of the human psychically in August 1946 through representations of a devastated humanity, the project takes on increasingly urgent and expanded legal form throughout the postwar occupation of Japan by US-led Allied forces. How is it that Germany is rendered eternal perpetrator through the judgment of history, even as Japan emerges as traumatized victim deserving of repair outside any such historical judgment? If, as I emphasized above, psychic and legal appropriations of trauma work together to maintain a strict boundary between victim and perpetrator, how is it that a vanquished Japan and a defeated Germany end up on opposite sides of this binary?

In the closing pages of "Hiroshima," Hersey observes that many citizens of the destroyed city "continued to feel a hatred for Americans which nothing could possibly erase. 'I see,' Dr. Sasaki once said, 'that they are holding a trial for war criminals in Tokyo just now. I think that they ought to try the men who decided to use the bomb and they should hang them all'" (67–68). Suffice it to say, a war tribunal against the American victors for their deployment of not just one but two atomic weapons on civilian populations in Japan in what Dower describes as a "war without mercy" was as unthinkable in 1946 as it is inconceivable today.[10] If Japan emerges as victim of atomic disaster, there cannot be an implicated perpetrator of this violence. To return to an insight from Scott, a victorious US nation-state fighting in "the good war," in Studs Terkel's words, can only be the adjudicator not violator of crimes against humanity. In this regard, we might speculate that the emergence of traumatized humanity in Hiroshima—indeed, the remarkable transformation of Japan from evil object into human subject—serves as a compensatory mechanism meant not to indict the US nation-state but rather to ensure its sovereign innocence and, in turn, that of Japan. What are the psychic and legal logics of this gesture?

In stark contrast to the Holocaust in Germany, the deployment of nuclear weapons in Japan has never been legally categorized as a "crime against humanity" or as "genocide." Among weapons of mass destruction—nuclear, chemical, biological—only nuclear weapons are not prohibited in international law, an arrangement, as legal theorist Antony Anghie observes, that highlights the fact that "sovereignty *is* nuclear weapons" (66; emphasis in original).[11] Like Clorinda's unheeded cries, Dr. Sasaki's impassioned outburst lamenting the total destruction of his hometown thus raises an unresolved problem of historical response and responsibility marking the dream of human rights. It invokes, that is, the subrogation of the sovereignty of the victorious nation-state in the service of protecting the sovereignty, the sanctity, of the devastated individual. This aborted dream comes to frame the entire legal proceedings of the IMTFE with significant consequences for the murdered and dead who remain eccentric to the judgment of history.

The IMTFE, or Tokyo War Crimes Tribunal, convened on May 3, 1946, and adjourned more than two and a half years later on November 12, 1948. It was modeled on the IMT at Nuremberg, whose earlier prosecutions of Nazi war criminals served as the legal template for proceedings in Tokyo. Comparatively streamlined, Nuremberg commenced on November 20, 1945, and concluded less than a year later on October 1, 1946. Nuremberg exemplified an unprecedented model of international cooperation as Allied forces, led by prosecutors from the United States, sought to account for atrocities committed by the top leadership of the Third Reich. At the same time, it developed new categories for prosecution in international law—aggressive war, war crimes, genocide, and crimes against humanity—through what Schmitt lamented in *The* Nomos *of the Earth in the International Law of the* Jus Publicum Europaeum as the increasing criminalization of war in the first half of twentieth-century Europe.[12] The IMT was overseen by judges from four Allied powers: France, Great Britain, the Soviet Union, and the United States. It effectively produced unanimous judgments on the German leaders and organizations charged before it, providing a "dream of deliverance," an image of Nazis as eternal perpetrators and Jews as eternal victims in the world imagination (Scott xii).

In contrast, this final judgment of history could not have been further from what was achieved in Tokyo. Following Japan's surrender, General MacArthur became the Supreme Commander for the Allied Powers (SCAP) that led the postwar occupation and reintegration of Japan into the (Western) family of nations. Although he was initially appalled by the various demands of the defeated Japanese empire for relief, it is a "great irony of the subsequent history," as legal historian Harry N. Scheiber observes, "that in MacArthur's oversight of Japan in the Occupation era, he became the controlling figure in a process that in fact did work with great effectiveness to 'relieve Japan of . . . the physical and psychological burdens of defeat'" (241).

In its efforts to suppress the spread of communism in Asia through rollback and containment of Soviet and Chinese insurgency, and in its determination to transform what had been long histories of Western domination through direct colonialism and extraction in the region into structures of political modernization and economic development, the United States came quickly to prioritize the establishment of a postwar US-Japan Cold War political alliance. To the extent that the atomic bombings documented by Hersey began psychically to transform the enemy nation from being perpetrators of violence to victims of atomic catastrophe for his Western audience, the IMTFE and the seven-year Allied occupation of Japan legally shifted the country's own self-image from that of colonizer to that of colonized. Here, the psychic and legal worked in tandem to produce in the Western imagination a traumatized Japanese populace largely innocent of any war crimes—indeed, to transform prewar Japan from enemy and stranger into postwar friend and ally. As a consequence of this transformation, Chen Kuan-hsing observes, Japan was not forced to engage in "the reflexive work of deimperialization within its own territory and from grappling with its historical relations with its former colonies (Korea, Taiwan, and others) or its protectorate (Manchukuo)" (7). To be sure, from the perspective of these prior colonial subjects, Japan is hardly innocent. The IMTFE and its legacy, Lisa Yoneyama elaborates, "might as well be regarded as a showcase not so much for 'Victor's Justice' as for 'Victor's Exoneration' . . . [a] Cold War culture of impunity under US regional hegemony" ("Traveling" 66).

At MacArthur's insistence, Emperor Hirohito, the wartime head of the Japanese nation-state, was granted special immunity from prosecution, and the 1951 San Francisco Peace Treaty normalizing relations between Japan and the Allied powers took an especially compromised position on Japan's responsibilities for reparations.[13] Unlike the top political leadership of Germany, Hirohito was not subject to trial at the IMTFE and was spared even from testifying. MacArthur believed that protecting Hirohito and permitting the Emperor system to continue into the postwar period was critical for stabilizing Japan politically and rehabilitating its economy for capitalist development as one critical bulwark against the spread of communism in Asia. While the Japanese Constitution was overhauled and many reforms were introduced to limit Hirohito's "divine" powers, he was not deemed a war criminal and was allowed to remain on the Chrysanthemum Throne. As Dower writes, "With the full support of MacArthur's headquarters, the [IMTFE] prosecution functioned, in effect, as a defense team for the emperor" (*Embracing* 326). Remarkably, unlike Nuremberg, the defense team for the Japanese leadership on trial in Tokyo was staffed, in part, by US lawyers.

In Hirohito's stead, select high-ranking military officials were prosecuted and held responsible for leading the Japanese people and the emperor himself astray. Hirohito was characterized as a victim of circumstance, a naïve and innocent ruler manipulated by a cadre of fanatical military leaders led by General Hideki Tōjō. In short, as Yuki Tanaka, Tim McCormack, and

Gerry Simpson observe, like the civilian populace, "the Emperor, too, was a victim of the war" (xxix). This image of traumatized innocence, as Alexis Dudden notes, would adhere to "how the Japanese people in general would eventually be described in the preponderance of national storytelling that took its cue from this decision" (37). We thus witness how psychic and legal appropriations of trauma worked to sustain an image of Japanese victimhood that served to prevent any reckoning of the country with its prewar history of colonization and violence, as well as their postwar effects, throughout the Greater East Asia Co-Prosperity Zone. In this regard, the postwar ascendancy of US empire is not dissociated from but rather converges with prewar histories of Japanese domination in the Transpacific region.

This history of the traumatized Japanese subject returns us to the enduring problem of sovereignty and the modern racial state. A reformulated US-Japan partnership in full bloom within only half a dozen years after the end of an unspeakably brutal war might be seen as quite remarkable. Nonetheless, as the prewar Japanese colonial empire was succeeded by postwar US military might through a series of brutal wars and partitions in Northeast (North and South Korea) and Southeast Asia (North and South Vietnam), American empire was grafted onto Japanese colonialism with grave consequences for a much longer history of unacknowledged violence across the region.

Unlike Nuremberg, the IMTFE consisted of judges and prosecutors from China, India, and the Philippines as well as eleven Western Allied powers (Australia, Canada, France, Holland, New Zealand, the Soviet Union, the United Kingdom, and the United States). The participation of these Asian countries made the Tokyo War Crimes Tribunal as much a multiracial as a multinational event, yet little commentary on the IMTFE's racial implications has been proffered by scholars in either international law or Asian studies. However, judges and prosecutors from Taiwan, Korea, Malaysia, Singapore, Indonesia, Burma, and Indochina—colonial protectorates and other sites of Japanese occupation from the late nineteenth century—were notably absent from the Tokyo War Crimes Tribunal.

Their omission, as historian Yuma Totani notes, led to accusations of racial bias, indexing the enduring problem of race, racism, racial reparations, and the inhuman in colonial Asia (13). By focusing on war crimes against white prisoners-of-war and civilians, the IMTFE ignored numerous aggressions committed by the Japanese Imperial Army against its Asian colonial subjects. According to Totani, Allied powers, in particular the United States, withheld evidence of certain sensitive war crimes cases, including the "'comfort woman' system, medical experimentation and the bacteriological warfare committed by Unit 731, and atrocities targeted at the Asian civilian populations" deemed less than human (3).

In other words, the IMTFE focused on war crimes committed by colonizers (Japan) against other colonizers (Western Allied powers) rather than war crimes committed by colonizers against the colonized—a closed-circuit of injury and repair predicated on the universalizing, self-same project of European humanism.[14] After all, what a colonizing Europe did to the world, a colonizing Japan did to Asia, earning in the process its exemplary status as the only modern nation-state in the region. From another perspective, as Takashi Fujitani observes in *Race for Empire,* Japan and the United States were not just mortal enemies in World War II but also parallel empires in their respective projects of total war. For instance, as the Japanese conscripted colonized Korean male subjects into their Imperial Army, racialized Japanese American males were coerced into enlisting in the US military as a way to prove their loyalty to the US nation-state and to secure release from the concentration camps in which they and their families were detained en masse throughout WWII. In the process, to refigure McCarthy's trenchant observations, Hersey's "insipid falsification of the truth of atomic warfare" raises the urgent question of exactly which murdered and sacrificed populations Hersey would have had to interview to bring justice to the dead.

Unsurprisingly, the verdicts reached at the IMTFE were riven with disagreement and dissent. Of the eleven members, eight judges delivered a majority opinion of guilt, qualified by two concurrent opinions, and opposed by three separate dissenting opinions. In contrast to Nuremberg, where the justices "overcame their differences" to deliver a unanimous ruling, there would be no final judgment of history in Tokyo (Totani 12). There was not even, as Marc Gallicchio observes, agreement on what to call the war (7). In the final analysis, without any consensual postwar history regarding Japanese empire in the Transpacific in the aftermath of atomic war, any prospects of making legal claims on the defeated nation-state for injury and redress on the part of its prewar colonial subjects were rendered moot.

In a 1,235-page opinion dissenting from each and every guilty verdict handed down by the Tribunal, Justice Radhabinod B. Pal of India, a forthright critic of Western colonialism, insisted that a judgment on Japan's war crimes could not be made in good conscience without first giving an account of prior atrocities committed by Western powers in Asia and Africa. To do otherwise would be legally untenable (Tanaka 27). "Was it not the West that had coined the word 'protectorate' as a euphemism for 'annexation'?" Pal asks. "And has not this constitutional fiction served its Western inventors in good stead?" (Tanaka 135). Pal argued that the Japanese Kwantung Army and

Western Allies were partners in crime. He condemned Western powers for prosecuting Japan while ignoring their own atrocities rooted in much longer colonial histories of Western dominance leading up to the atomic bombings (Tanaka 134). Indeed, Pal offered the unthinkable analogy between genocide in Europe and nuclear holocaust in Asia, directly connecting the "final solution" of a defeated Germany with the deployment of nuclear weapons on Hiroshima and Nagasaki by a victorious United States (Tanaka 295).

This, of course, is the precise analogy that the racial state and its judgment of history refuses to, indeed cannot, confront. However, it is an analogy that is exposed precisely by the (mis)alignments between legal and psychic theories of the history of the traumatized subject. As holocaust and genocide migrate from Europe to Asia, the coming together of psychoanalysis and law in a history of trauma circumscribes a Western limit to the figure of the human—to crimes against humanity and to war crimes—restricting their legal and ethical ambit. This history of the traumatized subject thus underwrites the subject of an unresolved colonial history of violence, one beginning with European exploration and expansion, extending to Japanese empire-building throughout East and Southeast Asia, and inherited by an ascendant US nation-state during the American Century. Indeed, in the larger project from which this article is drawn, I argue that the uneven distribution of the human to a devastated Japan after the atomic bombings, redress for the wartime internment of Japanese Americans in the name of the civil and civil rights, and unsuccessful postwar legal claims for reparations by comfort women conscripted into sexual slavery and rendered inhuman by the Japanese imperial army limn a Cold War history of what I describe as the problem of *racial* reparations and the human in the space of the Transpacific.

To be sure, as the comparison between the Holocaust and Hiroshima emphasizes—and as transitional justice movements across the decolonizing world such as South Africa's Truth and Reconciliation Commission underscore—when the sovereign integrity of the victorious nation-state is deemed to be the political priority, a juridical process of reckoning with violence and conflict will insistently recognize a proliferating chain of traumatized victims in the absence of clear perpetrators held to legal accountability. As a result, the psychic and legal arrogation of trauma come together not to uphold a strict boundary between designated victims and perpetrators but rather to generate a politics of recognition—a politics of individual suffering—that bypasses the judgment of history, the imperative for material redistribution, and the will to justice. If a politics of victim and perpetrator produced through the consensual judgment of history is the sine qua non of any legal claim for reparation—as the unresolved record of comfort women in the Transpacific and of chattel slavery in the Transatlantic highlight—we ought to begin theorizing how to reconfigure repair and redress outside paradigms of sovereignty altogether. We must do so neither for the sake of the victorious nation-state nor in the name of the human but rather on behalf of those rendered inhuman by their fraught political legacies and loaded psychic dynamics. ■

David L. Eng is the Richard L. Fisher Professor of English at the University of Pennsylvania, where he is also a professor of Asian American Studies, Comparative Literature and Literary Theory, and Gender, Sexuality, and Women's Studies. He is the coauthor (with Shinhee Han) of *Racial Melancholia, Racial Dissociation: On the Social and Psychic Lives of Asian Americans* (2019).

ACKNOWLEDGMENTS

Many thanks to Zahid Chaudhary, Ed Cohen, Takashi Fujitani, Teemu Ruskola, and the editors of *History of the Present,* especially Joan Scott, for their incisive comments on this article. Thanks as well to my Dissertation Workshop Group at the University of Pennsylvania—Melanie Abeygunawardana, Matthew Aiello, Thomas Conners, and Ava Kim—for their excellent insights on the project.

NOTES

1 See Lisa Yoneyama's *Hiroshima Traces* for a detailed analysis of the epigraph debate concerning the inscription on the Memorial Cenotaph, especially 16–18.

2 I borrow the following two paragraphs of my analysis of the death drive from my essay "Colonial Object Relations."

3 I want to thank Matthew Aiello for drawing my attention to the emergence of the collective represented by Clorinda's voice in this passage. I want to thank David Young Kim for his assistance with the original Italian.

4 Stef Craps makes an overlapping observation: "Given that this episode concerns the killing of an Ethiopian woman by a European crusader, an orientalist dimension which Caruth does not acknowledge, her reading of this tale can be seen to illustrate the difficulty of trauma theory to recognize the experience of the non-Western other" (15).

5 In addition to Craps and Rothberg, see Judith Butler's *Parting Ways: Jewishness and the Critique of Zionism* (New York: Columbia University Press, 2012).

6 Writing about modern-day Israel, Scott observes: "Jews were defined as potential victims in need of the protection of the Israeli security state. And, in an ironic twist, the achievement of their place in history came, for the Jewish victims of the Nazi genocide, in the form of an ethnically defined nation-state, which . . . rests on 'the notion that legitimate rule by *the people* over territory presupposed the absence (physically or culturally) of *other peoples* occupying that territory'" (20).

7   "Japanese Sign Final Surrender—1945." The National Archives.gov., June 16, 2021. youtu.be/4EqRTWMVqMY.

8   August 2021 marks the seventy-fifth anniversary of the magazine's publication of Hersey's article. Erin Overbey, the current archive editor at the *New Yorker,* reports that the editors of Hersey's essay realized "the cover they'd chosen for the issue—a vibrant, bucolic scene of children and families frolicking in a park—might not give readers enough warning about the devastating nature of its contents." So, they quickly added a white band to the forty-thousand newsstand copies of the issue that were being distributed in New York City. The band read: "HIROSHIMA: THIS ENTIRE ISSUE IS DEVOTED TO THE STORY OF HOW AN ATOMIC BOMB DESTROYED A CITY." See Erin Overbey, "A Rare Discovery on the Seventy-Fifth Anniversary of John Hersey's 'Hiroshima.'" the *New Yorker,* August 26, 2021, www.newyorker.com/books/double-take/a-rare-discovery-on-the-seventy-fifth-anniversary-of-john-herseys-hiroshima (accessed on August 27, 2021)

9   At the time of the bombing, Hiroshima's wartime population had been reduced to 250,000 from 380,000. Approximately, 90,000–146,000 people perished within two to four months of the atomic detonation, half of those casualties occurring on the first day. A sprawling military-industrial complex, Hiroshima was a hub for Japan's enormous war efforts, the base of the notorious Fifth Infantry deployed to Southeast Asia during the war, and a center for the production of ships, munitions, and other materiel for the Imperial Army. The city also relied on conscripted labor from Japan's various colonial possessions in East and Southeast Asia. Had the Imperial Palace in Tokyo come under threat, Emperor Hirohito was to evacuate to Hiroshima.

10 Consider, for example, President Barack Obama's 2016 visit to the Hiroshima Peace Memorial Park during which the president spoke at length about the costs of war and the need for peace and nuclear disarmament but without apologizing for any US actions during World War II, including the use of atomic weapons.

11 Alexis Dudden adds that the "chronic inability to confront how America's use of nuclear weapons against Japanese people in 1945 might constitute the kind of history for which survivors would seek an apology, let alone why the use of such weapons might represent a crime against humanity, is sustained by Washington's determination to maintain these weapons as the once and future legitimate tools of the national arsenal" (128–29). Hersey himself described the second bombing of Nagasaki as a criminal action.

12 It is ironic to note that, as Scott adds, "The London Charter listed aggressive warfare as one of the counts against the Nazis. It was signed by the Allies on August 8, 1945, the day [before] the United States bombed Nagasaki, two days after the bombing of Hiroshima; in February, the British and Americans had firebombed the city of Dresden—many thousands of civilians were killed in those raids. . . . Were these defensive operations or instances of aggressive warfare? And was it possible to insist that all war was a crime?" (12)

13 While the San Francisco Peace Treaty recognized that Japan should pay reparations, it also conceded that the Japanese government did not have the means to do so at the time, allowing the nation to prioritize its economic recovery over the needs of other nations. Japan eventually signed treaties with its East Asian neighbors to pay repa-

rations. However, these payments largely took the form of loans to its former colonies such as South Korea, which in turn allowed Japanese corporations to profit.

14 A diplomatic missive from the Australian Department of External Affairs to the United States Government reveals the colonial priorities and racial stakes of the human at the IMTFE: "many of the foulest [Japanese] atrocities in modern history [were] committed not only against the peoples of Eastern and Southeastern Asia but against nationals of Australia, the United States, and other Allied powers." Draft telegram to the Australian Embassy, Washington, DC, September 30, 1946, Department of External Affairs Records, A 1067/1, P 46/10/10/3, in the Australian National Archives, Canberra, Australia. Cited in Scheiber (246).

WORKS CITED

Anghie, Antony T. "Politic, Cautious, and Meticulous: An Introduction to the Symposium on the Marshall Islands Case." *AJIL Unbound* III (2017): 62–67. doi.org/10.1017/aju.2017.27.

Arendt, Hannah. *The Origins of Totalitarianism.* 1951; repr., New York: Harcourt, 1968.

Butler, Judith. *Frames of War: When Is Life Grievable?* London: Verso, 2009.

Butler, Judith. *Parting Ways: Jewishness and the Critique of Zionism.* New York: Columbia University Press, 2012.

Caruth, Cathy. *Unclaimed Experience: Trauma, Narrative, and History.* Baltimore: Johns Hopkins University Press, 1996.

Chen, Kuan-hsing. *Asia as Method: Toward Deimperialization.* Durham, NC: Duke University Press, 2010.

Craps, Stef. *Postcolonial Witnessing: Trauma Out of Bounds.* New York: Palgrave, 2013.

Derrida, Jacques. "The Force of Law." In *Deconstruction and the Possibility of Justice,* edited by Drucilla Cornell, Michael Rosenfeld, and David Gray Carlson, 3–67. New York: Routledge, 1992.

Dower, John W. *Embracing Defeat: Japan in the Wake of World War II.* New York: New Press, 1999.

Dower, John W. *War without Mercy: Race and Power in the Transpacific.* New York: Pantheon Books, 1986.

Dudden, Alexis. *Troubled Apologies among Japan, Korea, and the United States.* New York: Columbia University Press, 2008.

Eng, David L. "Colonial Object Relations." *Social Text* 34, no. 1 (2016): 1–19.

Freud, Sigmund, James Strachey, Anna Freud, and Carrie Lee Rothgeb. "Beyond the Pleasure Principle." In vol. 18 of *The Standard Edition of the Complete Works of Sigmund Freud,* 1–64. London: Hogarth Press, 1957.

Fujitani, Takashi. *Race for Empire: Koreans as Japanese and Japanese as Americans during World War II.* Berkeley: University of California Press, 2013.

Gallicchio, Marc. *The Unpredictability of the Past: Memories of the Asia-Pacific War in US–East Asian Relations.* Durham, NC: Duke University Press, 2007.

Hersey, John. "Hiroshima." *New Yorker,* August 31, 1946, 15–68.

Leys, Ruth. *Trauma: A Genealogy.* Chicago: University of Chicago Press, 2000.

McCarthy, Mary. "The Hiroshima *New Yorker.*" *Politics,* November 1946, 367.

Ross, Harold. "Letter to E. B. White." Wikipedia. en.wikipedia.org/wiki/Hiroshima_ (book)#cite_ref-New_7-0 (accessed June 16, 2021).

Rothberg, Michael. *Multidirectional Memory: Remembering the Holocaust in the Age of Decolonization.* Stanford, CA: Stanford University Press, 2009.

Rothman, Steve. "The Publication of 'Hiroshima' in the *New Yorker.*" www.hersey hiroshima.com/hiro.php? (accessed June 16, 2021).

Said, Edward. *Orientalism.* New York: Vintage Books, 1978.

Scott, Joan Wallach. *On the Judgment of History.* New York: Columbia University Press, 2021.

Scheiber, Harry N. "Taking Responsibility: Moral and Historical Perspectives on the Japanese War-Reparations Issues." *Berkeley Journal of International Law* 20, no. 1 (2002): 233–49.

Schmitt, Carl. *The* Nomos *of the Earth in the International Law of the* Jus Publicum Europaeum, translated by G. L. Ulman. New York: Telos Press, 2006.

Schmitt, Carl. *Political Theology: Four Chapters on the Concept of Sovereignty,* translated by George Schwab. Chicago: University of Chicago Press, 2006.

Spivak, Gayatri Chakravorty. *Outside in the Teaching Machine.* New York: Routledge, 1993.

Tanaka, Yuki, Tim McCormack, and Gerry Simpson, eds. *Beyond Victor's Justice? The Tokyo War Crimes Trial Revisited.* Leiden, Netherlands: Brill, 2011.

Tasso, Torquato. *La Gerusalemme liberata,* edited by Pietro Papini. Florence, Italy: Sansoni, 1917.

Terkel, Studs. *The Good War: An Oral History of World War II.* New York: New Press, 1984.

Totani, Yuma. *The Tokyo War Crimes Trial: The Pursuit of Justice in the Wake of World War II.* Cambridge, MA: Harvard University Asia Center, 2008.

Wald, Priscilla. "Cells, Genes, and Stories: Human Being Under the Microscope in the Aftermath of War." Paper presented at the Ward-Phillips Lecture Series "Human Being after Genocide," University of Notre Dame, Notre Dame, IN, April 1, 2009.

Yoneyama, Lisa. *Hiroshima Traces: Time, Space, and the Dialectics of Memory.* Berkeley: University of California Press, 1999.

Yoneyama, Lisa. "Traveling Memories, Contagious Justice: Americanization of Japanese War Crimes at the End of the Post-Cold War." *Journal of Asian American Studies* 6, no. 1 (2003): 57–93.

Michelle Stephens

Just In Time
Managing Fear and Anxiety at the End of the World

ABSTRACT In the early 2000s, Dipesh Chakrabarty powerfully defined the historical terms at stake in the shift from the postcolonial to the Anthropocene era, arguing that the posthuman image of a world without us profoundly contradicts historical practices for visualizing time. The notion of history that his essay foregrounded, however, can itself be historicized as a fantasy of modernity, one Édouard Glissant described as "History [with a capital H]." Using Glissant's psychoanalytically inflected insights as a starting point, this article argues that our dominant modes of historical thinking are always already colored by the anxieties and neurotic symptoms of the colonialist viewer. The argument then traces experimental hypotheses regarding the near and deep history of the human by key figures from the late nineteenth through the early twenty-first centuries—such as Sigmund Freud and Octave Mannoni, Paul Gilroy and Sylvia Wynter, and Frank Wilderson and Bruno Latour—as they grapple with two intimations: that the subject picturing a "world without us" is neurotic and that alternative historical sensibilities may lie on the other side of our apocalyptic imagination of the "end of the world."

KEYWORDS end of the world, Anthropocene, History [with a capital H], colonial misanthropy, Afro-pessimism

We have reached the end of a certain historical arc.

—Bruno Latour, *Down to Earth*

Folks cried and laughed and hugged each other and called out loud for the end of the world.

—Frank Wilderson III, *Afropessimism*

In his 2007 book on climate change and global warming, *The World without Us*, Alan Weisman posits a thought experiment: "Picture a world from which we all suddenly vanished," and then asks, would "the world without us . . . miss us?" (3–5). For historian Dipesh Chakrabarty, this image of a world

HISTORY of the PRESENT ▪ A Journal of Critical History ▪ 12:1 ▪ April 2022
DOI 10.1215/21599785-9547230 © 2022 Duke University Press

without us, a defining trope of the Anthropocene era, profoundly contradicts and confuses "our usual historical practices for visualizing times, past and future, times inaccessible to us personally" ("Climate" 197–98). As Chakrabarty asserts further in his canonical essay "The Climate of History: Four Theses": "To go along with Weisman's experiment, we have to insert ourselves into a future 'without us' in order to be able to visualize it" (201). However, framing our "historical sense of the present," *the now*, as threatened by pending catastrophe and the self-annihilation of the human, is "deeply destructive of our general sense of history" (201). A world without us, in other words, is a world without history, and without a historical sensibility we lose our framework for understanding the relationship between humans and the world, in the fullness of time.

Posthumanist announcements of the removal of the human in the Anthropocene era from the center of the global and historical narrative resonate with Chakrabarty's alarming conclusion that, "anthropogenic explanations of climate change spell the collapse of the age-old humanist distinction between natural history and human history" (201). As Jonathan Pugh notes, islands are often the metaphoric hyperobjects used to describe this setting of an Anthropocene "world without us" (65). Anthropocene writing affirms the "humbling powers of more-than-human relations," joining a discourse of the "more than human" that developed in the field of geography in the early years of the twenty-first century and spread throughout much of the social sciences. Focusing on the work of Timothy Morton, Pugh argues that scholars of the Anthropocene focus almost exclusively on "hyperobjects," such as global warming, that are "simply too great for the human intellect to grasp." The idea of a "world without us" becomes a metaphor for the deeper concern that "our transforming planet is revealing how humbled humans are by the overwhelming power and forces of the world" (65–67). Chakrabarty's fear of the collapse of human history and natural history, then, reflects a greater fear of that which is un-narratable in conventional historical terms, a "natural" history that involves forces and time scales well beyond the human imagination. We hear again the traces of Chakrabarty's lament, that this "more-than-human" world is a world without us, with forces at too grand a scale to be comprehensible with our historical understanding.

As powerful as Chakrabarty's analysis was for defining the historical terms at stake in the shift from, what we might call, the postcolonial to the Anthropocene era, the notion of history his essay foregrounds can itself be historicized.[1] In other words, what Chakrabarty fears—human and natural history collapsed—describes not necessarily history writ large, nor human sensibilities re history writ large, but rather a particular relationship to time reflecting a certain specific, dominant, historical sensibility. Carola Dietze describes this notion of history as a product of European modernity and modernization, whereby "Europe" becomes a signifier for "the concept of political modernity and the narratives of nation-building, rationalization, secularization, and so forth, connected with it—narratives used in the writing of history as well as in the social sciences" (70–71). For Bruno Latour, this is the historical worldview held by "the Moderns," the belief that "history [was] going to continue to move toward a common horizon, toward a world in which all humans could prosper equally" (*Down to Earth* 2).[2] While the anticipation of a "world without us" signals an awareness of planetary historical forces simultaneously precipitated by and beyond human control, the "end of the world" sensibility reflects an awareness of the consequences of this imagined future for our prior ways of understanding the past. The sense of apocalypse, in other words, is more accurately "the revelation of a certain regime of historicity," and Anthropocene fears reflect less the declining faith in history than a presentiment that history as we have known it may be undergoing revision and transformation (Latour, *Gaia* 196).

In the early 1980s, in a reflection titled, "Concerning history as neurosis," the Caribbean poet and theorist Édouard Glissant posited a different kind of thought experiment than Weisman's. "Would it be ridiculous," he asked, "to consider our lived history as a steadily advancing neurosis?" (65–66). Often when we think of the slave trade, colonialism, and slavery, we focus on their damaging effects on the histories and psyches of the colonized and enslaved. Glissant's speculation, however, includes European colonizers and their descendants in whom the "traumatic shock" of colonial modernity also produced repressions and "everyday fantasies as symptoms." One of these fantasies is the notion of an objective history of modernity itself: "History is a highly functional fantasy of the West, originating at precisely the time when it alone 'made' the history of the World" (64). Glissant names this idea of history "History [with a capital *H*]," the capitalization signaling a certain human notion, articulation, and narrativization of time that has been frozen, and which finds its origins in European colonialism (64).

Glissant's speculation is intriguing precisely for its implications. If the subject picturing a "world without us" is neurotic, caught up in fantasies that are symptomatic of a distorted view of world and self, then nothing about that picture can be understood as simply a forecasting or projection of and for *all* of humanity into a frightening anthropogenic future. The vision, in other words, always limited to a few "Moderns" even if globalized and performed as if for many, was always already colored by the anxieties and neurotic symptoms of the colonialist viewer. Glissant's hypothesis allows us to bring into view a hidden ontological frame obscured by Weisman's account and alarming to Dipesh Chakrabarty for the wrong reasons. A broader understanding of an intertwined human and natural past requires a profound reimagining of what it has meant, and what it will have meant, to be human during colonial modernity.

If the notion of history Chakrabarty is concerned about reflects a particular world view, then his concerns need to be placed side by side with an account of History such as Glissant's. Doing so moves our discussion from the framework of the subaltern's dialectical relationship with "History [with a capital *H*]," to that of a neurotic History's more entangled relationship with European modern, African diasporic, and other, multiple, worldly, nonhistories, *all* "characterized by ruptures" rather than narrative continuity (61). What this pairing with African diasporic and Caribbean traditions of decolonial thought brings into focus is less that the Anthropocene prefigures the loss of historical sensibility writ large. Rather, the Anthropocene is itself reflective of an emergent historical sensibility, an epistemic paradigm shift captured in the apocalyptic imagination of an "end of the world."

This paradigm shift shakes up our frozen narratives of the history of modernity and draws our attention to new structures of feeling and modes of engaging with the past, in *our* time of the present. The end to the human world, *as we have known it historically*, brings intimations of death to some, for example, to the Moderns Latour describes as experiencing a loss of faith in a declining historical arc. Psychoanalytic modes of inquiry and theory have provided, throughout the late nineteenth, twentieth, and early twenty-first centuries, some of the clearest indications of this anxious and melancholic state in the neurotic split subject of colonial modernity. However, there are other competing affects at the "end of the world," as captured in the Frank Wilderson quote used to open this article. Afro-pessimists are having a different experience of the end of modernity than the Moderns. For certain descendants of an anti-Black, racist, colonial modernity, an end to the neuroses of the past may help us to understand better other features of the history of the present emerging in their wake. This may be *just in time* to imagine, or prefigure, a futurity just beyond or on the other side of now.

As I write, we are living in a time of reckonings—with unchanging racial injustice, continued climate change, and nonhuman actors as the agents of a global pandemic that has killed, as of today's count, more than three million humans.[3] It is a time to reflect on our notions of the human, of history, and of the world as they relate to how we think about the history of the present. It is also time to assess what they reveal about the constitutive and instantiating terms of how we have been living our humanity. Our contemporary awareness of ourselves as humans, as a geophysical force with the ability to impact directly the future of the planet, has led for good and ill to an expansion of our notion of the human. Herein lies the rationale for thinking about our present conjuncture through the lens of psychoanalysis and history.

The Anthropocene can be seen not just as the geologic and historic era that reveals the consequences of man's egocentric relationship to the world. It could also be seen as a moment of awakening from a dream. In what follows, I track the traces of this dream of modernity through key twentieth and early twenty-first century writers and thinkers, across the fields of psychoanalysis (Octave Mannoni and Sigmund Freud) and Black diasporic studies (Paul Gilroy and Sylvia Wynter). These traces flesh out and build on Chakrabarty's, Glissant's, and Latour's framing and historicizing insights, illuminating new meanings of the history of modernity that have been emerging in the Anthropocene from the 1980s on. This article suggests a new structure of feeling in our time, emergent across multiple domains and discourses, appearing more regularly in the affect and tone of scholarship in the early twenty-first century. This structure of feeling, captured in an invocation of the end of the world, emanates from both our depressive fears (the Moderns) and our manic hopes (Afro-pessimistic subjects) that we are closer to the end of a dream or fantasy of history imagined and defined, hegemonically, by colonial modernity.

In the Time of Modernity

In 1945, three months into a psychoanalysis with Jacques Lacan, the French psychoanalyst in training, Octave Mannoni, found himself returning to the island of Madagascar, a place where he had lived since 1925 and held a number of civil servant positions. As director of the island colony's information services, in the 1940s Mannoni was an agent of the French empire, a European poised at the onset of decolonization. Just two years later, the Mouvement Démocratique de la Rénovation Malgache (MDRM) organized a widespread anticolonial revolt in Madagascar, leading to riots and their brutal suppression by the French. These events would inspire Mannoni to write *Prospero and Caliban: The Psychology of Colonization*, published in 1950.

In his account, Mannoni coined the phrase a "Prospero complex" to describe European colonizers' states of mind upon their arrival in new worlds. The colonizer-to-be approached the islands and mainlands he "discovered" in the Americas as pristine, blank spaces, wild, natural sites without historical sensibility. This approach reflected a certain psychic trait, "partly misanthropic, or at any rate anti-social," which led to a wish fulfillment fantasy of the new world as representing "the lure of a world without men" (101). Mannoni continued:

> It is the existence of this trait which makes the idea of the desert island so attractive, whereas in reality there is little to be said for it, as the real Robinsons discovered. The desert islands of the imagination are, it is true, peopled with imaginary beings, but that is after all their *raison d'être*. Some of the semihuman creatures the unconscious creates, such as Caliban or the Lilliputians, reveal their creator's desire to denigrate the whole of mankind. . . .
>
> The real attraction of solitude . . . is that if the world is emptied of human beings as they really are, it can be filled with the creatures of our own imagination: Calypso, Ariel, Friday. (101)

Mannoni described the ways in which the narcissistic or schizoid colonizer-self retreats into his own mind in the face of an encounter with an unfamiliar Otherness—both the otherness of the worlds themselves and of the people they may find there.

There is a historical line, and narrative, that connects Weisman's anthropogenic "world without us" back to Mannoni's "world without men," the Anthropocene era back to what Chris Lane has called the era of "colonial misanthropy" reflected in Mannoni's account (139). The Anthropocene can be seen not just as the geologic and historic era that reveals the consequences of Man's egocentric relationship to the world. Moreover, it is the extension, unseen at the time of its origin, of a profoundly *misanthropic* gaze as an underlying, determinative affective structure of modernity. In the "misanthropocene" of colonial modernity, certain historical groups have imagined ourselves, the human, as somehow able to be away and separate from the earth and our shared earthly being, therefore in flight toward death, toward species-death. We have been in a dream, constituting the rest of the world, of life, as somehow separate from ourselves, unaware that by denying the rest of the world's sentience and animacy, we were in danger of rendering ourselves, and possibly everyone and everything else along with us, inanimate. The setting of this dream has often been an island, "the island" as both a physical and epistemic setting for what Mannoni would insightfully recognize as the modern colonial's distorted, neurotic relationship to the world. Mannoni's Prospero complex was precisely an example of a psychic structure made visible when seen from the perspective of Glissant's thought experiment, that is, in the aftermath of a History seen by, projected, and recorded as if real through the eyes of the colonial neurotic.

Mannoni's Moderns were European colonial subjects in a profound psychic break with the modes of subjectivity possible in the European metropoles. In his mid-twentieth-century psychoanalytic theory of a neurotic colonialist structure of feeling, Mannoni linked this break to insecurities rooted in childhood. The European who travels from metropole to colony carries a "'primitive' image of the world" with him from childhood, held "in mind" as a fantasy of world and other:

> When the child suffers because he feels that the ties between himself and his parents are threatened and at the same time feels guilty because after all it is he who wants to break them, he reacts to the situation by dreaming of a world where there are no real bonds, a world which is entirely his and into which he can project the images of his unconscious, to which he is attached in the way which is to him the most satisfying. Now, it is this imaginary world which is, strictly speaking, the only 'primitive world' and it serves, so to speak, as the model of all other worlds. The dream-world in the child's mind exists side by side with the world of reality, it penetrates that world and organizes it emotionally and gradually it comes to coincide with it more or less exactly. (207)

Key European literary works revealed the ways in which this internal fantasy could be maintained and sustained, in conditions of physical, and/or psychic, isolation. In Daniel Defoe's novel *Robinson Crusoe*, for example, Crusoe's misanthropic neurosis requires isolation from others—European and otherwise—as the precondition for a form of psychological health: "In fact, Daniel Defoe's story recounts *the long and difficult cure of a misanthropic neurosis*. His hero, who is at first at odds with his environment, gradually recovers psychological health in solitude" (100). And Crusoe's dream— which is itself the condition for psychic health—was also Europe's dream: "Thence emerged the story of Robinson, in the way a dream might occur. When this dream was published, however, all Europe realized that it had been dreaming it" (103). The dream had begun more than a century earlier, in such iconic works as William Shakespeare's 1610–1611 play *The Tempest*, which revealed the shaping power of racialism in the colonial situation.[4]

The notion of a psychic complex that lies at the heart of white colonial European subjectivity, one that is embedded in the notion of the human we inherit from the European Enlightenment and colonial modernity, is not in and of itself original in Mannoni's work. Where Mannoni had an unusual insight was in his idea that the Prospero complex, as a colonialist structure of feeling, plays out a specific, neurotic fantasy or impulse "to rid the world of other people" (Lane 138). Mannoni was identifying as a constitutive feature of the Prospero complex a misanthropic impulse that, in his specific colonial context, he felt partially explained the brutal French response to the Malagasy revolt he lived through in 1947. Anthropogenic accounts that privilege a world without humans evade historical reality in eliding the fact that we got to here from there—from the misanthropic vision of a world without other "men" as a key semantic figure, an organizing signifier, in the psychic structure of European, colonial whiteness, to a world without us that yet reflects back to us some unknown truth about the dangerous implications and consequences of our earlier decisions.

The misanthropy at the heart of European colonialism included both a rejection of the world of real humans as one finds them in new and different parts of the world and a will to dominate those humans as subhuman or other. Collapsing the desire for a world without men into the will to dominate is an error, for it moves too quickly past the misanthropic desire, missing the ways in which the latter, the will to dominate, can operate as a defense against the former. The Prospero complex essentially describes the European colonial subject as carrying with him to the colonies a subjectivity already shaped by a specific neurotic complex inherited from childhood, one that translates into an inability to deal with the world of others. The world of others, in other words, produces anxiety. For Mannoni, this is partly a developmental issue involving attachment, but it is also cultural, creating a type of European cultural character. Translated into the framework of his psychoanalytic mentor Lacan, and parallel to Freud's identification of the Oedipus complex half a century earlier, the Prospero complex represented Mannoni's effort to identify a core psychic structure of the Symbolic and Imaginary orders of colonial modernity.

In the years leading up to and following *Prospero and Caliban*, Mannoni would become one of a generation of European intellectuals striving to bring into focus the implications of decolonization for European and global societies. In the early 2000s, Paul Gilroy diagnosed this trajectory as leading to a "postimperial melancholia," a particular structure of feeling shaping mid- to late-twentieth-century postcolonial modernity in the European metropole (2). Writing at the turn of a new millennium, Gilroy conveyed his sense that his time was also structured neurotically by profound repressions and denials (90). The line is not difficult to draw between Gilroy's twenty-first-century sufferers of postimperial melancholia in Britain, France, and the United States and Mannoni's early modern European colonial subjects, as Gilroy asserts: "The imperial and colonial past continues to shape political life in the overdeveloped-but-no-longer-imperial countries" (2). Was this colonial neurosis Mannoni diagnosed, whose effects Gilroy was still seeing more than fifty years later, also visible to the father of modern psychoanalysis and theorist of melancholia himself, Sigmund Freud?

Much earlier in the century, in his 1913 work *Totem and Taboo: Resemblances between the Mental Lives of Savages and Neurotics*, Freud identified neurosis as a psychic structure with striking similarities to the wishful impulses Mannoni described as undergirding European colonial racialism:

> The asocial nature of neuroses has its genetic origin in their most fundamental purpose, which is to take flight from an unsatisfying reality into a more pleasurable world of phantasy. The real world, which is avoided in this way by neurotics, is under the sway of human society and of the institutions collectively created by it. To turn away from reality is at the same time to withdraw from the community of man. (*SE* XXIV: 74)

For Ranjana Khanna, this convergence between Mannoni and Freud is not coincidental. Rather, it reveals the ways in which psychoanalysis itself "is a colonial discipline. . . . It brought into the world an idea of being that was dependent on colonial political and ontological relations," and "psychoanalysis and ethnology participate in the same episteme, one that sustains, through calm violence, the sovereign subject of Europe" (6, 68). It is within the neurotic structures of the sovereign subject that the links between psychoanalysis, colonialism, and modernity spring into view.

The Freud of his later years was well past the days of his youthful fascination with archaeology and the worlds of the colonial adventurer. As Khanna describes, "The age of colonial travel and exploration was that of Freud's youth. That of his old age was the moment of Nazi suppression" (64). *Totem and Taboo* coincides with Freud's significant loss of faith in the modern European subject, "brought about by his sense of despair at the violence of world war, and his own persecution in anti-Semitic turn-of-the-century Vienna" (Khanna 37). Khanna hews very closely to the articulation of Freud's melancholia to his disillusionment with the Austrian nation-state. It is in this context that, she argues, "Freud recognized the problem of European genealogy as the death of the synthetic European neurotic ego. He found in its place a destructive splitting" (27). My emphasis here is slightly different from Khanna's. Rather than analyzing Freud's mindset in relation to his ethnic shame and nationalist or racial despair, I would argue that Freud was experiencing the tendrils of a more profound ontological break. This break would lead to his questioning of the very terms of the human on which the psychoanalytic subject is predicated. To put it even more bluntly, under the early twentieth century ravages of war, Freud was losing faith in the advance of civilization, that is, in a notion of civilization advanced and exemplified in European modernity—while unable to let go of his foundational belief that leaving this civilizational trajectory could only be a movement toward death. Freud's concepts of melancholia and disavowal are symptomatic, one could argue, of his own declining faith in a human with its origins in that old, neurotic colonial vision, without the sense of a viable alternative.

Freud introduced the notion of the death drive in 1920 in *Beyond the Pleasure Principle*, the same year as his daughter's death from complications of both pregnancy and the Spanish flu. Given his own trauma, perhaps it is not so surprising that he describes the death drive as "an unconscious demonic principle driving the psyche to distraction [that] could be said to sabotage once and for all the vision of man in control of his mind" (Rose). Jacqueline Rose has provided a thoughtful take on Freud's controversial death drive, situating it in proximity to his experiences both during and immediately after two world wars and the death of his daughter. In the aftermath of these tragedies, we meet a Freud seeking his own personal escape into a world without men and a world without us. As he described in letters throughout 1914–1916 to such colleagues as Sandor Ferenczi and Lou Andreas-Salomé: "One has to use every means possible to withdraw from the frightful tension in the world outside." And a few years later, he offers an even darker take on Weisman's thought experiment of a "world without us": "Mankind was a doomed experiment and did not deserve to survive. 'We have to abdicate . . . and the Great Unknown, he or it, lurking behind Fate, will one day repeat such an experiment with another race'" (Rose n.p.). The reality of human mortality at a very personal level (death of a loved one) thrusts Freud into both a misanthropic desire to flee the society of others (the world without men) and a fear of humanity itself as a catastrophic failed experiment (the world without us). Taken together, this moment seems to represent a reckoning on his part with the mortal and unanticipated historical consequences of human actions. It is this reckoning that brings Freud to his own "end of the world" state of mind, one in which the glimmers of the regime of historicity he is living in, colonial modernity in *all* of its interconnected, intersectional, implications, slides briefly, affectively, into view.

If world war was the human-made death that interrupted the History that can be seen and grasped, the Spanish flu, as a harbinger of our earthly mortality, has no place in the mode of history Chakrabarty was outlining and lamenting the loss of in the early 2000s.[5] The Spanish flu exists instead in one of those nonhistories that Glissant described, the histories of breaks and ruptures that Europe has dissociated from, in terror of historical forces that cannot be grasped imaginatively or narrated symbolically. When Freud theorized that all organic matter feels a compulsion toward quiescence and death, was he sensing a desire in the modern European subject to separate from the (colonialist, neurotic) symbolic meanings underpinning one's sense of self? Could the drive toward death signal a structure of affect seeking release from the neurotic structures of a colonial misanthropic mind, a spectral unseen affect perceptible only as a deep anxiety, never able to be verbalized and traumatic thereby? In such a psychic state, the fear of symbolic death might keep one in denial of one's deathbound actions in life, one's fear of death serving as a depersonalized defense against one's human agency to be destructive in life—"Better death as a silent companion than a death that falls out of the skies. A remorseless law of nature is preferable to a death that should—might—not have taken place" (Rose). Could this be another aspect of the melancholic structure of the early twenty-first century, a misanthropocene in which our unwillingness, anxiety, and fear about grieving the traumatic death of a certain understanding of the modern self prevents us from seeing that it will have already happened by the time one becomes aware of it?

With the clear signs of an oncoming second world war, Freud's European dream of the human takes on an almost prophetic cast, an unconscious act of foresight premised on his developing ontological break. The turn in Freud's later writings to the death drive as a narcissistic injury, to studies of war, group psychology, biological processes, human predispositions, and historical accidents—all could be the signs of an unconscious hunt to ward off the symbolic death of one meaning of the human, while tracking down alternative meanings of human life (Rose).

In psychoanalysis, one traces one's history not so much to discover a past truth as to enable newly discovered, latent truths of our past experience to inform the present. Within aspects of "unformulated experience," as the American psychoanalyst Donnel Stern terms it, emergent structures of feeling can be generated from the repeated, meaning-making process of retracing the traumatic events of the past. The French psychoanalyst Jean Laplanche called this "afterwardsness," revising Freud's complex notion of *Nachtraglichkeit*, both of which we might consider as psychoanalytic approaches to history (222). *Nachtraglichkeit* or afterwardsness describes a view of history very much at odds with modernity's notion of a linear chronological movement through time. Rather, as Stern draws the contrast between *chronos* and *kairos*, in one temporality the subject creates a sense of self through the continuity of a linear, unifying narrative (501–2). In the other, selfness is constituted simply from what it feels like to just *be in time*, past, present, and future moving among and between one another in a repeating, cyclical way. The former can move into a dissociative mode by freezing time into narrative as a means of evading trauma. The latter creates room for a subject to stand in the spaces between the different times of their lives, identifying and learning from ruptures and breaks. Chakrabarty's fear that the events of the Anthropocene threaten to put the "future beyond the grasp of historical sensibility" could be understood in another sense then, as our reclaiming of the future from History, taking the future out of History (that is, seeing it as a preordained fixed narrative that "disciplines" us) and putting it back in time ("Climate" 197).

To the notion of afterwardsness, I would add one more psychoanalytic concept as a context for apprehending the sense of time we are living in now. Another interpersonalist American psychoanalyst, Edgar Levenson, describes a spiraling, repetitive form to the psychoanalytic encounter, a *"recursive,* isomorphic patterning of analytic content and transferential relationship that makes psychoanalysis work, recursive patterns being those that repeat themselves endlessly, like a hall of mirrors" (137). It is in the repetitions, as they transfer from past to present and from analysand to analyst and back, that various, multiple, and intersecting meanings of being in time emerge—what Glissant would also call transversal, as opposed to universal, histories (66). There is a similar, isomorphic mirroring of form in what, over the last seventy years or so, has been an emergent historical awareness countering the hegemonic narrative of modernity, an apocalyptic prefiguring of the end of the world as we have known it. This accelerating, intersectional sensibility of the present has been developing across multiple fields. And the scholars writing these histories have themselves been shaped by the histories of endings they are writing. From Chakrabarty through Gilroy, from Freud to Mannoni, wrestling with the meaning of the history of modernity for the present recovers an awareness of a deeper ontological break, a new awareness for *both* the postimperial *and* the postcolonial subject, with implications for both the sovereign subject of European modernity and the postcolonial subject of the politics of difference.

On the Being of the Human

The speculative style and interdisciplinary genres of recent forms of history-writing—thought experiments by Weisman (the world without us) and Glissant (history as neuroses), theses and hypotheses by Chakrabarty (four theses on history)—are filled with self-conscious rhetorical gestures that the writers use to show us the steps in their thinking. They produce geo-histories of the human that position themselves in the future anterior, in the "what will have been," once we are able to look back and reflect on History's disruptions and breaks, its spectral intimations. Freud also wrote such a geo-history, a thought experiment or "phylogenetic fantasy," in which he too projected a hypothesis to explain his feeling that "a link in the chain of being had been broken beyond repair" (Rose). His protagonist was Man of the Ice Age, an anxious animal for whom the outside world is threatening. Freud went on to describe how, in subsequent human generations "a portion of the children bring along the anxiousness of the beginning of the Ice Age" (Freud, "A Phylogenetic Fantasy" 13–14). Then, when egocentric man is born, "language was magic to him, his thoughts seemed omnipotent to him, he understood the world according to his ego" (15).

Freud's turn to geological fantasy only highlights the extent to which his concerns about the human went well beyond European ethnocentrism, indicating a crisis that seems more fundamental, at the level of a profound ontological schism. This is Freud writing from the future, when the ontological frameworks of modernity, "the affect of colonialism," reverberate as a kind of "spectral remainder," backward, from a time afterward (Khanna 12, 29). If the oedipal struggle against the divine father is the fantasy of the self with which the modern colonial subject enters modernity, what he disavows is a profound anxiety regarding his place in human history.

The meaning of this fantasy of the human past is its salience for Freud's present, less an anachronism than a kind of transgenerational haunting in reverse. This story of the transmission of anxiety in the species provides the foundation for his observations regarding the neurotic predispositions of the modern European subject: "The struggle with the exigencies of the Ice Age [and] their return after millennia become the disposition of the two groups of neuroses. Also in this sense neurosis is therefore a cultural acquisition. The parallel that has been sketched here may be no more than a playful comparison" (19). As Glissant also suggested, however, retracing this genealogy is not merely an intellectual game (65–66.) Freud and Glissant both moved beyond History, the official historical discipline and record, looking for side paths and "guideposts to orient the reader as the Argument struggles to think/ articulate itself outside the terms of the disciplinary discourses of our present epistemological order" (Wynter, "Coloniality of Being" 331). What these various fantasies, hypotheses, and stories—what Sylvia Wynter terms "the Argument"—are working through is a new story of the times we live in. This is a story based on the uncanny premonition of colonial modernity as the deathbound path to an Anthropocene future. And it has the potential to free up the imagination to do the work necessary for an alternative ending: "One major implication here: *humanness* is no longer a *noun. Being human is a praxis*" (Wynter, "Unparalleled Catastrophe?" 23).

Think of this article as another such thought experiment, another speculative hypothesis, a transversal tracing of guideposts to offer a different historiography of the Anthropocene in a history of modernity as neurosis. This neurosis is charted through the writings of scholars in Black diasporic and postcolonial studies, and "treated" from the perspective of a psychoanalytic approach to history. One can feel the first stirrings of alarm in the mid-1940s and 1950s, as decolonial revolts and the era of formal decolonization lit up across the colonial world, and efforts to think about the mental impact of decolonization on both colonizer and colonized began to be published—by Fanon, Memmi, and Césaire, but also Sartre and Mannoni. The 1940s and 1950s are also seen as one milestone of the Anthropocene, a "golden spike" evident between 1940 to 1965, the years bordering peak nuclear fallout along with the onset of the Great Acceleration (Subramanian). The recognition of cause for alarm stays submerged under the anticolonial, postcolonial politics of nationalism and statehood throughout the 1960s and 1970s, emerging again when the politics of postcolonial nationalism begin to run their course and writers, artists, and cultural producers in Black studies turn to cultural production as a new terrain in the 1980s. Unknowingly, this moment was also simultaneous with another Anthropocene milestone, since the 1980s was also the decade in which the term itself was coined and global warming began to emerge as a phenomenon of note in scientific discussions (Subramanian, "The Discovery of Global Warming"; Pavid).

This was also the height of postcolonial studies in the academy as Chakrabarty references, and of a conversation between Black cultural, African American, and Caribbean studies evident, for example, in the observations of Gates, Hall, and West regarding Blackness and the new cultural politics of difference. From the perspective of postcolonial studies, Chakrabarty has described this moment as a coming together of two notions and two politics of the human. The first, "the universalist-Enlightenment view of the human as potentially the same everywhere, the subject with capacity to bear and exercise rights," was met, as an outgrowth of the politics of decolonization, with "the postcolonial-postmodern view of the human as the same but endowed everywhere with . . . anthropological difference . . . differences of class, sexuality, gender, history, and so on" ("Postcolonial Studies" 1–2). The latter had evolved in the anticolonial movements of the early to mid-twentieth century, combining the discourse of rights and difference.

Psychoanalytic and postcolonial notions of the human came into dialogue with the 1986 reprinting of Frantz Fanon's *Black Skin, White Masks* (Lane 128). What postcolonial histories do not cite is the significance of Fanon's republication for Black diasporic cultural studies. While sometimes submerged within postcolonial studies, the Black diasporic cultural studies of the 1980s through the 2000s had a slightly different mandate than the postcolonialists of the postmodern era. Black diasporic scholars' engagement with

Fanon generated meanings not just about the psychic structure of white supremacy as the framework of imperialism and colonialism, nor even just about the colonial complexes created in the encounter between Europeans and old and new world subaltern populations. Rather, Fanon's reprinting also generated new meaning about the psychic structure of *anti-Blackness* in particular. This new meaning was generated less from an analysis of the effects of colonialism on the subaltern broadly conceived and more from an understanding of the ascription of Blackness itself, as a mode of the human, to a place of nonbeing and foreclosure.

The distinction I am drawing between postcolonial and Black diasporic cultural studies indicates an effort to untangle the conceptual overlap between the focus on colonialism and colonial subjectivity, on the one hand, and the focus on Blackness and anti-Black racism more specifically. If the subaltern populations of Africa and India, and in metropolitan Europe, were the focus of the first, the paradigm of anti-Blackness invoked more specifically the African-descended subject of New World slavery. As Frank Wilderson states more succinctly, "White supremacy and anti-Blackness are not the same" (170). If racism understood in relation to discourses of whiteness creates a sociocultural, discursive context for some of the world's modern nation-states, racism understood as a profound misanthropy that structures our understanding of the human raises it to the level of a deeper, underlying, sociogenic principle that has been globalized in a totalizing way—to shape language, historical consciousness, and structures of thought at an epistemic reach and scale. Anti-Blackness becomes one of the strongest manifestations of both versions of racism in an Anthropocene world, with racism itself serving as another name for that demonic unconscious principle underlying the death drive and the deathly fear of other humans. And if anti-Black violence "is a paradigm of oppression for which there is no coherent form of redress, other than Frantz Fanon's 'end of the world,'" one can see why for Afro-pessimists "the end of the world" is a possible occasion for celebration (170).

For many Black female writers, for much of the late nineteenth and twentieth centuries the history of anti-Blackness has been framed as a Manichean battle between the Black male enslaved ego and the white male master self (hooks). Maybe this is why the Caribbean philosopher Sylvia Wynter has stepped back further in time to characterize the history shaping the twentieth-century conjuncture. Wynter's profound contribution was to reframe the politics of both sovereignty and difference as symptoms of a deeper, structuring, epistemic break whose effects, and affects, would continue to repeat throughout the time of modernity. Wynter's canonical 2003 essay on "Unsettling the Coloniality of Being," represents a comprehensive laying out of arguments developed over many years, which describe a fundamental breach in historical epistemology (262). Posited as a set of hypotheses concerning the "Big Bang" processes that constituted modernity, Wynter dives deep into the early modern archive to provide a record substantiating the claim here, and held by Wynter herself, that the Anthropocene and the colonial stories are linked in a shared, destructive notion of the human.

For Wynter, this history's golden spike is not industrial man of the nineteenth century but colonial man of the fifteenth, and more specifically, his act of establishing a secular notion of the human founded, as she terms it, on the "degodding" of the subject. Wynter names secularization itself as the source of a series of traumatizing decisions regarding human subjectivity catalyzed and developed further in the European by the colonial encounter. As she states, it is "this first degodded (if still hybridly religio-secular) . . . human in history," "Man1" as she names him, that is "foundational to modernity" and it is this specific split in being—prior to any ego splits in the Freudian subject of the nineteenth- and early twentieth-century nation-state—that serves as the defensive formation that founds modernity ("Coloniality of Being" 281, 299, 265).

What has made Wynter's writings on the coloniality of being so helpful for Black and decolonial scholars is her modeling of what it means to tell a "deep" history of modernity founded on a break, founded in trauma. And like Glissant and Mannoni, Wynter's traumatized subject is the early modern European. Mannoni's Prospero complex, the splitting of the ego that Freud was tracking in relation to the death drive, Gilroy's postimperial melancholics, and Latour's Moderns; the interweaving of these strands produces an emergent, intersecting account of modernity in contemporary social theory and cultural thought. Wynter's hypothesis brings these stories together. Man1 represents the moment when a new symbolic order founded on a new sociogenic principle of the human comes into being, with religio-cultural structures of feeling from the past transferred and harnessed to the narratives of the early modern colonial present, regarding race, Blackness, and gender. The splitting of the modern European from the divine requires a reconfiguration of the chain of being. If the degodded is ego-bound, bound to a certain notion of the human on a trajectory toward becoming a sovereign rational self, the indigenous of the Americas and Africa, the exploited, massacred, transported, and enslaved are also subject to a profound transference—deathbound as the nonsubjects of modernity, bare life (JanMohamed).

For Wynter, it is the totalizing power and globalizing reach of this historical narrative that is truly frightening. In more psychoanalytic terms, within the frame of this concept of the human, anti-Blackness is a form of acting *in* that, while ever-present in the time of modernity, is not timeless. It evolves and adapts to the discourses of subsequent eras, transferring and transmuting through various regimes of modern knowledge and epistemes of the symbolic order.

The turn of the second millennium marks the emergence of an anxious apprehension that a fundamental misanthropy undergirds the decolonial, Anthropocene present, necessitating critical second takes on the cultural politics of difference so celebrated by postcolonial and decolonial subjects in the 1980s. The suspicion or "afro-pessimism" of scholars writing against the cultural politics of race and difference, against sovereignty, and about the turn to death and other notions of the human are just in time to converge, even if not yet to be in direct dialogue with, an uncanny and disavowed sense of the deathbound historical structure of the Anthropocene.[6] This is one meaning of Wilderson's provocative statement: "Human life is dependent on Black death for its existence and for its coherence. . . . There is no world without Blacks, yet there are no Blacks who are in the world" (42). The world without us is preceded by our world, a world without Blacks. The ego-bound subject *is* a deathbound subject, whose existence depends on the symbolic and physical death of others and of their life-worlds.

Wynter's Man₁, Freud's Ice Age Man, Mannoni's colonial Prosperos, Chakrabarty's and Gilroy's postcolonial and postimperial multicultural subjects of difference all emerge and evolve in relation to the ego-bound subject of colonial history. Haunting them, as seen afterward, from a perspective on the other side of now, are new structures of feeling, nonhistories based in trauma, discernible in the affects of a new millennium. Melancholic and afro-pessimistic specters of colonial affect, of the "godding" and "degodding" of man, leave their traces in grim modes of history telling that also point to paths beyond a misanthropic trauma that impacts not just the meta-psychological but the ontological itself. The word *Anthropocene* is derived from combining anthropo- from the Ancient Greek *anthropos* meaning "human," and -cene from the Ancient Greek *kainos* meaning "new" or "recent." *Kairos*, the Ancient Greek word for a more liminal rather than chronological way of being in time, can also mean the right, critical, or opportune moment. A call to action is the steady drumbeat of Wynter's writings on "the coloniality of being," a call for us to notice that this apocalyptic moment provides an opportunity.

In a 2015 interview with Katherine McKittrick, Wynter asserts:

So this is what gives me the urgency, do you see what I mean? For we cannot allow ourselves to *continue* thinking in this way. This way of thinking is linked to the *same* ethno-class mode of behavior-regulatory and cognitively closed order of knowledge that has led to our now major collectively human predicament: the ongoing process of global warming, climate instability, and ecosystemic catastrophe. ("Unparalleled Catastrophe?" 20)

My hypothesis here is not that this has not been said or thought before, but rather, that it is now, in the Anthropocene, that the meaning of that observation is being felt. Feeling the dark ecologies of the Anthropocene as a trauma to the human may be just what the humanities, the human sciences, need to see to imagine a way forward. What Chakrabarty misses is that the history that led us to the Anthropocene is ungraspable because it is traumatic, our historical narratives frozen in a state of anxiety not unlike that of Freud's Ice Age Man. Discerning other, entangled strands of the present requires modes of history-writing with the epistemological creativity of hypotheses and speculative experiments, a tuning in to hidden structures of feeling. Wynter is an artist and poet as much as a historian, tuning in to the epochal Zeitgeist the way Freud attempted to when, in theorizing a death drive, he foresaw with melancholy the rupture in the glorious history of modernity and the sovereign ego that was coming on the other side of now. ■

Michelle Stephens is a professor of English and Latino and Caribbean Studies at Rutgers University, New Brunswick; the founding executive director of the Institute for the Study of Global Racial Justice; and a practicing psychoanalyst. She is the author of *Skin Acts: Race, Psychoanalysis, and the Black Male Performer* (2014) and three recently coedited collections of archipelagic studies, the most recent of which is *Contemporary Archipelagic Thinking* with Yolanda Martínez-San Miguel (2020).

NOTES

1   For more of Chakrabarty's discussions of the impact of climate change and the Anthropocene on postcolonial studies, see "Postcolonial Studies," 1–18.

2   In *Facing Gaia*, Latour further historicizes the apocalyptic sensibility of "the Moderns" as a group for whom "the ground on which their history had always been played out, has become unstable" (2–3).

3   As reported on Friday, May 14, 2021, at www.google.com/search?client=firefox-b-1-e&q=worldwide+pandemic+death+count.

4   See Peter Hulme's discussion in "Hurricanes in the Caribbees," 55–83.

5   As Rose contextualizes, the Spanish flu has become "a silent stalker of history, barely included in lists of the world's modern afflictions, even though its death toll came close to the combined toll of the two world wars" ("To Die One's Own Death" n.p.).

6   This link is foregrounded in the alternative name for the era as the Plantationocene, with an origin now dated back to the Columbian "exchange" itself, that is, in the traumatic colonial encounter.

WORKS CITED

Césaire, Aimé. *Discourse on Colonialism: Présence Africaine*. Paris: Dakar, 1955.

Chakrabarty, Dipesh. "The Climate of History: Four Theses." *Critical Inquiry* 35, no. 2 (2009): 197–223.

Chakrabarty, Dipesh. "Postcolonial Studies and the Challenge of Climate Change." *New Literary History* 43, no. 1 (2012): 1–18.

Dietze, Carola. "Toward a History on Equal Terms: A Discussion of *Provincializing Europe*." *History and Theory* 47, no. 1 (2008): 69–84.

Fanon, Frantz. *Black Skin, White Masks*, translated by Charles L. Markmann. 1967; repr., London: Pluto Press, 1986.

Freud, Sigmund. *Beyond the Pleasure Principle*, translated by C. J. M. Hubback. London: International Psycho-Analytical, 1922.

Freud, Sigmund. *A Phylogenetic Fantasy: Overview of the Transference Neuroses*, edited by Ilse Grubrich-Simitis and translated by Axel Hoffer and Peter T. Hoffer. Cambridge, MA: Harvard University Press, 1987.

Freud, Sigmund, James Strachey, Anna Freud, and Carrie Lee Rothgeb. "Totem and Taboo: Resemblances between the Mental Lives of Savages and Neurotics." In vol. 13 of *The Standard Edition of the Complete Psychological Works of Sigmund Freud*, translated and edited by James Strachey, 1–255. London: Hogarth Press, 1953.

Gates, Henry Louis, Jr., and Kwame Anthony Appiah, eds. *"Race," Writing, and Difference*. Chicago: University of Chicago Press, 1986.

Gilroy, Paul. *Postcolonial Melancholia*. New York: Columbia University Press, 2005.

Glissant, Édouard. *Caribbean Discourse: Selected Essays*. Charlottesville: University of Virginia Press, 1989.

Hall, Stuart. "Cultural Identity and Diaspora." In *Identity: Community, Culture, Difference*, edited by Jonathan Rutherford, 222–37. London: Lawrence and Wishart, 1990.

Hall, Stuart. "Minimal Selves." In *The Real Me: Post-Modernism and the Question of Identity*, edited by L. Appignanesi, 44–79. London: Institute of Contemporary Arts, 1987.

hooks, bell. "Feminism as a Persistent Critique of History: What's Love Got to Do With It?" In *The Fact of Blackness: Frantz Fanon and Visual Representation*, edited by Alan Read, 76–85. London: Institute of Contemporary Arts, 1996.

Hulme, Peter. "Hurricanes in the Caribbees: The Constitution of the Discourse of English Colonialism." In *1642: Literature and Power in the Seventeenth Century*, edited by Francis Barker, Jennifer Stone, andPeter Hulme, 55–83. Essex, UK: University of Essex, 1981.

JanMohamed, Abdul R. *The Death-Bound-Subject: Richard Wright's Archaeology of Death*. Durham, NC: Duke University Press, 2005.

Khanna, Ranjana. *Dark Continents: Psychoanalysis and Colonialism*. Durham, NC: Duke University Press, 2003.

Lane, Christopher. "Psychoanalysis and Colonialism Redux: Why Mannoni's 'Prospero Complex' Still Haunts Us." *Journal of Modern Literature* 25, nos. 3–4 (2002): 127–50.

Laplanche, Jean. *Jean Laplanche: Seduction, Translation, Drives*, edited by John Fletcher and Martin Stanton and translated by Martin Stanton. London: Institute of Contemporary Arts, 1992.

Latour, Bruno. *Down to Earth: Politics in the New Climatic Regime*. Cambridge, UK: Polity Press, 2018.

Latour, Bruno. *Facing Gaia: Eight Lectures on the New Climatic Regime*, translated by Catherine Porter. Cambridge, UK: Polity Press, 2017.

Levenson, Edgar. "Show and Tell: The Recursive Order of Transference." In *How Does Treatment Help: On the Modes of Therapeutic Action of Psychoanalytic Psychotherapy*, edited by Arnold Rothstein, 135–43. Madison, CT: International Universities Press, 1988.

Mannoni, Octave. *Prospero and Caliban: The Psychology of Colonization*, translated by Pamela Powesland. 1950; repr., Ann Arbor: University of Michigan Press, 1990.

Memmi, Albert. *The Colonizer and the Colonized*. Boston: Beacon Press, 1967.

Morton, Timothy. *Hyperobjects: Philosophy and Ecology after the End of the World*. Minneapolis: University of Minnesota Press, 2013.

Pavid, Katie. "What Is the Anthropocene and Why Does It Matter?" Natural History Museum. www.nhm.ac.uk/discover/what-is-the-anthropocene.html (accessed December 7, 2020).

Pugh, Jonathan. "The Affirmational Turn to Ontology in the Anthropocene: A Critique." In *Contemporary Archipelagic Thinking: Towards New Comparative Methodologies and Disciplinary Formations*, edited by Yolanda Martínez-San Miguel and Michelle Stephens, 65–82. Lanham, MD: Rowman and Littlefield, 2020.

Rose, Jacqueline. "To Die One's Own Death: Jacqueline Rose on Freud and His Daughter." *London Review of Books*, November 19, 2020. www.lrb.co.uk/the-paper/v42/n22/jacqueline-rose/to-die-one-s-own-death.

Sartre, Jean-Paul. "Black Orpheus." *Présence Africaine*, 1951, 219–47.

Stern, Donnel B. "Unformulated Experience, Dissociation, and *Nachträglichkeit*." *Journal of Analytical Psychology* 62, no. 4 (2017): 501–25.

Subramanian, Meera. "The Discovery of Global Warming." history.aip.org/climate/timeline.htm (accessed December 7, 2020).

Subramanian, Meera. "Humans versus Earth: The Quest to Define the Anthropocene." *Nature*, August 6, 2019. www.nature.com/articles/d41586-019-02381-2.

Weisman, Alan. *The World without Us*. New York: Picador, 2007.

West, Cornel. "The New Cultural Politics of Difference." *October* 53 (1990): 93–109.

Wilderson, Frank, III. *Afropessimism*. New York: Liveright Publishing, 2020.

Williams, Raymond. *Marxism and Literature*. Oxford: Oxford University Press, 1977.

Wynter, Sylvia. "Unsettling the Coloniality of Being/Power/Truth/Freedom: Towards the Human, after Man, Its Overrepresentation—An Argument." *New Centennial Review* 3, no. 3 (2003): 257–337.

Wynter, Sylvia, and Katherine McKittrick. "Unparalleled Catastrophe For Our Species? Or, to Give Humanness a Different Future: Conversations." In *Sylvia Wynter: On Being Human as Praxis*, edited by Katherine McKittrick, 9–89. Durham, NC: Duke University Press, 2015.

Max Cavitch

In the Interest of History

ABSTRACT Psychoanalysis is often wrongly perceived to be uninterested in history. Yet, as the most comprehensive and sophisticated basis for the exploration of human consciousness, the field of psychoanalysis, from its inception to the present, has continued to offer unprecedented insights into how we perceive, record, and share the complexities of temporality. The aim of this article is to demonstrate, with the help of various works by Walter Benjamin—works in which his attunement with psychoanalytic concepts is of special interest—that all historical writing must yield, in one way or another, to the post-Freudian description of the unconscious and its role in elaborating historians' interest in the historical as such.

KEYWORDS psychoanalysis, historiography, critique, autobiography, interpretation

You do not think. You dream. Dream all day long. Dream everything.
Dream maliciously and incessantly. Don't you know that by now?

—Patrick Hamilton, *Angel Street*

Psychoanalysis began as an attempt to help patients who were, as Sigmund Freud and Josef Breuer put it in 1893, suffering "from reminiscences" (*SE* II: 7). The significance of this starting point for further psychoanalytic understandings of neurosis, trauma, dissociation, desire, fantasy, knowledge—and of mental functioning generally—cannot be overstated. Indeed, psychoanalysis inaugurated a new historical episteme—a new era of consciousness, in which individual and collective relations to the past, present, *and* future were permanently transformed. Along with the mentally ill, *all* of civilization's discontented—nostalgics, revanchists, melancholics, utopians, ideologues, reactionaries, reformers, dreamers, revolutionaries, misanthropes, and fantasists—have come to be understood, and have often been able better to understand themselves, as struggling with various aspects of the complex temporality of experience that psychoanalysis has introduced into the thought of history, including the historical present and the historical future.

HISTORY of the PRESENT ▪ A Journal of Critical History ▪ 12:1 ▪ April 2022
DOI 10.1215/21599785-9547239 © 2022 Duke University Press

Freud did not "discover" the unconscious. As he himself liked to say, the poets always "got there" before him. Saint Augustine, for example, in the fourth century CE, was well aware of the unconscious: "There are some things in man which even his own spirit within him does not know" (210– 11). But what Freud and those after him have done is to help us learn to question "the very idea of the self as an object of knowledge." In other words, psychoanalysis provides both the obligation and many of the best tools with which to live our lives as subjects (in every sense of the word) of uncertainty. Before Freud, the "self" most often *seemed* to be a problem of knowledge; so it seemed to Saint Augustine. After Freud, knowledge is itself the problem, and the ancient dictum "Know thyself!"—which had so often been questioned before—finally gives way, as Adam Phillips puts it, to "a radical and formative insufficiency, something that cannot be solved by knowledge. With the post-Freudian description of the unconscious, the idea of human completeness disappears. We are not in search of wholeness . . . we are in search of good ways of bearing our incompleteness" (7).

The aim of this article is to demonstrate, with the help of various works by Walter Benjamin in which his attunement with Freudian psychology is of special interest, that all historical writing must yield, in one way or another, to this "radical and formative insufficiency," even as it often quite anxiously seeks to preempt potentially endless elaborations of the historian's unruly, subjective investments in the past. The early insights of psychoanalysis helped Marxist and Progressive historians, including Benjamin, to dispel the Rankean naivete that had come to dominate Western historiography since the late nineteenth century. Yet, more recently, the prestige of the social sciences, the dawning of the computer age, and a lamentable mistrust of narrative history have all aided the widespread institutional entrenchment of social historians' empiricist fixations. These fixations have continued, into our own time, to make the animations of subjective interest seem like insurmountable but unfortunate limitations on the historical enterprise, rather than what psychoanalysis helps show such interest to be: the project of history itself.

Very Interesting

In economical, psychological, and philosophical terms, "interest" is often a trope for desperation: for a lack or surplus of interest, for interest's malfunctioning or impotence, and for the tenuity both of interested self-states and of what is of interest to them. Regarding the phenomenology of interest, Heidegger (in what was originally a lecture delivered in 1951) complained about a lack of contemporary readiness to "learn thinking," which in his view ought to begin, not with "thinking" as such but with affect or mood (*Thinking* 5).

Thinking should begin, that is, precisely with that which interrupts and frustrates all efforts (for example, in political or economic theory) to equate rational (self-)interest and disinterested (self-)knowledge. In Heidegger's own psychoanalytic formulation, interest must always be a matter of contestation, for how can we be certain of our interests when our ability to know *ourselves* is so limited and uncertain? How can we reliably judge our own interests when we cannot reliably judge our own desires, fears, and resistances? We cannot. Thus Dean Mathiowetz, following Heidegger, has aptly characterized "interest" as a medium of "contested self-constitution" (9).

One sign of this aptness is the sprawling interest in counterfactuals in contemporary discourse, from novels and films to philosophy, sociology, computer science, and history—an interest driven by the ramped up stakes of questions about both causation and contingency. Never before our postnuclear, posttruth, post-Holocenic era has the relation between past, present, and future seemed so uncertain to so many. Never before has the authority of counterfactuals seemed more legitimate in so many different disciplines. Humanity's pressing concerns, not only with what might have been but also with what might otherwise be, range from the political and economic to the environmental and existential, and its tides of regret and longing have become tsunamis, straining the material resources of the planet along with the conceptual resources of semantics, epistemology, and metaphysics.

In the field of history, one of the reactions to these conceptual strains has been a resurgence of ontological realism—a resurgence, that is, of faith in an objective reality that exists independently of our modes of accessing it. This faith expresses itself in historiographical endorsements of naïve empiricism and in history writing that seeks its footing in events understood to exist prior to transcription and narration. Of course, no serious historian doubts that transcription and narration are subjectively conditioned—that historical "facts" are produced through interpretation. But many serious historians hold fast to the conviction that events themselves precede interpretation and thus that historical causation proceeds in a strictly linear, chronological fashion, from the event to interest in the event, including the historian's interest in transcribing and narrating it.

The Specularity of Interest

These days, so many contemporary historians and historiographers espouse neo-Rankean forms of ontological realism—as if history were nothing more than narrativized data and as if historical method were nothing more than what Adorno calls "reconstruction, mere technique" (247)—that even the most persuasive, archive-based speculative histories, such as those by Saidiya Hartman, tend either to be exiled to the remote precincts of intellectual history or to be exceptionalized as maverick or virtuoso. Indeed, Hartman herself anticipates this sort of reception in her recent essay on Esther Brown—an African American woman living in New York in the early twentieth century—by identifying her own work of speculative history with the accusations of "wayward" and "riotous" activity that fill the official archive of Brown's life: "State violence, surveillance, and detention produce the archival traces and institutional records that inform the reconstruction of [lives like Brown's]; but desire and the want of something better decide the contours of the telling." Hartman's own narrative, that is, "emulates the errant path of the wayward and moves from one story to another by way of encounter, chance meeting, proximity, and the sociality created by enclosure. It strives to convey the aspiration and longing of the wayward and the tumult and upheaval incited by the chorus" (470).

To tell the history of Esther Brown and of the "chorus" of women with whom she chanted and cried, in what was mere "din" to outsiders and to agents of the state, Hartman practices a method she dubs "critical fabulation" (470). This "wayward" term challenges both the fear of imagination (Lat. *fābula*: "story-telling") and the resistance to critique that, together, characterize the forms of naïve empiricism currently dominating the profession of history writing—not to reject or obscure the "cold hard facts" (477) of the newspaper articles, personal correspondence, institutional documents, testimonies, prison records, interviews, and other archival materials Hartman's research uncovered but rather to challenge the material and ideological premises (many of them quite factitious) of their matter-of-factness. To do so in the absence of a rich counterarchive requires imaginative labor of the sort that many historians are still all too quick to resent and to discredit as "literary," as if "literary" were a synonym for "falsified," or—to put a sharper, psychoanalytic point to it—as if identification and projection were akin to psychosis.

Insistence on ontological realism—and on the transparent meaning of what is simply "there"—functions among many contemporary historians like a reaction-formation: a defense, not only against the fear of being accused by other historians of wearing their psyches on their sleeves but also against the anxiety generated by the unconscious knowledge that telling anyone's history means telling some version of one's own. The critique of objectivity—in Kantian terms, the critical investigation of the perceived need to distinguish between objectivity and subjectivity—has been a collective working-through of the defensive reaction-formation that insists on cleaving to ontological realism in the writing of history. Modern historiography was inaugurated in the simultaneously enabling and constraining context of the critique of objectivity, and, ever since the late eighteenth century, the vicissitudes of critique have kept the fate of the past from falling permanently into anyone's hands. This has been unsettling for all concerned, and various consequential contestations have been staged. The one that has occupied us most strenuously in recent decades pits the desire to drive a wedge between the empirical and the theoretical against the desire to harmonize them. As in every such contest, there are skilled players on both sides as well as those who persist in trying to change the rules of the game.

The crucial point is that all such players are actual existents—human beings with full subjectivities of their own. For there will always be those who will forget or deliberately ignore the fact that behind every history there is a *histōr*, someone giving an account of their inquiries, and that both the inquiry and the account are conducted by people in particular social and historical circumstances. The historian is not, as some enjoy pretending, a figure of pure immediacy and disinterestedness but an individual with a specific history of subjectivation for which that historian (just like anyone else) is and will remain accountable. This accountability, when recognized, very understandably generates ambivalence, even among players on the side of the "harmonizers"—such as Joan Wallach Scott, for example, as she contemplates the fate of the papers she herself has contributed to Brown University's Feminist Theory Papers archive: "When I think about the uses to which my artifacts could be put, I become the worst kind of objective historian, insisting on the transparent meaning of what's there . . . a legitimacy I want preserved on my terms" (*Fantasy* 146). But Scott knows that others, including other harmonizers, are likely to resist such awareness of their own defense mechanisms, and this prompts her, elsewhere and in a more urgent tone, to inveigh against the sidelining of critical theory by the "wedge-drivers" and thus

> to call attention to what seems to me to be an increasingly evident tendency among scholars who know they have been influenced by poststructuralist theory to minimize that critical influence, to describe it as simply one among many "methodologies" that has been used to advance empirical projects that are now taken to be the primary object of research and writing. The minimization of poststructuralist influence and the denial of its epistemological position (one that, among other things, insists on *the necessary interconnection between the theoretical and the empirical*) takes place under the sign of eclecticism. ("Against Eclecticism" 114; emphasis added)

Scott's term, "poststructuralist theory," designates a very large and unfixed canon of post-WWII theoretical (i.e., interrogative and propositional) writings that share, if nothing else, a commitment to reflect on the (shifting) grounds of their own possibility.

In Scott's essay, Derrida is the representative figure for what she and others also call "critique." But many other suitable figures could be invoked, including Roland Barthes, Judith Butler, Gilles Deleuze, Umberto Eco, Michel Foucault, Julia Kristeva, Jean-Luc Nancy, Richard Rorty, and Bernard Stiegler—figures who, for all their idiosyncrasies and clashes with one another, tend to be strategically homogenized by the "wedge-drivers" in service of their defense mechanisms. One such historian (like Scott, a skilled player and a leading scholar of Native American history) worries that "to go all the way with the postmodernists is to reject the *entire* historical enterprise—not just Indian history—as a hopeless discourse of meaningless texts talking to meaningless texts; no document or oral tradition could ever provide useful evidence about the world outside itself" (Richter 386). Richter's skittishness about "going all the way" and his hyperbolic rhetoric of *rejection, entirety, hopelessness,* and *meaninglessness* are familiar signs of the anxiety that can beset even the smartest wedge-driver's unconscious resistance to the wish to relinquish, as Scott is more or less able to do, the cumbersome fantasy of control.

In her embrace of other kinds of fantasy, Hartman, one of the rule-changers, goes so far as to make her own imagined accountability the primary subject of her accounts of the past. Speculation, fantasy, identification, projection, and countertime all have both evidentiary and methodological significance for her historical work, which resolutely defies the generic boundaries between history and autobiography that much recent historiographical work, such as Jaume Aurell's monograph on "historians' autobiographies," seeks to maintain, not least by commending the effort to preserve "epistemological distance" from the subjects of their properly historical writing. In Aurell's view, "historians turn to autobiography, as philosophers do to poetry and literary critics to history, to learn not only about other people and the past but also about themselves and the present" (2)—as if these "turns" were matters of recreation or truancy. When, one wants to ask, have literary critics had to "turn" to history? And is the writing of philosophy, from Empedocles to Nietzsche, not frequently poetic in both substance and form? As an objectivist, Aurell is surprised and impressed to discover that so many eminent historians have elected to face "the difficulties that practicing this new genre—and a very subjective one—has brought them" (3). Yet he seems unwilling to engage—and does not even mention—

scholarship, such as Hartman's *Lose Your Mother: A Journey Along the Atlantic Slave Route* (2007), that participates in both genres simultaneously. Nor does he offer any account of the prodigious work of recent speculative historians, such as Robert N. Bellah's *Religion in Human Evolution: From the Paleolithic to the Axial Age* (2011) and Steven Mithen's *After the Ice: A Global Human History, 20,000–5000 BC* (2004).

Walter Benjamin's Dream of Tme

Remarkably, Aurell also bypasses Benjamin, one of the twentieth century's greatest historiographers, critical theorists, *and* autobiographers, who famously observed that one might "speak of an unforgettable life or moment even if all men had forgotten it. If the nature of such a life or moment required that it be unforgotten, that predicate would not imply a falsehood but merely a claim not fulfilled by men, and probably also a reference to a realm in which it *is* fulfilled" (*Illuminations* 70). As Benjamin fully appreciated, one such realm of forgotten fulfillment is the unconscious. Indeed, for Benjamin, history is to be understood as a dream of time, and historians have to be willing to take on "the task of dream interpretation" (*Arcades* 464). By making a fetish of genre, scholars like Aurell not only suppress the fundamental intersectionality of history and autobiography but also seek to shore up the objectivist's barrier between the psychodynamics of autobiography and the "real empirical research" (Aurell 187) of history.

In contrast, Scott, Hartman, and other nonobjectivist historians understand that the task of interpreting history's dream of time cannot begin unless and until the events, texts, and other artifacts of "real empirical research" are recognized as being just as overdetermined, in the psychoanalytic sense, as the historian's interest in interpreting them. That is, ceremonies, ledger-entries, and fossils are as fully overdetermined as a historian's fantasy or projection; fossil and fantasy alike are condensations of multiple ideations, images, associations, and meanings that exceed their ipseity. A fantasy is as real as a fossil, even though the fantasy cannot be grasped in the same manner; and a fossil is as potent as a fantasy in its resistance to disaffected objectification. History itself, understood as the narration of events that have taken place, cannot, as Freud argued, be fully explained by "impersonal factors." For "each event," he continues, "seems to be overdetermined and proves to be the effect of several convergent causes. Frightened by the immense complication of events, our investigations take the side of one correlation as against another and set up contradictions which do not exist but have only arisen owing to a rupture of more comprehensive relations" (*SE* XXIII: 107–8).

Freud makes it quite clear, here and elsewhere, that he is not espousing the sort of radical, amoral relativism that many detractors of "postmodernism" have sought to wield as a blunt weapon against critical theory. He is writing about the historiographic need to properly recognize and account for the overdetermination of "each event"—which is precisely what, even before Freud published the passage above (in *Moses and Monotheism* [1939]), Benjamin had already described in the following way, employing a very Freudian archaeological analogy for what he called the historians' need

> to return always and again to the same body of fact, scattering it about as you scatter about earth, turning it over as you turn the earth. For bodies of fact are but strata, layers, which disclose to the most painstaking investigation alone whatever constitutes the true valuables hiding within the interior of the earth: The images which, once having been pried free of all earlier contexts, lie as precious objects *in the sober chambers of our late understanding*. . . . [T]he cautious touch of the probing spade in dark soil remains indispensable, and whoever preserves in his notes only the inventory of finds and not *this dark joy at the very site of his finding*, too, denies himself the best part of it. (*Berlin Chronicle*, 52–53; emphasis added)

Contemporary speculative historians take their cue, one way or another, from these always-ready-to-be-returned-to sources. Christopher Tomlins, for example, in his recent speculative history of Nat Turner and the Turner Rebellion, describes marshalling "empirical evidence" to "conjecture" with scrupulous reflexivity about the phenomena whose oft-told history he seeks to write anew (xvi–xvii). Conjecture and speculation, as practiced by scholars like Tomlins and Hartman, have become at least partially legitimized historical methodologies because, from a psychoanalytic perspective, they are *predicates* of understanding.

The Necessity of Psychoanalysis

The notion that our current episteme is fundamentally psychoanalytic remains controversial, and not only among historians. Such controversy is healthy, to the extent that it is well informed—not least because psychoanalysis is no unified, static model of the mind but rather a complex system of thought in which constantly evolving schema of clinical practice and metapsychological insight continue to be subject to revision, retesting, and reconceptualization. As Joan Scott admits, she herself came quite late to the serious study of psychoanalysis. Once having done so, however, she quickly recognized how crucial psychoanalytic thinking is to any historical methodology that would refuse "the conflation of social construction with subjectivity"—a necessary refusal, because social construction "presumes an external causality for the constitution of subjects that is challenged by the operations of the unconscious in the formation of individual subjects" ("Psychoanalysis"). Still, far too many otherwise capable intellectuals persist in equating psychoanalysis with Freud's (largely unread) corpus, or they assume that psychoanalytic theory has remained more or less unchanged since the epoch of Lacan's seventh seminar. Even those scholars of history and literature who are devoted to critique often fail to recognize that psychoanalysis is, in one way or another, the epistemic foundation of the oeuvres of all the critical theorists they most admire (see, e.g., Allen). Very few twenty-first-century literature departments (in the United States) ask their students to read further than Freud and Lacan, and even fewer history departments offer courses on psychohistorical methodologies. (The discipline of psychology, having recast itself as an empirical social science, has almost entirely banished psychoanalysis from the curriculum.) And only a handful of humanists have been paying close attention to the dramatic reconvergence, over the past three decades, of psychoanalysis and neuroscience (Freud's original field), giving rise to the new field of neuropsychoanalysis.

For the more objectively minded and/or temperamentally self-effacing historians who remain thoroughly skeptical of psychoanalysis as our best-yet descriptive and dynamic model of the mind, it will perhaps come as welcome news that, since the 1990s, advances in neurophysiology and neurochemistry have harmonized with many aspects of the psychoanalytic model. Freud, a neurologist by training, was forced in the late nineteenth century to break from what was then an extremely rudimentary science of the mind—one that had yet to understand even the most basic workings of neurons themselves, and that, until quite recently, has perversely refused to study the single most important aspect of human mental functioning: subjectivity. But, at last, neuroscience—and, specifically, the field now known as neuropsychoanalysis—has begun to do what Freud always predicted it someday would: help confirm the clinical findings and theoretical propositions that he and others have been expanding and refining for well over a century. For example: the fundamental psychoanalytic premise that most of our thoughts and feelings are unconscious has both prompted and helped describe the findings of recent neurological investigations of the brain's limbic system; examination of the workings of the brain's frontal lobe executive control systems provides a neurological groundwork for what psychoanalysis understands as conscious, or "secondary-process" thinking; the brain's dopaminergic seeking systems behave much like operations of what Freud called "libido"; and lapses or losses in frontal executive control of mesocortical and mesolimbic seeking systems manifest in what Freud dubbed the royal-road to the unconscious—dreams—and in other forms of "primary-process" thinking.

Speaking and working across the fields of neuroscience and psychoanalysis continues to be challenging, and many professionals in both fields remain skeptical of the endeavor. Yet, whatever else it is, neuropsychoanalysis is not a zero-sum game: contemporary neuroscience has not set out to "replace" psychoanalysis nor is psychoanalysis merely waiting for neuroscience to "catch up" with what it already knows. Rather, researchers in both fields have begun in earnest to unite their efforts in reciprocal, mutually enhancing work on clinical, scientific, and theoretical fronts, better to pursue the study of human subjectivity in ways unfettered by the rigidity of earlier mind/brain distinctions.[1] And psychologically inclined historians who want to avoid the functionalist opportunism of neurohistorical speculators like Daniel Smail and Lynn Hunt can now look to the field of neuropsychoanalysis for evidence-based insights into *interest itself* as an evolutionary achievement—one that affords us the *pleasurable anticipation* of discovering resources necessary for survival and success and, as such, is the foundation of our brains' meaning-making activities. As Heidegger put it long ago, "understanding is grounded primarily in . . . anticipation" (*Being and Time* 321). Much more recently, Jason Wright and Jaak Panksepp, whose research on the neural mechanisms of emotion helped establish the field of "affective neuroscience" and the foundations of neuropsychoanalysis, posited the existence of a neural "seeking system" that, when chemically or electronically aroused, promotes a psychological state "of positive euphoria accompanied by increased engagement with all of the life-supporting 'affordances' of the world" (9). This psychological manifestation of neural "seeking" is what we, like Heidegger and Benjamin, mean by "interest," which we experience as a combination of spontaneous excitation and the purposeful maintenance of a state of heightened awareness of and openness to various internal or external objects.

One of Panksepp's crucial observations is that this seeking system—which links emotions, thoughts, sensations, and internal and external objects—is subject to vicissitudes that can lead away from, as well as toward, what might be considered in a given time and place, cogent, shared representations of reality. And extreme overstimulation and overtaxing of the seeking system, Wright and Panksepp note, are associated with hypomania, delusion, and even psychosis (29). For, like all mental processes, interest—as manifested by neural seeking systems—operates on a continuum and is associated with a wide variety of subjective states, or self-states, and it helps condition the affective linkages at play in the storage, retrieval, and reconsolidation of memories in and through language.

Benjamin's History of His Own Making

Of his early discovery of the pliancy of words in relation to external objects and of his fervent interest in perceiving similarities, Benjamin writes: "If, in this way, I distorted both myself and the world, I did only what I had to do to gain a foothold in life" (*Berlin Chronicle* 131). Such "distortions," in other words, are both adaptive and meaningful. The "line" of history, along with all of its potentially meaningful "affordances" (or "footholds"), is always already "distorted," which means that the work of history must proceed with an awareness—an awareness best articulated in psychoanalytic terms—of our subjective interest in redeeming those distortions. "We can never entirely recover," Benjamin writes, "what has been forgotten. And this is perhaps a good thing. The shock of repossession would be so devastating that we would immediately cease to understand our longing. But we do understand it; and the more deeply what has been forgotten lies buried within us, the better we understand this longing" (140). To understand our "longing," our interest, is the work of history—thus Heidegger's interest in history, not as mere antiquarianism but as a vital concern for *unrealized possibilities in the past* and their relation to *unresolved problems of living in the present*. For Heidegger, thinking is always a form of remembrance, a remembrance of what has yet to be thought, an effortful overcoming of what he calls *Seinsvergessenheit*.

In his autobiographical work, *Berlin Childhood around 1900*, Benjamin describes walking through the city as a child and "planting" himself in various places where calamitous "events" had recently occurred. He did so, he tells us, "in order to steep my senses in the evanescent breath which the event had left behind" (106). His autobiographical interest in the Berlin of his childhood leads him to this (and other) recollections of the history of his interest as such, which he experiences—and recalls experiencing—in one or another particular, contingent self-state whose transience or evanescence is a sign, not of its facticity but of its authenticity. Benjamin's autobiography teaches us that it is in the interest of history to approach the past from a psychoanalytic—and, latterly, neuropsychoanalytic—perspective, precisely because history, all history, is the history of our interest in it.

Yet the genre of autobiography still occupies an uneasy place with respect both to history and to psychoanalysis: to the field of history, because of the tensions it amplifies regarding the nature and relation of the objective and the subjective; to the field of psychoanalysis, because of the legal and ethical demands of privacy and the need to preserve the integrity of clinical experience. Yet this same uneasiness is also an index of autobiography's pervasive implication in the narratives both fields generate, including the historiographical and metapsychological stories they tell, as it were, about themselves. In our own time, psychoanalysis no longer occupies the authoritative position it once, briefly, did in certain domains of literary and even historical studies. Societal and cultural changes help account for this—changes that include the economically driven shift away from psychodynamic psychotherapies toward behaviorism and psychopharmacology, the resurgence of identity politics, and the superannuation of the psychoanalytic profession. In clinical and academic environments, psychoanalysis has been driven to the margins by the prestige of the physical sciences, the "post"-postmodern reaction against critical theory, and, especially, the widespread intellectual clamor for empirical, evidence-based research in the humanities. Yet at the disciplinary margin of history, autobiography (in which literary, popular, and commercial interest has never been higher) pushes back against naïve empiricism and, precisely in the interest of history, could further help illuminate the participation of contemporary historicisms in what Jacques Derrida calls "resistances of psychoanalysis" (*Resistances*)—that is, both the nature of the resistances that psychoanalysis seeks to understand and to work through the various forms of resistance to psychoanalytic inquiry manifested by so many contemporary historians themselves.

Indeed, many of Derrida's own efforts to deconstruct logical positivism begin with autobiography, including his exacting readings of Jean-Jacques Rousseau's *Confessions* as a work that is at once literary, historical, and philosophical and that participates in—that has an *interest* in—each of these discourses and in the *interested*, often counterfactual, thinking that governs not only its signifying structure but also both its writer's and reader's relation to what may go "unperceived" (*Of Grammatology* 158). What may go unperceived, along with what comes to be acknowledged to have been perceived, are operations of the unconscious that must themselves be recognized as historical. That is, they are fully immanent to what Walter Benjamin calls "the concrete historical situation of the *interest* [*Interesse*] taken in the object" (*Arcades* 391). In other words, the "interest" of the historian in an object of study—like that of the philosopher and the literary critic—is a consequence of the historian's own subjectivation, including the formative consequences of the "epistemophilic instinct" that Freud postulated in his theories of childhood sexuality and obsessional neuroses (*SE* X: 245). By itself, Freud's own epistemological project does not, of course, define or delimit historicism as such. But it does offer compelling support for a practice of history that eschews what Georg Lukács, shortly before Freud's death, rebuked as "the pseudo-historicism of the mere authenticity of individual facts" (166). Here, Lukács is referring to the genre of the historical novel, but his critique of both the scientistic reduction of qualitative experience to quantitative data and the naïve historicism of relentless temporal separation is framed, like psychoanalysis, in service of the *interests* of actual, not merely or nominally fictive, persons.

The complexity of Benjamin's appeal to "interest" has never been fully acknowledged. Indeed, Benjamin's other fundamentally psycho-historical concepts of "dream," "phantasmagoria," and "awakening" have only recently begun to receive serious attention (see, e.g., Stewart). His understanding of the historian's "interest" is that it is neither wholly endogamous nor wholly exogamous; it arises and exists in relation to both social structure and individual consciousness; it is neither the deep spring of the historian's desire nor is it a shallow reflection of some common good. Instead, Benjamin unites the perspectives of the psychoanalytic thinker and the historical materialist, blasting apart the rigidly doctrinaire historicism of "collective *versus* individual" history and bringing together historical materialism and the ethics of subjectivation. As Marx puts it: "Men make their own history, but they do not make it just as they please in circumstances they choose for themselves" (32). For Benjamin, in his unique synthesis of Marxism, psychoanalysis, and messianism, the historian's relation to the past exists by way of "interest," which, as a word—in Benjamin's and Marx's German as in English—derives from the Latin word *interresse* ("to concern, make a difference, be of importance"), meaning literally "to be between" (*inter + esse*). Interest, in this radical sense, finds its meaning not merely in the calculating form of its rationality but also in the contestatory form of its subjectivity—for example, in Freud's Oedipal scenario, in which the child's interest in both mother and father is at once self-regarding and irrational; driven instinctually to interest (seduce, please, satisfy, obey, challenge) both parents, the child seeks to drive them apart from each other, to interrupt their interest in each other ("I hate their love," writes Mohamed Choukri of his parents in his autobiography [26]), so as "to be between" them, to survive rather than to be dangerously and frustratingly excluded from the bright circle of *their* interest, despite the various risks that captivating parental interest always entails.

One of these risks has to do with both parents' responses to the child's "epistemophilic instinct." Children's efforts to pursue their interest in their parents (their bodies, their relationship with each other, their sexual behaviors, etc.) may be either inhibited or encouraged, punished or rewarded, in ways that are potentially of tremendous consequence for their future intellectual lives. That the desire for knowledge is a developmental achievement of early childhood is one of the insights into the historian's "interest" that Benjamin ruminates in his reworking of the contents of his *"Berlin Chronicle"*

Notices into his more conventionally autobiographical account, *Berlin Child-hood around 1900*, completed in 1938. Many of Benjamin's vignettes, or images, of his earliest memories illuminate the sorts of protractions and interruptions that constitute any child's fitfully advancing knowledge of the parental world. For example, in the *"Berlin Chronicle" Notices*, Benjamin reports being awakened one night by his father, who had entered his bedroom to deliver—"half against his will, I believe"—news of the death of a cousin, "an older man who meant nothing to me" (131). His father shares with him a very detailed account, and Benjamin implies that it is the meaningfulness of some aspect of the man's death that prompts or compels his father to tell him far more than he can, or cares to, absorb. Still, Benjamin recalls storing away "an impression of my room and my bed . . . the way you scrutinize a place with greater care when you sense that one day you will have to search there for something you have forgotten" (132). The child, in other words, registers that something is odd and thus notable, not *in* his father's discourse, but *about* it, something "half against his will," something "forgotten" that will have to be retrieved. It was only many years later, Benjamin tells us, that "I learned what that was. Here, in this room, my father had 'forgotten' one piece of the death-news: That the disease was called syphilis." (132). Benjamin's ironizing of the word "forgotten" draws full attention to his sense of the overdetermined nature of the forgotten piece of information. In the later, *Berlin Childhood* version, Benjamin omits this direct reference to his father's amnesia. However, he adds the rather disaffected speculation that his father, "in order not to be alone," had sought out "my room . . . and not me" (86) as if to hint at their later alienation from each other.

The vignette stirs up many questions: What is his father's interest in the salacious detail, or in telling his son the story from which it is omitted, or in his son's future discovery of what he had "forgotten" to include? And what is the relation between Benjamin's own interest, as a child, in the inferred significance of the otherwise unmemorable story and Benjamin's later interest in the recollection and narration of this particular memory? If, in Benjamin's own words, "the mysterious work of remembering" is nothing less than "the power of making endless interpolations into what has been" (*Berlin Chronicle* 28), then what is his interest in exercising such power in this instance? Indeed, what remnants of a child's phallic striving might stir such an interest, not only in the past but also in the present of the past, in relation to a father with whom he had been (prior to his death in 1926) so frequently at odds?

Such remnants are found in the comical sketch of his father's frustration with their newly installed telephone, which is cast in distinctly Oedipal terms: the schoolfriends who call young Walter in the afternoon turn the phone's ring into "an alarm signal that menaced . . . my parents' midday nap," as if the son himself had burst in on them, in the manner of a primal scene. Yet it is not only the "nap" that is "menaced," he tells us, but also "the historical era that underwrote and enveloped this siesta" (*Berlin Childhood* 49)—a historical era (the nineteenth century) that, for Benjamin, "contains the whole distorted world of childhood" (133). This, his own former "abode . . . now lies hollow before me like an empty shell." "I hold it to my ear," he tells us, as if it were a kind of telephone receiver and the voice on the other end of the wire, not his father's, but his own future voice, calling to awaken him from the world in which he remains his father's child (132).

The trope of awakening concentrates Benjamin's thoughts on memory and conscious knowledge of the past in his *Arcades Project*, where its structure "yields," as he puts it, "before an unending variety of concrete states of consciousness conditioned by every conceivable level of wakefulness within all possible centers" (389). His explicitly psychoanalytic analysis of the structure of awakening anticipates, here, what later psychoanalytic theorists would call "self-states" and for whom, as for Benjamin, the trope of awakening would help account for the dynamics of intersubjective (social) as well as intrapsychic experience. The concept of "self-states" emerged in the clinical practice and theoretical writing of (chiefly) Philip Bromberg, Jody Messler Davies, and Donnel Stern, building on a number of much earlier, underdeveloped concepts including Pierre Janet's emphasis (in 1889) on the primacy of dissociation, Freud's notion of "part-egos" (*SE* IX: 150), and W. R. D. Fairbairn's observations on the multiplicity of ego states. Since the 1990s, Bromberg, Davies, Stern, and others have published numerous clinically grounded and metapsychologically astute books and articles premised on a nonmonadic, dissociative model of subjectivity. As Bromberg puts it most fundamentally: "Self-states are what the mind comprises. Dissociation is what the mind does" (*Awakening* 2).

Bromberg elaborates an understanding of the self "as decentered, and the mind as a configuration of shifting, nonlinear, discontinuous states of consciousness in an ongoing dialectic with the healthy illusion of a unitary selfhood" (*Standing* 270). And he suggests that what we have long been used to calling "the unconscious" might be more usefully described as a "suspension or deterioration of linkages between self-states, preventing certain aspects of self—along with their respective constellations of affects, memories, values and cognitive capacities—from achieving access to the personality within the same state of consciousness" (*Standing* 182). Intersubjectively, as well as intrapsychically, self-states are engaged in a form of dialogue that Bromberg, like Benjamin, associates with the structure of awakening. Indeed, one of Bromberg's books is called *Awakening the Dreamer,* by which he does not mean to evoke the rousing of a benighted patient's slumbering unconscious by a classically alert and controlling analyst but rather "a multitude of processes whereby shifting self-states in the patient, and in the analyst, come forward onto the stage of intersubjective dialogue, generating greater self-state coherence in both parties" (22). In Bromberg's structure of "awakening," the dissociative gap between a sleep state and a waking state is only one among innumerable possible dissociative gaps between different self-states, and it is in the spaces *between* different self-states that we may most often find ourselves "standing"—not rigidly, but actively taking our stand, as we seek to know the tenebrous forms of continuity we require to live in and with the world.

Benjamin's account, in *Berlin Childhood around 1900,* of his experience of distorted relations between ego and world (e.g., his projection and identification with inanimate objects and his difficulty finding or producing an image of himself) is not a mere recollection of the past—a notion of memory he himself eschewed—but a coming forward onto Bromberg's "stage of intersubjective dialogue" of a childhood self-state and a recollective self-state. In this light, the narrated continuity of a life, or what we call "autobiography," is an account of one's contingent efforts to generate sufficient self-state coherence, where "sufficiency" can only be judged subjectively and where "life" consists largely of casting about for ways to realize, often retrospectively, the pursuit of one's interests.

Conditional Interest and Historical Imagination

All "lives," like all lives, are, of course, largely counterfactual. Human beings are engines of irrealities: fantasies, confirmation-biases, psychic defense mechanisms and dissociative states, ideologies and belief-systems, states of desire, disgust, ecstasy, optimism, and shame, vicissitudes of temperament, genetic predispositions, "unformulated experience" (Stern), and even "unexperienced experience" (Blanchot 67). We make the world, and one another, up as we go—not as fiction but as what Jacques Lacan calls the "symbolic order," the term by which he refers to the social world generally and, more specifically, to that world as it is ordered by language. Focusing on the symbolic dimension of lived experience can help us to understand more keenly the "made up" (but not "fictive") quality of human experience, as Benedict Anderson did so influentially in his study of modern nation-states as "imagined communities." Lacan's theory of the symbolic order, as he himself came to realize late in his career, was hampered by its underestimation of the centrality to human experience of all that resists, thwarts, or escapes signification, including the ways in which the intelligibility of the symbolic is forever being subverted by the gaps, or aporias, inherent in language itself—the instances of recalcitrance to meaning to which meaning-making systems can help us testify, but which they cannot necessarily solve (with laws) or even cogently formulate (with symbols). Yet, even though our relation to the symbolic order is less passive and more complex than Lacan initially thought, we nevertheless remain its subjects, and thus there can be no certain way of understanding any utterance, sensation, judgment, symptom, triumph, relationship, satisfaction, or ordeal *that is predicated on its facticity*. Indeed, facticity, or matter-of-factness, is the slipperiest of predicates. As Robert Frost puts it: "The fact is the sweetest dream that labor knows" (26)—a line that rings true, despite making (or perhaps because it makes) mincemeat of commonsense distinctions between the concrete and the abstract—neatly epigrammatizing imagination's centrality to our manipular contact with the world, including the concretions of language itself. To live in a world of pure facticity (as if it were possible even to imagine such a thing) would be to enter the maw of fire that some of us still picture as hell. Without the symbolic order, there would be nothing but conflagration. Hell would be real.

Instead, we have the hellishness of regret to contend with. In his essay on the shortness of life, "De brevitate vitae," Seneca asks us to "look back in memory and consider . . . how many have robbed you of life when you were not aware of what you were losing" (295). For most of us, this is a superfluous injunction; we already spend far too much time looking back in precisely this way, scanning the past for someone else to blame for our missed opportunities. Autobiographical writing is uniquely susceptible to this all-too-human, all-too-serious frivolity. Indeed, many autobiographies function chiefly as its alibi—Oscar Wilde's *De Profundis*, for example, with its perseveration on the series of larcenies, both petty and grand, by which Lord Alfred Douglas robbed him of his splendid life and, ultimately, his liberty. Sooner or later, we all discover that to recount a life is to be brought face-to-face, repeatedly, with what once would have been better choices, better paths. If only one had known! If only the right person had been there to light the way! Anticipating the rekindling of regret, Rousseau ends the perambulatory opening of his *Confessions* with a wistful meditation on "the lot that would naturally have been mine if I had fallen into the hands of a better master," advising the reader that the rest of his book is one long dilation on "*instead of which*" (42–43; emphasis added). Edmund Gosse has less patience with his second-guesses, reprimanding himself for what he calls, in *Father and Son*, his "vain and trivial speculations"—speculations on how much happier his mother's life might have been had she not repressed her story-telling instinct and perhaps, implicitly, on what his own life would have been like, had he not largely repressed certain sexual instincts of his own (49). Similarly hard on himself, Behrouz Boochani, in *No Friend but the Mountains*, condemns as "worthless" his desire, while contemplating his mortality, "to interpret a counterfactual occurrence; that is, reflect deeply on something that might have occurred in the past—but in fact didn't" (76).

Other autobiographers are less prone to condemn in themselves what is so common to all: the desire that life could yet be something we had differently lived. "Somewhere in the world," Lauren Slater writes, "if you pressed the right keys, or the right combination of keys, there would be thunder and Mozart, and more; there would be all you'd craved but been too clenched to take, soft songs you could sleep to, chords like a hammock, maybe, and a hand to hold, the way time slows in a tub. If you knew the right notes" (19). In *Lying*, of course, Slater revels in what might or might not be her pathological tendency to blur all distinctions between what might have been and what actually was. But one may also confer on lying the presumptive dignity of literary fiction—an ethical sleight-of-hand nowhere better exposed than in Toni Cade Bambara's "A Sort of Preface" to *Gorilla, My Love*:

> It does no good to write autobiographical fiction cause the minute the book hits the stand here comes your mama screamin how could you and sighin death where is thy sting and she snatches you up out your bed to grill you about what was going down back there in Brooklyn when she was working three jobs and trying to improve the quality of your life and come to find on page 42 that you were messin around with that nasty boy up the block and breaks into sobs and quite naturally your family strolls in all sleepy-eyed to catch the floor show at 5:00 A.M. but as far as your mama is concerned, it is nineteen-forty-and-something and you ain't too grown to have your ass whupped. . . . So I deal in straight-up fiction myself, cause I value my family and friends, and mostly cause I lie a lot anyway. (ix–x)

Bambara's "straight-up fiction" is a sly oxymoron, evoking the undiluted strength of whiskey without ice: not watered-down truth masquerading as a liquor never brewed but life right from the bottle, on which a misleading label has been slapped ("cause I lie a lot anyway"). Bambara implies that her lying, unlike Slater's, is intentional, volitional; she lies because she can, not because she cannot help it or because she cannot distinguish between lies and truths. But both writers are taking a similar kind of pleasure in shaking the reader's tree, with the slightly scandalous reminder (as reminders of the obvious usually are) that prevarication is part of the truth of everyone's experience and, thus, that autobiography, as Derrida puts it, always "takes place between fiction and truth" (*Demeure* 16).

This "place," or "taking-place," "between fiction and truth" is strongly associated, not only with the tradition of confession but also with the testimonial place or space of sufferance and suffering where people are engaged to tell the truth of their experience and, thus, the place or space of all the forms of perjury, falsification, lying, silencing, amnesia, and denial to which all testimony remains forever open (*Demeure* 29–30). Every autobiographer who testifies to her ipseity is a witness to her own testimony—perhaps a secret witness, perhaps a multitude of witnesses, each in its own time, situation, and mood; each in its own relation to each of the other witnesses, if we regard them, as contemporary psychoanalysis invites us to do, as individual self-states, who may or may not trust or even believe (in) one another.

Nostalgic self-states protect us from thinking too exclusively in terms of remote conditionals. By dwelling sentimentally on what was, we can avoid perseverating on what might have been, which is an especially handy defense for autobiographical writers, who must somehow face, or efface, the various ill-considered actions and lamented outcomes that populate all of our pasts and that scar so many of us with the lacerations of regret. Benjamin Franklin— a man who seems never to have suffered very keenly from regret—observed that an autobiography may be thought of as an opportunity for "a Repetition of the same Life from its Beginnings, only asking the Advantage Authors have in a second Edition to correct some Faults of the first" (9). Franklin's preferred term for such faults was "errata," and, skilled printer that he was, he often likened living to the composition of a book. For the most part, the "errata" of his life—the ones, at any rate, that he shares in his autobiography—are trivial. The greatest exception is his account of the death of his son Francis: "In 1736 I lost one of my Sons, a fine Boy of 4 Years old, by the Smallpox taken in the common way. I long regretted bitterly and still regret that I had not given it to him by Inoculation. This I mention for the Sake of Parents, who omit that Operation on the Supposition that they should never forgive themselves if a Child died under it; my Example showing that the Regret may be the same either way" (96). The poignancy of loss is compounded here by Franklin's uncharacteristically glum implication that the correction of an erratum may be just another erratum; even if he could have gone back in time to inoculate his son, the boy might still have died.

Franklin's own death, in 1790, left his autobiography unfinished. Around the same time, the neologism "autobiography" itself began to migrate from German to English, French, and other European languages, just as—one notes with interest—the term "nostalgia," which had been coined (also in

Germany) in 1688 by the Swiss physician Johannes Hofer, began to lose its distinctly nosological categorization as a disease. Hofer had first identified the disease among Swiss soldiers serving abroad who, in his view, exhibited a manic or melancholic longing for their homeland that could in some instances be seriously debilitating and even fatal. For almost a century, doctors debated the possible physical and psychological causes of the disease until reaching the consensus that what had seemed, at least in the most grievous cases, like pathological homesickness was, in fact, misdiagnosed tuberculosis (see Boym). Thus, as "autobiography" entered the modern lexicon of literary genres, medical science began to relinquish the term "nostalgia" to a modern language of emotion keyed to particular ways of understanding time and place. That is, a crippling longing to revive some object, event, or quality of the past came to be recognized as a psychological condition rather than a physical malady—a condition in which the nostalgic failed, even refused, to forge or sustain a personally tolerable relation to the past.

"Autobiography" names a mode of historiography by which writers seek—and often very interestingly fail—to forge for themselves a personally tolerable relation to the past, and also by which they contribute to the historical record of what and how human beings remember, both consciously and unconsciously. Psychoanalysis has always been in the interest of (this) history because it helps keep history, as a discipline of writing (about) the past, *open to the intolerable*, to what Michel Foucault—in his praise of psychoanalysis as a counterpositivist methodology—describes as the "perpetual principle of dissatisfaction, of calling into question, of criticism and contestation of what may seem, in other respects, to be established" (373). For almost a century, the idea of studying "internal" or subjective states seemed intolerable to those who devoted themselves to understanding the human brain—until one of history's characteristically unanticipated shifts in perspective occurred. Is it too much to hope that, after the past several decades of empiricist retrenchment, historians might, in the interest of history, embrace a similar shift? ▪

Max Cavitch is an associate professor of English at the University of Pennsylvania, where he is also codirector of the Psychoanalytic Studies Program, a faculty affiliate of the History Graduate Group, and a member of the Executive Committee of the McNeil Center for Early American Studies.

ACKNOWLEDGMENTS

For their astute readings of earlier versions of this essay, thanks to Brian Connolly, Edward Larkin, and Joan Wallach Scott.

NOTES

1   As Elizabeth A. Wilson observed in an early issue of this journal, there has been a tendency among some neuropsychoanalysts to idealize as "a strong, polished alloy" what has been and might yet be forged "out of various elements of neuroscience and psychoanalysis" (149)—an idealization that has had the effect of masking or suppressing, she argues, their mutually deconstructive potentials. While I agree that historical antagonisms, steep learning-curves, and skeptical funders have induced many neuropsychoanalysts to minimize all that remains (and might always remain) noncongruous and incommensurate between psychoanalysis and neuroscience, the decade since Wilson voiced her concerns has seen a breathtaking expansion and diversification of this still-emergent field. The work of Mark Solms (2015; 2021), George Northoff (2011), and Jaak Panksepp and Lucy Biven (2012), for example, has already pushed far beyond the empirical and the medically verifiable both conceptually and in relation to the treatment of neurologically and psychologically compromised patients. Even in the area of sexuality—much neglected by psychoanalysis in recent decades, as Wilson rightly observes (161)—rekindled interest in drive theory, within and beyond the field of neuropsychoanalysis, has energized important new debates regarding the relationship between functionalist and nonfunctionalist theories of libido.

WORKS CITED

Adorno, Theodor. *Minima Moralia: Reflections on a Damaged Life*, translated by E. F. N. Jephcott. London: Verso, 2005.

Allen, Amy. *Critique on the Couch: Why Critical Theory Needs Psychoanalysis*. New York: Columbia University Press, 2021.

Anderson, Benedict. *Imagined Communities: Reflections on the Origin and Spread of Nationalism*. London: Verso, 1983.

Aurell, Jaume. *Theoretical Perspectives on Historians' Autobiographies: From Documentation to Intervention*. London: Routledge, 2016.

Bambara, Toni Cade. *Gorilla, My Love*. New York: Random House, 1972.

Benjamin, Walter. *The Arcades Project*, translated by Howard Eiland and Kevin McLaughlin. Cambridge, MA: Harvard University Press, 2002.

Benjamin, Walter. *Berlin Childhood around 1900*, translated by Howard Eiland. Cambridge, MA: Harvard University Press, 2006.

Benjamin, Walter. *The "Berlin Chronicle" Notices*, translated by Carl Skoggard. Madrid: Pilot Editions, 2015.

Benjamin, Walter. *Illuminations: Essays and Reflections*, edited by Hannah Arendt. New York: Schocken Books, 1969.

Blanchot, Maurice. *The Writing of the Disaster*, translated by Ann Smock. Lincoln: University of Nebraska Press, 1995.

Boochani, Behrouz. *No Friend but the Mountains: Writing from Manus Prison*, translated by Omid Tofighian. Toronto: Anansi, 2019.

Boym, Svetlana. *The Future of Nostalgia*. New York: Basic Books, 2001.

Bromberg, Philip M. *Awakening the Dreamer: Clinical Journeys*. Mahwah, NJ: Analytic Press, 2006.

Bromberg, Philip M. *Standing in the Spaces: Essays on Clinical Process, Trauma, and Dissociation*. Mahwah, NJ: Analytic Press, 1998.

Choukri, Mohamed. *For Bread Alone*, translated by Paul Bowles. London: Telegram, 2006.

Derrida, Jacques. *Demeure: Fiction and Testimony*, translated by Elizabeth Rottenberg. Stanford, CA: Stanford University Press, 2000.

Derrida, Jacques. *Of Grammatology*, translated by Gayatri Chakravorty Spivak. Baltimore: Johns Hopkins University Press, 1997.

Derrida, Jacques. *Resistances of Psychoanalysis*, translated by Peggy Kamuf, Pascale-Anne Brault, and Michael Naas. Stanford, CA: Stanford University Press, 1998.

Fairbairn, W. R. D. *From Instinct to Self: Selected Papers of W. R. D. Fairbairn, Volume 1: Clinical and Theoretical Papers*, edited by David E. Scharff and Ellinor Fairbairn Birtles. London: Jason Aronson, 1995.

Foucault, Michel. *The Order of Things: An Archaeology of the Human Sciences*, a translation of *Les Mots et les choses*. New York: Vintage Books, 1994.

Franklin, Benjamin. *Autobiography*, edited by Joyce E. Chaplin. New York: W. W. Norton, 2012.

Freud, Sigmund, James Strachey, Anna Freud, and Carrie Lee Rothgeb. "Creative Writers and Day-Dreaming." In vol. 9 of *The Standard Edition of the Complete Psychological Works of Sigmund Freud*, 141–53. London: Hogarth Press, 1959.

Freud, Sigmund, James Strachey, Anna Freud, and Carrie Lee Rothgeb. "Moses and Monotheism: Three Essays." In vol. 23 of *The Standard Edition of the Complete Psychological Works of Sigmund Freud*, 1–137. London: Hogarth Press, 1964.

Freud, Sigmund, James Strachey, Anna Freud, and Carrie Lee Rothgeb. "Notes Upon a Case of Obsessional Neurosis." In vol. 10 of *The Standard Edition of the Complete Psychological Works of Sigmund Freud*, 151–318. London: Hogarth Press, 1955.

Freud, Sigmund, James Strachey, Anna Freud, and Carrie Lee Rothgeb. "On the Psychical Mechanisms of Hysterical Phenomena: Preliminary Communication." In vol. 2 of *The Standard Edition of the Complete Psychological Works of Sigmund Freud*, 1–17. London: Hogarth Press, 1955.

Frost, Robert. *Collected Poems, Prose, and Plays*, edited by Richard Poirier and Mark Richardson. New York: Library of America, 1995.

Gosse, Edmund. *Father and Son: A Study of Two Temperaments*, edited by Peter Abbs. London: Penguin, 1989.

Hamilton, Patrick. *Angel Street: A Victorian Thriller in Three Acts*. London: Samuel French, 1942.

Hartman, Saidiya. "The Anarchy of Colored Girls Assembled in a Riotous Manner." *South Atlantic Quarterly* 117, no. 3 (2018): 465–90.

Heidegger, Martin. *Being and Time*, translated by Joan Stambaugh. Albany: State University of New York Press, 1996.

Heidegger, Martin. *What Is Called Thinking?*, translated by J. Glenn Gray. New York: Harper and Row, 1968.

Janet, Pierre. *L'automatisme psychologique: Essai de psychologie expérimentale sur les formes inférieures de l'activité humaine*. Paris: Félix Alcan, 1889.

Lukács, George. *The Historical Novel*, translated by Hannah and Stanley Mitchell. Lincoln: University of Nebraska Press, 1983.

Marx, Karl. "The Eighteenth Brumaire of Louis Bonaparte." In *Later Political Writings*, translated by Terrell Carver, 31–127. Cambridge: Cambridge University Press, 1996.

Mathiowetz, Dean. *Appeals to Interest: Language, Contestation, and the Shaping of Political Agency*. University Park: Pennsylvania State University Press, 2011.

Northoff, Georg. *Neuropsychoanalysis in Practice: Brain, Self, and Objects*. Oxford: Oxford University Press, 2011.

Panksepp, Jaak, and Lucy Biven. *The Archaeology of Mind: Neuroevolutionary Origins of Human Emotions*. New York: W. W. Norton, 2012.

Phillips, Adam. *Terrors and Experts*. Cambridge, MA: Harvard University Press, 1996.

Richter, Daniel. "Whose Indian History?" *William and Mary Quarterly* 50, no, 2 (1993): 379–93.

Rousseau, Jean-Jacques. *Confessions*, translated by Angela Scholar. Oxford: Oxford University Press, 2008.

Saint Augustine. *Confessions*, translated by R. S. Pine-Coffin. Harmondsworth, UK: Penguin, 1961.

Scott, Joan Wallach. "Against Eclecticism." *Differences: A Journal of Feminist Cultural Studies* 16, no. 3 (2005): 114–37.

Scott, Joan Wallach. *The Fantasy of Feminist History*. Durham, NC: Duke University Press, 2011.

Scott, Joan Wallach. "Psychoanalysis and the Indeterminacy of History." In *Situation Critical! Critique, Theory, and Early American Studies*, edited by Max Cavitch and Brian Connolly. Forthcoming.

Seneca. *Moral Essays, Volume II*, translated by John W. Basore. Cambridge, MA: Harvard University Press, 1932.

Slater, Lauren. *Lying: A Metaphorical Memoir*. New York: Penguin, 2000.

Solms, Mark. *The Feeling Brain: Selected Papers on Neuropsychoanalysis*. London: Karnak, 2015.

Solms, Mark. *The Hidden Spring: A Journey to the Source of Consciousness*. New York: W. W. Norton, 2021.

Stern, Donnel. *Unformulated Experience: From Dissociation to Imagination in Psychoanalysis*. New York: Taylor and Francis, 2003.

Stewart, Elizabeth. *Catastrophe and Survival: Walter Benjamin and Psychoanalysis*. London: Bloomsbury, 2012.

Tomlins, Christopher. *In the Matter of Nat Turner: A Speculative History*. Princeton, NJ: Princeton University Press, 2020.

Wilson, Elizabeth A. "Another Neurological Scene." *History of the Present* 1, no. 2 (2011): 149–69.

Wright, Jason S., and Jaak Panksepp. "An Evolutionary Framework to Understand Foraging, Wanting, and Desire: The Neuropsychology of the SEEKING System." *Neuropsychoanalysis* 14, no. 1 (2012): 5–39.

Zahid R. Chaudhary

Paranoid Publics

ABSTRACT This article takes up the recent insurrection in Washington, DC, and the paranoid politics of QAnon. It analyzes the gamification of paranoia across QAnon and related
paranoid publics. Taking seriously Sigmund Freud's insight that delusional formations are
attempts at recovery, this article reads QAnon as a part of a symptomatology of the social
world.

KEYWORDS conspiracy, paranoia, QAnon, play, neoliberalism

There is no freedom without opinions that diverge from reality, but such
divergence endangers freedom.
—Adorno, "Opinion Delusion Society"

Disinformation is necessary.
—Q

Witness the self-professed QAnon influencer and shaman, shirtless, with
painted face and feral hat who took to howling in the Senate chamber
after breaking into the Capitol building along with the rest of the mob on
January 6, 2021, to "stop the steal": a surreal display of a primitivist fascism
in its experimental and speculative form. What are the conditions of this
scene's possibility? The shaman concretizes the storming of the Capitol as
an elaborate spectacle, intended to "stop the steal" but also intended for the
eyes of ubiquitous digital cameras. There is the mixed crowd of Trump
supporters—small business owners, middle managers, white supremacists,
ex-military personnel—from which the shaman emerged; there are the
multiple politicians who tacitly or explicitly lent support to the crowd
and the narrative of election fraud that galvanized it. The theatrics of January 6 shocked in part because scenes of play-acting, phoniness, and collective fun appeared dissonant with an event that demonstrated all too

HISTORY of the PRESENT ▪ A Journal of Critical History ▪ 12:1 ▪ April 2022
DOI 10.1215/21599785-9547248 © 2022 Duke University Press

spectacularly the damage to democracy that had been ongoing in less visible ways over the last three decades.

The imagined injury—a stolen election—is all the more galvanizing for being unreal and is a cipher for multiple other investments: being wronged, of seeking justice, acting in the interests of an aggrieved self, and of feeling dispossessed in one's own country. Indeed, a recent study of the demographics of those arrested or charged with participating in the Capitol attack found that 95 percent were white, 85 percent were male, and most came from regions that have seen an increase in nonwhite populations (Pape). The actually dispossessed could not afford a trip to Washington, DC. Since almost all charged or arrested were professionals, narratives of economic immiseration, of being "left behind," are not sufficient explanations for what motivated their radicalization. I want to argue that so-called radicalization took forms of misrecognitions and conjuring—of injury, grievance, and malevolent enemies—that constitute paranoid ideation. When an imagined injury, or an injury to one's fantasies of nationhood or collective belonging is the effectual element in one's political participation, we are clearly in the presence of powerful psychodynamics. It is the transit from paranoid ideation to political action that interests me in this article.[1]

The January 6 crowd represented an amalgamation of paranoid publics: QAnon, antivaxxers, various militia groups, and so on. The insurrection was also a carnival, a logical endpoint for the libidinal and spectatorial politics that installed Trumpism as a political symptom of American politics. The oft-repeated QAnon dictum, "Enjoy the Show," is key both to Trumpism as well as to the media ecology in which QAnon germinated. The combination of performance and fun (posing for pictures, playing dress up) with deadly intent (killing a person with a fire extinguisher), the conjuncture of paranoia and political mobilization, and the spontaneous collective effervescence of the crowd coupled with a premeditated effort by some participants to monetize the digital livestreams of themselves at the Capitol all suggest that the psychodynamics of this event are indissociable from their economic and political aspects.

In this article, I am interested in reading paranoia's collective political life as an element of a larger symptomatology of the social world. Instead of assuming false consciousness on the part of paranoid publics, or dismissing them as merely delusional, I consider paranoia as a symptom illuminating the social formations that produce it. Paranoia and anxiety are not in themselves pathological, but they can become the outlets for pathology. If my analysis risks pathologizing paranoid politics, I hope it will be clear that such an analysis is aimed at taking these politics seriously if only because collective pathologies are a serious business. Limning the terms of these mass psychological phenomena and the forms of subjectivation, self-cultivation, and world-building they mean to make possible is critical for understanding the contemporary conjuncture of right-wing extremism, the devaluation of truth, and the increasing exposure of the polity to various forms of risk.

I will repeatedly return to QAnon as my example not because it is the most effectual or exceptional form of contemporary paranoid politics but for the following reasons: it has assimilated other conspiracies into its multiverse, making it a "big tent conspiracy"; it has grown organically out of the mediascape in which it germinated and its growth is instructive for understanding the powers of new media; it shares features with other paranoid politics such as antimask, antilockdown, antivaxxing movements but also with evangelical Christianity and millenarian movements; its membership overlaps with extremist movements such as Proud Boys and Boogaloo Bois; QAnon is one product of Trumpism and a valuable lens on this political strain that is likely to outlive Donald Trump himself and also likely to outlive QAnon itself.[2] Like all historical phenomena, there is something about contemporary conspiracy thinking that is unique to its historical conditions but also invokes (often literally) other golden ages of conspiratorial fantasy.[3] Paranoid politics are wayward forms of counterknowledges involving scrutiny of the self and also of the world, discharging psychic tension even as such scrutiny stimulates it. The conspiratorial explanation represents a fear that is simultaneously a desire; it is a wish-fulfillment doubling as a warning. As Robyn Marasco puts it, "conspiracy theory is a love affair with power that poses as its critique" (238). However irrational its own forms of reasoning, it assumes that the powers and authorities it is exposing operate rationally and are not merely powerful but all-powerful—that is to say, ideal and pure forms of power.

One of the guiding principles of my exploration of paranoia's recent mass psychological forms is Sigmund Freud's insight in his analysis of Daniel Paul Schreber—whose 1903 *Memoirs of My Nervous Illness* would become an urtext for later psychoanalytic accounts not only of paranoia but also psychosis, proto-fascism, and delusional ideation—that paranoia represents an effort at holding together a world that seems to be disintegrating. Noting that ideation around "world catastrophe" attends many cases of paranoia, Freud writes:

> we shall not find it difficult to explain these catastrophes. . . . The end of the world is the projection of this internal catastrophe; his subjective world has come to an end since his withdrawal of his love from it. . . . He builds it up

by the work of his delusions. *The delusional formation* [wahnbildung], *which we take to be the pathological product, is in reality an attempt at recovery* [heilungsversuch], *a process of reconstruction.* (*SE* XII: 69–70)

Paranoid delusions are a *heilungsversuch*, or a "healing attempt" that entails a reworking and refashioning both of the self and the world. Delusional formations (*wahnbildung*), insofar as they are a type of *bildung*, entail not only projecting idealized fantasy images on to the world but also transforming and cultivating oneself by means of such projection. Paranoia, in its obsessive scrutiny of external signs and patterns, might appear to be directed outwards, but it is at the same time a form of self-recuperation and self-cultivation. Even the paranoid are not the radically autonomous and voluntarist subjects of liberalism; they too are subject to historically particular limits and practices of self-formation and moral solicitation. Paranoid formations are not a break from reality as such but an accentuation and intensification of its features.

Critiques of paranoid publics expressing alarm at the fact that distortions and untruth have entered the sphere of politics, supposedly inaugurating a new "posttruth age," are not helpful for understanding what is at stake in paranoid politics. These accounts, even when not delivered in a nostalgic or elegiac tone, nevertheless remain tone deaf both to the historical existence of other eras of truth-demolition and also to the fundamentally adversarial relationship between truth and politics. Theodor Adorno observed that mass delusions arise from opinions that have sedimented into a semblance of truth. Reason, like opinion, has its subjective origins: "The moment called cathexis in psychology, thought's affective investment in the object, is not extrinsic to thought . . . but [is] rather the condition of its truth" (*Critical* 109). This suggests that the discursive, ideational, and affective traffic between the real and the unreal, the rational and irrational, the past and the present already exists in one's navigation of social relations. We operate with all manner of normative delusions, some of them "healing attempts" akin to Schreber's. There are no easy correctives to mass delusions, then, if one understands the problem of mass delusional formations as only an epistemological one, shorn of its historical and psychological conditions.

Politics of the LARP

History and psychology, therefore, point us to extra-epistemological dimensions of mass delusions; political economy does so as well. In this section, I will develop the psycho-historical and political economic groundwork for understanding contemporary paranoid publics. My wager is that we are witnessing the gamification of paranoia. The ludic grounds of paranoid ideation include new forms of economic necessity as well as psycho-historical processes entailing the constitution of enemies. The problem of collective paranoia persists stubbornly in the inequities of an administered world that promises the good life; but for QAnon, the question concerning epistemology is transformed in light of the ludic tendencies of contemporary paranoid publics. "Delusion" derives from the Latin root, *ludere*, meaning "to play." From this perspective, the paranoid publics of previous eras might also appear in a new light, as collective formations activated by what Roger Caillois called the "play instincts."

LIVE ACTION ROLE PLAY

These instincts are now solicited from users of contemporary digital platforms, which are not mere tools that preexisting paranoid publics deploy; rather these new media solidify paranoid publics. They may not originate paranoia but feed it, sometimes lending credence to delusionary ideation because the algorithms favor more extreme content that has some resonance with previously engaged content. QAnon's central doctrines seem designed for the clickbait era: politicians, the film industry, Jews, and "elites" form a cabal that thrives on ritual sexual abuse and murder of children, whose blood these elites drink to renew their vitality; Trump plans to put an end to all this by arresting or executing the cabal; the day this happens is called "The Storm." As QAnon began to grow and received significant press coverage,[4] Q opined on media critiques of QAnon, questioning why resources were being spent on discrediting something that mainstream media claimed was a conspiracy theory: "ALL FOR A LARP?" The acronym stands for "live action role play," a kind of game in which players assume an identity and perform scenarios in real life (think "Dungeons and Dragons"). In internet parlance, LARP has accrued an additional meaning: it refers to someone whose online persona paints them as privy to an exciting secret or an interesting life though in reality they may be Mr. Generic who lives next door. For users of 4chan—where QAnon initially took hold as a collective phenomenon—a LARP is someone pretending to have inside governmental or political information. Before Q there were other well-known LARPs posting on 4chan, with names such as "CIA Anon," "High Level Insider," and "Highway Patrolman." Their pronouncements on 4chan were delivered as aggressive truth-telling, and the necessity of both aggression and truth-telling presupposed a hostile world of opaque signs, duped citizenry, and oblivious politics. The persona of the truth-teller would become a central libidinal attachment for QAnon participants.

The term "LARP" performs important interpretive work, suggesting a host of relationships between performance and community formation, play and reality, and between public, private, and anonymous selves. A LARP assumes not only a make-believe subject position but also a make-believe world in which that newly assumed identity resides: its environment, its web of relationships and their orders of hierarchies, and the possibilities of action in the alternate universe. LARPing fuels the attention economies of platforms like reddit, the chans, and alt-tech platforms, not only at the level of content (users pretending to be fictional people) but also as economic exigency. Deployed as a theoretical formulation, what I am calling "the politics of the LARP" can provide critical sightlines into formations of paranoid publics and the conditions of emergence they share with other related cultural and political phenomenon. Such an understanding of LARP as a conceptual category helps us to see the conjoint operations of economic necessity, affective commitments, and subjectivation. In D. W. Winnicott's account of play, make-believe blends the real with the fantastical to train the self to be able to tell them apart—this game mediates distinctions between fantasy and the real. In the world of LARP, this distinction is lost.

Mimicry and role-playing are the LARP's fundamental techniques. The original LARPers—communities of sword-carrying real-life role-players—dress up in costumes they often make themselves and together act out a narrative whose key points are decided in advance but whose central themes are fodder for improvisation and elaborate play-acting. This close imbrication of theater and spectacle with gamification—play in all of its senses—endures in all the multiple meanings and practices of LARPing taking place not just on fringe platforms like 4chan but regularly on mainstream platforms. The selfie, the thirst trap, the vlog confessional, the well-observed nature scene, the photograph of the airline wing in air, the viral tweet are all fodder for LARPing. Thus LARPing itself is a phenomenon far larger than 4chan or QAnon. Paranoid publics emerge out of such familiar everyday LARP practices of digital life: Twitter and Instagram users, YouTube personalities, and of course influencers, regularly engage in a game of pretend, meeting the demands of increasing user engagement and donning the required persona for followers. The fact of knowing that online life is often filtered, enhanced, and contrived for the spectacle changes nothing in the fundamental operations of the LARP. The self is dispersed between the real one and the online image, which is further split between the anonymous and the nonanonymous persona, and variegated across the moods and protocols of different online platforms. Such dispersal of subjectivity is taken as given and is key to paranoid subjectivation because even as one participates in make-believe the knowledge that one's environment is the product of others' make-believing is never successfully repressed.

Influencers are more likely to be aware of their own participation in a world of playacting than the average user of Instagram, because they are fully aware of their roles as content providers. One can participate in a LARP without having any awareness that one is participating in a LARP, and even if one has such an awareness, the power of LARPing is not much diminished for the cultivation of personal and collective worlds of make-believe. Influencers, for all their awareness of the staginess of the life they represent online nevertheless must not call out this online existence as a LARP, not because it would break the spell but precisely because it is assumed that online life is contrived, yet such contrivances continue to exert influence nevertheless. Indeed, when LARPing becomes a generalized phenomenon, no opprobrium attaches to the figure of the influencer; this figure's mysterious powers of influence have become an aspiration. LARPing is a quotidian solicitation and practice for users of new media and definitely not restricted to the fringe regions of the internet. The horned and winged LARPers of yore had a clear demarcation between the space of play and the space of reality; digital platforms blur this distinction. Such a convergence of the unreal with the real is critical for the formation of paranoid publics.

The sense of community offered up through play is another mechanism for such convergence. QAnon is first and foremost a community, however diffusely and heterogeneously constituted.[5] The user interface on 4chan, where QAnon began, is deliberately low-tech and user-un-friendly, reinforcing a sense among users that they are a part of the 4chan community, with unique skills to navigate the platform. People outside of this community are "normies." Q encouraged community formation by indicating in parentheses that certain words, such as "timberwolf" and "warlocks" were "inside terms," codes for particular people or particular alliances.[5] 4chan threads are up-ranked based on user engagement, which in /pol/ (politics) and /b/ (random) boards indexes how incendiary or offensive the remark or meme is found by other users. This may or may not, however, be someone taking actual offense at a post, since a mood of supreme irony rules all terms of engagement and anyone taking a meme or post at face value can and often is publicly shamed by other users. A spirit of the LARP already underwrites participation in the chans, whether or not one is a part of QAnon. A given member of QAnon might hold fast to some or none of the core doctrines. The game, such as it is, entails sharing content that either creates an overall mood of outrage or moral panic or offers new interpretations of the Q's cryptic posts. Insofar as the Anons are participating in a LARP, paranoia marks the affective script of the game or the mood in which this game is to be played. Put simply, the game solicits paranoia from its participants, whether as performance or as "true belief."[6]

In a LARP, the participant is both actor and audience, aiming to fascinate themselves, other participants, and anyone on the outside looking in. In QAnon land, the outrage and offense expressed by "normies" is a part of the show. Thus, even the nonparticipants in the LARP are included in it, and the scope for play expands far *beyond* the boundaries of the playground or the stage, if you will.[7] For this politics, the ordinary world has the character of being itself temporary, and the people in it all players in spite of themselves. Since the whole world has now become a play space, the LARPers of QAnon insist they are not a LARP. Q's mocking statement, "All for a LARP?" suggests that the powers ranged against QAnon understand its central doctrines as the truth rather than make-believe, and this rhetorical flourish interpellates those powers as players. "All for a LARP?" has become a refrain in QAnon forums. As an utterance, it is a feat of paranoid projection and an invitation into the rabbit hole: QAnon knows the truth, and this knowledge is imputed to those who seek to criticize or de-platform QAnon precisely because they do not want the truth to come out. Thus "All for a LARP?" reaffirms the truth QAnon already knows and suggests that none of this is a game. The world is reduced to a belief already suspected, but at the same time this utterance also belies the anxiety it is intended to repress, that all is in fact make-believe. The Anons are often fascinated with their newfound role as truth-tellers and search for opportunities to develop it further, all the while being ready to discard or transform it as the requirements of the performance shift. QAnon does not require belief in the sense of an enduring conviction whose propositions can be taken at face-value; instead, belief is a provisional matter, like the temporary world of the game, held in relation to the demands of the game and discarded or revised as these demands shift. The adventure of the game and corollary to this, the cultivation of the self, are the primary drivers of participation.

The fun in LARPing consists of a simultaneous break from one's ordinary self—its expansion and assumption of another identity—and the release of one's true self. Its power resides in the existence of the true in the guise of the false. Arguably, this is the case for all fictions and fictionality, but in a LARP, this power is focalized around self-making and world-making. The real world is a cipher for a hidden world that exists alongside it, and one's actions in that hidden world—now magically visible everywhere—consolidate the true (previously hidden) self and reaffirm the terms of the game. Such are the adventures of QAnon-style healing attempts: this entire endeavor is a feat of collective projection and all the more riveting and fun for being so.

Projection is a psychic defense against the limits imposed on one's life-world by reality. It names a neutral operation by means of which people rid themselves—often unconsciously—of a desire, thought, or feeling by displacing it onto an external entity, where it appears changed from its original form. LARPing entails projection in the sense that all play involves projection: the world is reinvented through make-believe while simultaneously "found" anew, as if it existed there all along (Winnicott 712). An internal excitation is experienced as an external perception; this can become pathological, curative, or remain simply neutral depending on the context in which it occurs. Projection can be at work in paranoiac experiences but it is not reducible to paranoia, which itself makes use of projection as one among other psychological mechanisms. By means of paranoid projection, the subject masters an original unease, and paranoid desire aids in orienting oneself in the world, however temporarily. Freud suggests that paranoid projection entails shifts within ego formation, often giving rise to a sense of megalomania, ego aggrandizement, paired with epistemic certainty (*SE* XII: 62–63).

"LARP-ONOMICS"

Such are the psychodynamics of the LARP at the level of subjectivation, but as I suggested earlier, LARPing also entails political-economic processes that feed the expansion of paranoid publics. Contemporary paranoid ideation is riveted to dominant forms of neoliberal governance, not only in the existence of literal revenue streams but also in the often-deleterious ludic dynamics of economic calculation. The influencer represents the gamification of performance, of the imbrication of economic logics with the realm of performance and make believe—of "LARP-onomics," if you will.[8] It was Friedrich A. Hayek, the arch-priest of neoliberal thought, who described economic operations as a game—"namely, a game partly of skill and partly of chance" (71). This "game of catallaxy" depends on liberty and encourages improvisation, and although "undesigned," it still proliferates information and advances progress. Naturally Hayek's vision of this game is a utopian one, deriving as he does the word "catallaxy" from the Greek word *katallattein*, "which meant, significantly, not only 'to exchange' but also 'to admit into the community' and 'to change from enemy into friend'" (108). Grounded on agonism (competition), the game nevertheless delivers a reconciliation or adequation of diverse needs. Crucially, the game rewards not effort but strength, skill, or discernment: "It would be nonsensical to demand that the results for the different players be just" (71).[9] Hayek refers to calls for the redistribution of wealth as "unjust" because these calls invoke an authority other than the inexorable laws of the market. By figuring market imperatives as the impersonal and objective demands of a game, Hayek explicitly sequesters these imperatives—emanating from the oracular diktats of the market—from the sphere of ethics. In a game, just as "truth" is the result of the game's various rules, and "belief" is a lever for improvisation and subject to reinvention, "justice" can only be understood as an end that conforms to the operations of the game. In the attention economy, "gaming" the algorithm to increase engagement is a mark not of the cheat but of the skilled player. Gamification cedes ethics in the service either of rule-bound action or of improvisation, depending on the kind of game at hand. In either case gamification—like politics—is fundamentally inimical to factual truth.[10]

The algorithmic up-ranking of posts, the clamor for user attention, the desire to be viral all feed into circuits of monetization that make participation in the LARP a central necessity not only for the influencers within paranoid publics but also for tech companies that profit from the platforms and the advertisers the platforms serve. LARPing is therefore a cultural, political, and economic logic. QTubers perform alongside influencers, Qvangelists, entrepreneurs, online-only warriors, vigilantes, interpreters (known in QAnon parlance as "bakers") for user attention. Participation options abound and are always flexible. Increasingly, as QAnon has entered the world of the wellness industry ("pastel QAnon"), it can resemble lifestyle marketing. There is always merchandise and swag to consume and multiple books for sale describing The Great Awakening or The Coming Storm. QAnon has also seen success at the ballot box, in Georgia (Marjorie Taylor Greene), Colorado (Lauren Boebert), and Oregon (Jo Rae Perkins, who did not win the election but won the Republican primary). Its growth into multiple positions of institutional and cultural influence is a mark of successful improvisation, with its attendant willingness to bend the rules. Caillois described games of make-believe as being fundamentally free of strict rules—as he put it, "*mimicry* is incessant invention" (23). The flexibility of the QAnon multiverse—its accommodation of all past conspiracy theories and openness to new ones, its adaptation to various political and economic spaces—is nevertheless underwritten by norms that entail a fundamental adherence to a political game that tacks right.

On January 6, 2021, some people erected a scaffold with a noose on the mall outside the Capitol building, suggesting a prehistory of the LARP in the American tradition of lynching, complete with its carnivalesque forms of enjoyment. The storming of the Capitol was a LARP similar to the white supremacist march on Charlottesville in August 2017 that had marked the spiritual inauguration of Trump's regime. The specter of the noose haunted, as well, the scene of the hapless St. Louis couple anxious to defend their property against imagined BLM threats, taking the opportunity to act out the fantasy that attends gun purchases. The noose also hangs over incidents too numerous to count of an enraged white person threatening a person of color. Karen, that perennially anxious and enraged figure of contemporary racial capitalist modernity, has elective affinities with the QAnon shaman. LARPing gives rise to the expression of latent desires and wishes.

One member of the January 6 melee had brought homemade napalm in his truck for the fight. Another texted his friends a picture of himself in blackface with the note "I'm gonna walk around DC FKG with people by yelling 'Allahu ak Bar' randomly" (NBC Washington Staff). Such are the Schreber-like healing attempts that aim to rebuild the world: manifestations of the political unconscious of the American gothic—crafts made by tinkering in the garage, the nostalgia for blackface and playing dress-up, the enjoyment of adolescent sadism. These LARPs involving napalm, blackface, and "Allah ak Bar" are of a piece with the hanging noose—all components of a fever dream in which violence against racial minorities at home is a project contiguous with American imperial wars abroad, including its ongoing "war on terror." Cold War paranoia, which had authorized American imperial wars since the Second World War, had morphed into hysterical anxiety about the so-called "New World Order" in the nineties and eventually returned after 9/11 to the classic paranoid form it had in the Cold War: an anxiety that persecutes the entity it claims to be persecuted by. Concurrently, voter suppression, the rise of incarceration rates, and the persistence of police impunity eroded civil rights gains. These associative links were apprehended by the January 6 rioters in their zeal to oppose Black Lives Matter, Jews, Muslims, and "communism." In their political theology, these profanities all require elimination. Hence, some members mockingly reenacted the murder of George Floyd even as the Capitol was stormed a short distance away. The LARP involving racialized murder is a part of the same game that attacks democratic symbols. At stake in these performances is the "making real" of forms of aggression cultivated over time, often online.

A wished-for performance, including one of losing self-mastery, took the opportunity for embodied action. As Jim Watkins, the owner of websites that hosted QAnon, said at the scene of the Capitol's storming: this began as a LARP and "it became real. It's American history now" (Hoback).

By means of its rhetorics of extreme unseriousness, irony, and pastiche, overlaid on a current of aggressive ideation, QAnon forums reproduce aspects of what Theodor Adorno analyzed as psychological features of fascist propaganda: the glib jokiness that "is not so much an obstacle as a stimulant in itself" (*Psychological Technique* 80). The deindividuating experience of being in a group facilitates destructive forms of disinhibition, but with the addition that for a politics of the LARP such disinhibition also meets the requirements of the game.[11] The online culture of "lulz," with its conscious attempts at offending sensibilities combined with the cultivation of extreme irony and the drive to outperform other posts in sheer engagement through a greater show of aggression or prurience all appeal to conscious and unconscious wishes and affective needs of the users. Such demonstrations of the violations of norms—often for the sake of the performance—serve to bind the audience as a paranoid community, with access to otherwise opaque truths and now linked to one another by the libidinal glue of shared aggression, made permissible because the game requires it.

As a form of play, LARPing aids in integrating oneself to a larger whole, with all the libidinal comforts and tensions that come with such integration. The gaps in logic, the phantasmatic nature of friends and enemies, and the associative links across different claims, personages, and events, all indicate a deferred plenitude that is the endgame for QAnon participants. The piecemeal nature of the information available on the internet is enticing for would-be Anons because it extends the experience of half-conscious accrual of a conspiratorial plot. The repetition of stock tropes, the expressions of nationalist sentiment, and the insistence that the world is in a sorry state as a result of the cabal's activities all take place in the half-light of conscious conviction similar to the state of consciousness Freud discovered in his experiences in hypnotizing patients. Subjects under hypnosis are prone to a strange regression in which the emotions they are experiencing under hypnosis are both fully present and yet understood as phony: "Some knowledge that in spite of everything hypnosis is only a game, a deceptive renewal of these old impressions, may, however remain behind and take care that there is a resistance against any too serious consequences of the suspension of the will in hypnosis" (*SE* XVIII: 127). Adorno would read this moment in Freud's account of group psychology as an account of how the phoniness at the heart of fascism becomes integrated into the social world.[12] QAnon demonstrates that such phoniness results from the operations of the game but this is so because the game is not "only a game."

Group Psychology as Mass Psychosis
ANXIETY AND PROJECTION

What accounts for the destructiveness at the heart of the politics of paranoia? How does play become oriented toward a twofold destruction, of the world and of oneself? While answers to these questions are already implied in the account given above of the dangers of make-believe, I would like to draw out the implications of the LARP's psychodynamics more explicitly. In *Group Psychology*, Freud indicated that fundamentally group psychology is akin to the psychology of the individual because "only rarely . . . is individual psychology in a position to disregard the relations of this individual to others" (*SE* XVIII: 69). Freud concerned himself in this book not with aberrant or exceptional social organizations but mundane ones, including the army, the family, and the church. To such ordinary forms of collective experiences we might add the nation and nationalism. Benedict Anderson's classic account of nationalism, though not explicitly addressing group psychodynamics, highlighted a critical affective and psychological need that imagined communities have served. Nationalism takes over from religion as a form of collective imagining, a secular belief in transcendence. The political theology of nationalism is "a secular transformation of fatality into continuity, contingency into meaning" (Anderson 11). Such collective imaginings—not specific to nationalism—are forms of psychic suturing that allow accidental and contingent facts to become significant for collective life. Anderson puts it well in his pithy statement, "it is the magic of nationalism to turn chance into destiny" (Anderson 12). It creates continuity between the dead and the unborn, inserting both into national history. It also integrates one's immediate experience with collective history.

Already in Anderson's account, nationalism resembles a collective delusion, or to put it more specifically, a collective projection. The continuity it forges between the self and the group allows one to transmute one's own powerlessness and contingent existence into a supreme force understood as collective will and destiny. The same dynamics are present in a formation like QAnon. Such an installation of authority arises in tandem with the rise of capitalism. For Adorno, it was precisely this confluence of capitalism with collective being that prepared the political and affective ground for fascism, since capitalism demands that people submit to its economic necessities, resulting in a gradual repudiation of the very subjective autonomy that democratic ideals foster (*Critical* 98). Critical to such an experience is that repudiation itself *feels* like subjective autonomy; the middle classes have long provided support for atavistic and counterrevolutionary politics, yet their reasons for doing so are historically contingent.[13] Hence the dubious itineraries of "freedom"—reconceived in our contemporary political climate as the right to "free speech" even when such speech is a ruse for the suppression of social critique and social change or sometimes an outright call for violence. Daily adaptation or identification with the status quo—even when it poses as its demolition—prepares the ground for the acceptance of authoritarianism. As in a LARP, people are incentivized "to preserve themselves only if they renounce their self" (*Critical* 98). That is, the dissatisfactions and disappointments of capitalist reality, in stark opposition to what democracy had promised, means that "people remain indifferent to democracy, if they do not in fact secretly detest it" (99).The psychodynamics of the group offer intoxicating possibilities of projection, introjection, and the surrender of freedom.

Ressentiment, which imagines that others steal the rightful satisfaction of one's own desires, seeks gratification by destroying the perceived enemy through the same actions that rebound on the self's own destruction, names one dynamic for channeling collective anxiety, and there are others. Freud understood anxiety as a vital component of survival mechanisms because it prepares one for situations of danger, priming the organism for its fight/ flight reactions in response to an anticipated external danger. When danger is present in the external environment, anxiety is a natural and even necessary response. Neurotic anxiety, on the other hand, is triggered not externally but internally; it suggests a libidinal disturbance causing sensations that feel like danger but the effect of which is far in excess of any reasonable external danger (*SE* XVIII: 396). Franz Neumann, a contemporary of Adorno, was among the first thinkers to consider the political, mass psychological implications of anxiety. Neumann suggests that if Freud is correct that for masses of people identification with a leader is a means of identification with one another as well, it means identification is a mechanism for mastering anxiety. The leader is idealized as being capable of addressing one's distress, and corollary to this is the positing of certain others as the source of distress (618). Neumann argues that the word "scapegoat" is inaccurate for describing the subject-position of the enemy whose elimination promises to assuage a shared collective anxiety, because scapegoats are "substitutes whom one only needs to send into the wilderness" (619). The libidinal cathexis involving the-enemy-within spells the end of figuration and the hardening of conviction, what Neumann refers to as "false concreteness." True historical anxiety—the result of inequality, hunger, or war—transmutes into neurotic anxiety, which is then assuaged by renouncing the ego through a false concreteness secured through identification. Since the enemy is fundamentally evil, singular, and therefore un-substitutable and exempt from the play of signification, one's conviction about the enemy's guilty and rotten nature cannot be shaken. Projection entails a conjuring of such truths to which one must hold fast because their certainty is the grounds not only of the self but also of the group. The noose erected in front of the US Capitol stood as a warning to Black people, Muslims, Jews, immigrants, "globalists," and the "cabal" of elites. These enemies, for all the differences among them, constitute a single facticity against which the mob constituted itself as united in order to "Stop the Steal."

The slogan "Stop the Steal" serves a tripartite purpose: it is a projective utterance that disavows its own kleptomania; it marks a libidinal cathexis with Trump as leader; it is a cry for political action. In all three functions it serves as a form of ego aggrandizement. While attachment and identification with Trump as leader might aid such aggrandizement, as in Freud and Neumann's reading, a leader is not a necessary condition for the sense of megalomania that attaches to paranoid formations like QAnon. This might seem a surprising claim given Q's scriptural authority and Trump's halo, but following the projective itinerary of the Anons will clarify what I mean.

Projection is a defense against an originary anxiety for Melanie Klein, who also emphasized play as a critical feature of psychoanalytic practice. Crucially, for Klein it is the pressure of the death drive (understood not as a vague biologistic notion but as a mode of social relation) that gives rise to anxiety, which is "felt as fear of annihilation (death) and takes the form of persecution" (4).[14] Such a fear becomes externalized—projected, for babies, onto the mother's breast (the object at hand). Should the breast be withheld when it is needed—an inevitable course of events—it is experienced as a bad object; when it gratifies physical need, it is introjected as a good object and idealized, as capable of delivering limitless gratification. Such is the experience of what Klein calls the "paranoid-schizoid" position. Key to understanding Klein's account of projection is to understand that both extreme idealization of the good object and demonization of the bad object are forms of repression. Idealization represses the unease created by the bad object, and demonization of the bad object represses the persecutory anxiety that this object had unleashed. Thus, both idealization and demonization are forms of adaptation to changing realities, and such splitting of the world into idealized Manichean forms entails a split within the ego itself. Such extreme forms of splitting weaken the ego itself, increasingly bereft of a sense of self which it now experiences as disintegrating, "falling to bits," and dispersed and dissociated. Such dispersal of the self and de-individuation that attends projective identification is an experience of psychosis that can be overcome if the good object had been successfully introjected, but even so, it remains an ever-present potential in interpersonal relations. Ego integration is an ongoing project, and the stark appearance of the polarized world— divided between those who are good and those who are evil—originating in psychic splitting, remains an ever-present danger.

PSYCHOSES

Whether in the form of nationalism, racist hatred, delusional paranoia, or conspiratorial explanation, projection marks a narrative reversal for the subject caught in its thrall, who can then guarantee itself the upper-hand. Such a position longs to remake the world in the image of the psychotic illusions it has already deemed to be truth. Even a cursory consideration of the recent political discourse in light of collective projection brings to mind the denigration of truth as "fake news", the longing to consolidate executive state power by invocations of a shadowy "deep state", railing against "cancel culture" while ensuring that some viewpoints or voices do not find a home in the public sphere, trying to "Stop the Steal" by attempting to steal the election, proclaiming a conspiracy at work to conspire, and so on. Projection is a psychological mechanism that operates in an obscure zone between epistemology and phenomenology; when indulged in the grip of paranoia, it replaces knowledge with knowingness. In the internet age, its privileged genres are the headline and the meme. Destructive forms of mass projection are an elaborate LARP, investing the world with forms of the group's psychic needs and wishes, but such a solution spells disaster because it ensures that the image of the world reflected back to the paranoid subject is a repetition of itself, caught now in pathological forms of symbol formation that assure certitude but fail to relieve anxiety. New data is easily assimilated into the schema as a repetition of the self-same because for the paranoid all evidence confirms what is already known[15] and all that is contingent becomes necessary.

Freud's account of group psychology turns on his account of authority and its surrogates: totemic forms, collective ideals, and the figure of the leader provide focal points for an otherwise dispersed collectivity. These forms of authority appeal to the individual's narcissism insofar as identification with these forms promises the fulfillment of narcissistic fantasies (aiming at becoming an ego-ideal, being in the know and therefore superior) and binds the individuals to one another. Authority does not operate in group psychology as a form of coercion or brute power but rather as a promissory note or a lure. For the Anons, the failed prophecy is always about to come true, if only you "Trust the Plan." Adorno follows Freud even as he revises him in his analysis of the group psychology of fascism: "The leader image grat-ifies the follower's twofold wish to submit to authority and to be authority himself. . . . The people who obey the dictators also sense that the latter are superfluous. They reconcile this contradiction through the assumption that they are themselves the ruthless oppressor" (*Culture Industry* 142). This assumption of ruthless capacities is the beginning of the LARP. The ego aggrandize-ment entailed in these psychodynamics relies on the transfer of authority from the leader (an external reality) to the self's internal capacities and pow-ers. Thus begins the adventures of paranoia in the realm of self-cultivation. Trump is simultaneously just like his followers and also positioned as an ideal. It is not that leaders are adept at techniques of mass psychological manipulation in any conscious way such that one has to impute brilliance and calculation to leaders who are indeed often incompetent and even faintly ridiculous. Rather, it is the repeated voicing of an uninhibited latent wish of the group that proves so effective for mass mobilization. This explains why the fascist and quasi-fascist leaders' arguments operate not by means of rationality but rather by means of association, as in paranoid formulations. Wearing one's unconscious on one's sleeve becomes a strength for the leader—what Adorno refers to as making "rational use of his irrationality"— and language serves as a form of magic rather than rational signification (*Culture Industry* 148). It provides cathexes even as it signifies.

Leaders and demagogues function, therefore, as phantasmic forms. In libidinal politics, the putative powers of the leader do not require military control, intellectual prowess, and certainly not a life already lived according to the group's shared ideals. It would therefore be fruitless to search for expla-nations for libidinal politics in the personalities of particular historical lead-ers. The logical conclusion to be drawn from Freud and Adorno's accounts is that the leader or demagogue's necessity to a group is short-lived at best, and specific leaders are superfluous with respect to the libidinal politics that they might have helped to focalize.

The psychoanalyst Wilfred Bion went as far as to posit a leaderless the-ory of group formations, locating group psychology not in the centrality of a shared locus of authority but in the (Kleinian) dispersive and self-disintegrating mechanisms of psychosis. Leaders and figures of authority that might seem to draw to themselves collective projections are, Bion ar-gues, merely symptoms of a preexisting psychotic social formation. Bion's critical insight into group psychology—key to understanding contempo-rary paranoid publics—is that the requirements of a leader is "to be devoid of contact with any reality other than the reality of the basic-assumption-group demands" (178). In other words, the leader is a placeholder for the emotions of the group; leaders are like phantasmatic forms, invented and reinvented over the history of the group. For QAnon, insofar as LARPing is a game, the hierarchies within its formations are necessarily contrived and subject to reinvention. A dispositional psychosis attends all collective actions, Bion suggests, and while such psychotic experiences can be necessary steps for an eventual integration of the self with reality, such integration is not guaranteed. In groups, emotional release and spontaneous action correspond to psychotic anxieties similar to primal object relations. Bion states categorically that it is this *earlier* form of object relations, in the paranoid-schizoid mechanisms of infantile anxiety, that the "the ultimate sources of all group behaviour" reside (189). Bion's reflections on group psychology are particularly helpful for understanding contemporary paranoid politics, whose invocations of messiahs, leaders, or demagogues are less vociferous than their insistence that the unreal is real, and also whose fundamental forms of understanding are nimble enough to incorporate contingency (as in QAnon).

The End of the World

Recall that infantile anxiety in object relations theory stems from the intrusion of the death drive, which, in an elaborate and shuttling drama of projection, introjection, and splitting, results in the division of both the ego and the objects it encounters. Such splitting, an attempt at channeling the disturbances of the death drive, makes possible the expressions of sadistic and masochistic release. Projection, introjection, and splitting are, in other words, mechanisms of recovery central to the project of reparation that would follow in Klein's account of the depressive position that ensues when, in the fantasies of the paranoid-schizoid position, the ego's objects have been damaged. The deliberate flouting of norms and the ratcheting up of offense as a collective project for QAnon has imbued this paranoid formation with a psychotic anxiety always at the ready for fight/flight. This has persisted well past QAnon's de-platforming. To follow QAnon channels on Telegram means to enter a Manichean world in which an immediate fight/flight response is necessary. QAnon shares this aggressive quality with militia groups such as The Oath Keepers, Proud Boys, and Boogaloo Bois, who have installed aggression more explicitly as their raison d'être; anti-lockdown protests and antivaxxing demonstrations not only share members with some of these other groups but also they increasingly occupy the same psychodynamics. The Boogaloo Bois do not have a leader and are a decentralized group, unlike the Proud Boys, with whom they share an apocalyptic sense that the United States government needs to be overthrown, a new civil war fought, and new forms of freedom therefore made possible. Although Anons looked to Q for "crumbs" that would help them play the game of paranoid truth-seeking, Q was only one node in the game that took on a life of its own and continues to evolve in spite of his extended silence. Although adherents of QAnon exalt Donald Trump, their arcane interpretations of everything from Trump's misspellings to Melania Trump's wardrobe only underscores the truth of Bion's understanding of group leaders as phantasmic part-objects that conform to collective projection. Not being beholden to a specific leader is a strength rather than a weakness to such a politics of the LARP. Such politics are equally available to extreme groups as well as mainstream politicians, industrialists, funders of "dark money," and political parties who encourage extremists and feel energized by them.

Considering the conjoint problems of paranoid publics, posttruth, political polarization through group object relations illuminates several key points. The alarm over the neoliberal corrosion of communication systems and information ecologies—a staple of discussions of posttruth—conceals a longing for an order of authority that was itself an invention of group psychological dynamics. The catastrophes of the twentieth-century invent not only their own forms of abolishing factual truth but also the latent psychoses within the mass delusion of nationalism that consistently find expression in the constitution of new enemies, internal and external. This was the case not only for Europe and the United States but also for recently decolonized countries whose own intellectuals presciently warned of the pitfalls of nationalism. The Cold War division of the globe into blocs—a profoundly paranoid-schizoid formation—was all the more effective for channeling collective aggression and building the conditions for ongoing aggressions in the form of capitalist exploitation. So while the contemporary crises of democratic rule are not exceptional, they differ from twentieth-century crises in that the forms of idealization-as-repression are undergoing a change. After the fall of competing Cold War utopias, the pretext for new wars in Afghanistan and Iraq claimed "freedom" and "democracy" as the reasons for aggression. Domestically, the roll-back phase of neoliberalism extolled the virtues of "choice" and "freedom" as it stripped workers of basic protections. The idealizing of freedom as well as democracy in these instances served to undermine both, domestically as well as globally. Still, such idealization appealed to utopian aims even if it did so cynically. QAnon and the militias that have surfaced in recent years seem attached to such fascist utopias. Their endgame is "the storm" or some similar vision of catastrophe that is not simply to be welcomed passively but rather to be actively precipitated as quickly as possible.[16] The overriding affect of their politics is the thrill of vengeance paired with the practice of a scandalous freedom that evades accountability, destroys existing law, and overturns the existing order—such are the pleasures of *jouissance* as proferred by QAnon. The imminent "storm" is also a world-historically entertaining show.

Such LARP fantasies are collectively cultivated through performative iterations of memes and expressions of outrage; the performative LARP of online projection prefigures the politics of the LARP to be embodied on the ground: tiki torches carried by white supremacists in Charlottesville, the storm arriving in an attack on the Capitol, the GOP closing party ranks to ensure impunity for Trump's actions. As Freud explained long ago, the death drive operates in a fugitive manner, often appearing in forms that can feel freeing. "Question Authority" shows up regularly as an exhortation on QAnon paraphernalia, and Lauren Boebert, a QAnon congresswoman recently tweeted, "Never let anyone tell you that you shouldn't speak up for what you believe in. The 'powers that be' fear our voice more than anything. That's exactly why we need to be more vocal than ever." These exhortations are not subversions of the freedom-seeking impulses at the heart of well-worn American platitudes but expressions of the fascist apocalypticism that had always underlain their banal repetition.[17] In the QAnon multiverse, the world to come is only possible after the fearsome yet desirable cataclysm, one that can be hastened with increased calls to punish the evildoers. Such calls are simultaneously expressions of ego aggrandizement. To be sure, dystopian visions are also a form of idealization and enact their own forms of psychological and political repression, but it is dystopian imagination that undergirds the unease of contemporary politics. Even social movements that aim for a more genuinely egalitarian world express their protests by holding up a mirror to contemporary forms of inequality: "We are the 99%"; "Black Lives Matter." For the occupy movement, for BLM, and also for climate activists the storm is already here and has been brewing for decades. "I Can't Breathe" expresses racial injustice, and it also speaks—emblematically—of all manner of uninhabitable worlds. World catastrophe, then, is a critique of the existing order for one politics and the solution to worldly ills in another. Whether it is an orientation toward a dystopian cataclysm or a mirror held up to one already occurring, it is dystopia that lends politics its charge.

In Freud's analysis of Schreber, he notes that megalomaniacal ideation tends to become haunted by images of world catastrophe, of everything being burned to the ground, of the world falling away to make room for a new order, and so on. Such visions of the ruined world are an acknowledgment of an unconscious withdrawal of libido: "The projection of this internal catastrophe; his subjective world has come to an end since his withdrawal of love from it." Recent news images of climate disasters and even more recently the footage of COVID-19 lockdown-induced emptiness in world cities have not only demonstrated that classic filmic tropes of dystopian fantasy are now available in the form of reality—the objective world appearing in the garb of the LARP—but also intimated how the storm might look for an imagination given to delusional paranoia. A recent QAnon meme showed the face of Donald Trump pasted on the head of a US soldier in full body armor, leading his prisoner (Joe Biden) across a blighted landscape. The figure of the US soldier remains heroic in the mythology of QAnon and the militia groups— indeed the militia groups in particular have a significant membership drawn from former members of the US armed forces. "Support our Troops," the jingoistic imperative of post-9/11 America that was often weaponized against critiques of American imperial wars, has in some memes come to mean support the overthrow of the US government, in the most literal-minded way of bringing the war home. The Anons are as phantasmic as Richard Nixon's "silent majority"—a phrase they have begun to recirculate—and no less powerful for being so. They are even infected with similar moral panics. They are least delusional when they refer to themselves as the storm. For all their putatively fringe existence, they share in the same forms of idealized subjectivation that neoliberalism makes available: the entrepreneur, the influencer, the Instagram and YouTube star, and the hustler who has mastered the art of "pivoting" (in neoliberal parlance, an injury displayed as virtue or skill). The forms of subjectivation—not specific to extremist groups—is how the politics of the LARP transit from the virtual to the real. The Anons claim the certainty but also the challenge of conspiracy, whose Latin root we would do well to recall in the age of COVID-19 and the cracks in democracy it has accentuated; *conspīrāre* means "to breathe together"—provided that one can breathe. ∎

Zahid R. Chaudhary is an associate professor of English at Princeton University. This article is drawn from his forthcoming book, *Unruly Truth: Libidinal Politics and Crises of Authority*.

ACKNOWLEDGMENTS

I have benefited from the wisdom of the following readers: the editors of *History of the Present*, Ben Conisbee Baer, Rey Chow, David Eng, Asli Igsiz, Jarrett Moran, Gayle Salamon, Robyn Wiegman, Joanna Wuest, and seminar participants at the CUNY-Graduate Center's Committee of Globalization and Social Change and Princeton's Society of Fellows. I am grateful for their guidance and insights.

NOTES

1   As Richard Hofstadter noted in his 1964 analysis of what he called "paranoid style" in American politics, paranoia has a life outside the sphere of psychology, as a tendency of political thought. Hofstadter draws too sharp a distinction, however, between the

pathological and nonpathological, and his designation of "paranoid style" as an explicitly pejorative term assumes liberalism (and moderation) as a grounding and normative principle. See Hofstadter, *The Paranoid Style in American Politics*.

2   Even as I write, QAnon, banned by mainstream platforms, is fragmenting across alt-tech platforms such as Gab and Telegram, among others.

3   Fredric Jameson has read conspiracies as attempts to solve the aesthetic-political problem of representing an increasingly complex social totality (Jameson 3). Following on his provocation, Timothy Melley reads conspiracy as a manifestation of what he calls "agency panic" (Melley 14). For both Jameson and Melley, conspiracy represents a solution to an impossible problem: representation of social totality (Jameson) or the apprehension of individual autonomy (Melley).

4   A May 2021 poll found that 15 percent of Americans believe that a cabal of satan-worshipping pedophiles are in control of the world, and 20 percent believe that a cataclysmic storm would wipe out these evil elites. QAnon beliefs have become as popular as some religions (Russonello).

5   It is notoriously difficult to assess how many people are adherents of QAnon (Kight).

6   Commentators have increasingly noted the resemblance between QAnon participation and role-playing games (Berkowitz; "QAnon Is an Alternate Reality"; "QAnon"). These analyses miss that LARPing is a generalized phenomenon not specific to QAnon but a part of an emerging cultural and political logic.

7   What Johan Huizinga in his classic 1938 study, *Homo Ludens*, referred to as the "consecrated spot" or "temporary worlds within ordinary worlds" in which the rules of the game obtain, is no longer distinguishable as such for a politics of the LARP (Huizinga 10).

8   Thanks to Ben Conisbee Baer for suggesting this neologism. The recent corporate scandals of WeWork and Theranos involved LARPing tendencies that have become increasingly normalized for start-ups.

9   Seemingly unaware of the affinities between deluding and playing, and the resulting contradiction between truth and gamification, Hayek deludes both himself and his adherents. On Hayek's profound antipathy to those he called "social justice warriors," see Wendy Brown's insightful discussion in *In the Ruins of Neoliberalism*, 30–39.

10   Hannah Arendt explains that the hostile relationship between truth and politics is an ancient conflict, explained by qualities intrinsic to each: the work of politics requires a reduction of truth, and truth requires impartial investigation free of self-interest. See "Truth and Politics" in Arendt.

11   For the classic account of de-individuation and group psychology (see Le Bon).

12   See "Freudian Theory and the Pattern of Fascist Propaganda" in Adorno, *The Culture Industry*.

13   Wendy Brown's discussion of repressive desublimation brilliantly explains how this occurs under neoliberalism (see Brown).

14   Klein's most sustained discussion of projection is her essay, "Notes on Some Schizoid Mechanisms" (1946).

15   Such a sense of epistemological certainty and mastery is the grounds for new fantasies of dominance. Adorno and Horkheimer describe this well: "The closed circle of perpetual sameness becomes a surrogate for omnipotence. It is as if the serpent which

told the first human 'Ye shall be as gods' had kept his promise in the paranoiac. . . .
His will permeates the whole universe; nothing may be unrelated to him" (Adorno
and Horkheimer 157).

16   For an insightful account of conspiratorial apocalypticism (see Guilhot). Guilhot's
argument that the QAnon shaman seeks to rebuild a destroyed world resonates with
my argument here, though Guilhot and I differ on our assessment of psychosocial
explanations.

17   For recent accounts of the resurgence of fascism (see Harootunian; Toscano).

WORKS CITED

Adorno, Theodor. *Critical Models: Interventions and Catchwords*, translated by Henry Pick-
    ford. New York: Columbia University Press, 2005.

Adorno, Theodor. *The Culture Industry: Selected Essays on Mass Culture*, 2nd ed., edited by
    J. M. Bernstein, London: Routledge, 2001.

Adorno, Theodor. *The Psychological Technique of Martin Luther Thomas' Radio Addresses*.
    Stanford, CA: Stanford University Press, 2000.

Adorno, Theodor. W. *The Stars Down to Earth*. 2nd ed. London: Routledge, 2001.

Adorno, Theodor W., and Max Horkheimer. *Dialectic of Enlightenment*. 1st ed. Stanford,
    CA: Stanford University Press, 2007.

Anderson, Benedict. *Imagined Communities*. 6th ed. New York: Verso, 1983.

Arendt, Hannah. *Between Past and Future*. New York: Penguin Books, 2006.

Berkowitz, Reed. "A Game Designer's Analysis of QAnon." The Street/Phil's Stock
    World, January 22. www.thestreet.com/phildavis/news/a-game-designers-analysis
    -of-qanon.

Bion, W. R. *Experiences in Groups and Other Papers*. London: Routledge, 1991.

Brown, Wendy. *In the Ruins of Neoliberalism: The Rise of Antidemocratic Politics in the West*.
    New York: Columbia University Press, 2019.

Caillois, Roger. *Man, Play, and Games*. Champaign: University of Illinois Press, 2001.

Freud, Sigmund, James Strachey, Anna Freud, and Carrie Lee Rothgeb. "Psycho-Analytic
    Notes on an Autobiographical Account of A Case of Paranoia (Dementia Para-
    noides)." In vol. 12 of *The Standard Edition of the Complete Psychological Works of Sig-
    mund Freud*, 1–82. London: Hogarth Press, 1958.

Freud, Sigmund, James Strachey, Anna Freud, and Carrie Lee Rothgeb. "Group Psychol-
    ogy and the Analysis of the Ego." In vol. 18 of *The Standard Edition of the Complete
    Psychological Works of Sigmund Freud*, 65–144. London: Hogarth Presss, 1955.

Guilhot, Nicolas. "Bad Information." *Boston Review*, August 23, 2021. bostonreview
    .net/politics/nicolas-guilhot-bad-information?utm_source=Boston+Review+Email+
    Subscribers&utm_campaign=1e97b2b0bf-MC_Newsletter_8_26_21&utm_medium
    =email&utm_term=0_2cb428c5ad-1e97b2b0bf-40733269&mc_cid=1e97b2b0bf&mc_
    eid=20bc04a1d1.

Harootunian, Harry. "A Fascism for Our Time." *Massachusetts Review*, January 6, 2021.
    www.massreview.org/node/9428.

Hayek, Friedrich A. *Law, Legislation, and Liberty, Volume 2: The Mirage of Social Justice*. Chi-
    cago: University of Chicago Press, 1978.

Hoback, Cullen, dir. *Q: Into the Storm*. New York: HBO, 2021.

Huizinga, J. *Homo Ludens: A Study of the Play Element in Culture*. Boston: Beacon Press, 1950.

Jameson, Fredric. *The Geopolitical Aesthetic: Cinema and Space in the World System*. Bloomington: Indiana University Press, 1995.

Kight, Stef W. "Poll: One-Third of Americans Are Open to QAnon Conspiracy Theories." *Axios*, October 21, 2020. www.axios.com/poll-qanon-americans-belief-growing -2a2d2a55-38a7-4b2a-a1b6-2685a956feef.html.

Klein, Melanie. *The Collected Works of Melanie Klein, Volume 3: "Envy and Gratitude" and Other Works*. London: Hogarth Press, 1955.

Le Bon, Gustave. *The Crowd: A Study of the Popular Mind*. London: T. Fisher Unwin, 1895.

Marasco, Robyn. "Toward A Critique of Conspiratorial Reason." *Constellations* 23, no. 2 (2016): 236–43. doi.org/10.1111/1467–8675.12222.

Melley, Timothy. *Empire of Conspiracy: The Culture of Paranoia in Postwar America*. Ithaca, NY: Cornell University Press, 2000.

NBC Washington Staff. "Armed Man Threatened Violence against DC Mayor in Texts to Family, Friends: Feds." NBC4 Washington, January 13, 2021. www.nbcwashington .com/news/local/armed-man-threatened-violence-against-dc-mayor-in-texts-to -family-friends-feds/2540682/.

Neumann, Franz L. "Anxiety and Politics." *Triple C: Communication, Capitalism, and Critique* 15, no. 2 (2017): 612–36. doi.org/10.31269/triplec.v15i2.901.

Pape, Robert A. "Opinion: What an Analysis of 377 Americans Arrested or Charged in the Capitol Insurrection Tells Us." *Washington Post*, April 6, 2021. www.washingtonpost .com/opinions/2021/04/06/capitol-insurrection-arrests-cpost-analysis/.

"QAnon: A Game That Plays People." *Think*, January 21, 2021. think.kera.org/2021/01/21 /qanon-a-game-that-plays-people/.

"QAnon Is an Alternate Reality, But It's No Game." New Yorker Radio Hour, January 15, 2021. www.wnycstudios.org/podcasts/tnyradiohour/segments/qanon-alternate -reality-its-no-game.

Russonello, Giovanni. "QAnon Now as Popular in US as Some Major Religions, Poll Suggests." *New York Times*, May 27, 2021. www.nytimes.com/2021/05/27/us/politics /qanon-republicans-trump.html.

Toscano, Alberto. "Notes on Late Fascism." *Historical Materialism*, April 2, 2017. www .historicalmaterialism.org/blog/notes-late-fascism.

Winnicott, D. W. "The Use of an Object." *International Journal of Psychoanlysis* 50 (1969): 711–16.

Alex Colston

Left Freudians
The Psychoanalytic Politics of Disobedience

ABSTRACT Are the limits of psychoanalytic politics the limits of the politics of psychoanalysis's founding father, Sigmund Freud? This article offers an answer to this question by discussing Freud's political affinities and then recounting a short history of the "Left Freudians," psychoanalytic thinkers who broke with Freud's old-style liberalism. Freud was neither a communist nor a political radical, but he was the figurehead of a tradition of inquiry and body of knowledge that lent itself to radical political thought and practice. How does psychoanalytic thinking justify this ideological break? Beginning with anarchist Otto Gross, this article traces a genealogy of radical psychoanalytic thinkers through the historical depoliticization and repression of political psychoanalysis, unearthing its more radical proponents and critiques and substantiating Gross's assertion that psychoanalysis is preparatory work for the revolution. At the end of the genealogy, the article turns to psychoanalyst Jacques Lacan's infamous and emblematic encounter with provocateurs from the radical student movement. Neither as domineering nor paternalistic as he seemed, Lacan's diagnosis of the revolutionaries as hysterical helots should be read as his own provocation for them to clarify their desire, because the purpose of political psychoanalysis is to understand the unconscious desire involved in political acts.

KEYWORDS political psychoanalysis, Marxism, Jacques Lacan, revolution, ideology

There are three impossible professions—educating, healing and governing.

—Sigmund Freud

Psychoanalysis is like the Russian Revolution: we don't know when it started going bad.

—Anti-Oedipus

Intervention: "Lacan, is psychoanalysis revolutionary?" Lacan: "Now, there's a good question!"

—Dialogue between a protestor and Jacques Lacan

HISTORY of the PRESENT ▪ A Journal of Critical History ▪ 12:1 ▪ April 2022
DOI 10.1215/21599785-9547257 © 2022 Duke University Press

Ernest Jones gave Sigmund Freud the title of "immortal sire" in the dedication of his multivolume biography, suggesting Freud might forever loom as a paternal imago over psychoanalysis. (1: v)[1] In a similar vein, Lionel Trilling later said that the history of psychoanalysis had already been "made actual and dramatic in the person of Freud," affirming that generations recapitulate their origins as a matter of course (Zaretsky, *Secrets* 293). Accordingly, psychoanalysts relived, with wide variation, the epic of its founder. Trilling praised this as an advantage, but as Eli Zaretsky has noted, this encomium concealed an obscene prohibition: "do nothing of which Freud would have disapproved" (*Secrets* 293). To this day, demonstrative obedience to the father of psychoanalysis is commonly how analysts justify their interpretation and technique. Yet, if Freud's life provides content to the discipline, in every sense of that word, then when it comes to politics, one's beliefs, principles, and course of action are anything but clear. So what were Freud's politics? If they could be followed, should they be, as if tantamount to psychoanalytic practice? And how did leftists, with or against Freud's own sympathies, come to inherit psychoanalysis? Finally, who were these left Freudians and what legacy did they leave?

There is perhaps something historically inapt, even anachronistic, in speaking of Freud's politics in today's personalized manner, which can proceed as if politics were a possession, attribute, or passionate identity rather than an institutional affiliation, world-historical cause, mode of action, or circumstantial identification or disidentification.[2] Be that as it may, prominent biographers and historians have differed over Freud's politics. Peter Gay has argued that Freud's politics were typical of Viennese Jews, writing "Freud became a liberal because the liberal world view was congenial to him and because, as the saying goes, it was good for the Jews" (17), but Eli Zaretksy has taken particular exception to this, asserting that Gay "(mis)described" Freud's politics: "like almost all European analysts of the time, [Freud] was a social democrat, not a classic free-market liberal" (113). Philip Rieff disagreed with both accounts, saying Freud was "a neutralist with respect to all political forms" (300). These competing determinations are each a partial truth of a naturally overdetermined reality.

Finding an explanation *between* Freud's Judaism and anti-Semitic Viennese culture, the vocational community of analysts and the apolitical posture of analytic neutrality, Carl Schorske's depiction is the most psychoanalytic. Expanding on Freud's own dream analysis, Schorske traces how Freud's antiaristocratic and antiauthoritarian instinct, his professional frustration because of institutional racism, and his ambivalent identification with his socialist peers ran parallel with working through a disappointing memory of his father. Attempting to convince his son that liberalism had made the world safe for the Jewish people, Freud's father, Jacob Freud, told young Sigmund about how an anti-Semitic Christian once publicly humiliated him. Because his father did not fight back, Sigmund deemed his father's behavior "unheroic," and he vowed to take revenge on his behalf, as a reincarnated Hannibal, who swore to avenge his father against the Romans (Schorske 337; Roudinesco, *Freud*: 196–97).

Thus, Freud was generally in concert with Viennese intellectuals, which meant sharing a desire for a "generational revolt against the fathers [that] took the specific historical form of rejection of their fathers' liberal creed," but the ultimate effect of his self-analysis was depoliticizing (Schorske 337). According to Schorske, a desire for revenge against the Austrian aristocracy—figured symbolically in Hannibal's vengeance against Rome—eventually fulfilled a wish for patricide in a dream and a desire for professional assimilation into Vienna's professoriate (and a disappointing trip to Rome) in waking life. Along the way, not only does "patricide replace politics," but by way of Freud's retreat from political conflict into academia and the founding of psychoanalysis, "psychoanalysis overcomes history" (342). Conceived as wish-fulfillment, "politics is neutralized by a counterpolitical psychology" (342). The son, in a baroque way, had recapitulated his father's capitulation.

Schorske's conclusion is that the *Interpretation of Dreams* provided Freud a substitute language to understand his fraught relationship with the social and political realities of Austrian society. "As scientist and Jew, as citizen and son," Freud gave priority to fantasy solutions to political problems (329). He goes so far as to say that Freud's theory of mind was "an epoch-making interpretation of human experience in which politics could be reduced to an epiphenomenal manifestation of psychic forces" (329–30). So, when Elizabeth Roudinesco recounts that Freud called himself an "old-style liberal" (20) one should hasten to add that the designation was a fantasized formulation that reconciled himself to his father and his fatherland and produced the means to psychoanalytic knowledge, the science of patriarchy. Knowledge had appeared to set Freud free from politics, but that was hardly the consequence. There is something tragic about this wishful reconciliation: The forces of fascistic Christian anti-Semitism, under the sign of the Nazi party but of a piece with those that humiliated his father, would knock on Freud's door late in life, and though Freud did not let them in, they eventually invaded and forced him and his kin to flee his home. Liberalism, moreover, did not protect him from this fate, though it proved a refuge again in London (Gay 611–29). While Schorske's analysis is ironclad in many respects, it is necessary to qualify his conclusion: fantasy is a fateful politics, too.

The amount of dispute over Freud's political affinities is equal to the complex turns Freud's unconscious took to produce them. Crucially, the account of politics in Freud's personal life is a circular one, as Schorske neatly summarizes: "He defined his oedipal stance in such a way as to overcome his father by realizing the liberal creed his father professed but failed to defend" (337). But this was not simply a personal affair: Freud's oedipal journey is, fittingly enough, a local instantiation *avant la lettre* of what he eventually theorized as the mythic origin of patriarchal society in *Totem and Taboo*, which doubles as a myth of political revolution. Therein, Freud weaves a just-so tale of brothers who murder their "primal" father, but in their contrition and emotional ambivalence they institute a rule-bound society to prevent repetition of the crime. (*SE* XIII: 142–46) For Herbert Marcuse, this is a prehistorical mold out of which historical revolts are shaped: "The crime is reenacted in the conflict of the old and new generation, in revolt and rebellion against established authority—and in subsequent repentance" (69). Freud's politics, all told, were a labyrinthine metapsychology of the snares of intergenerational revolt, rebellion, assimilation, and compliance with respect to established authorities.

Questions arise with respect to our present concerns: Are left Freudians condemned to Freud's circular ambit of fantasized rebellion and to repeat the cycle of failed revolt waged against, yet ultimately with, established authorities? Can we speak of a father complex—embedded in the origins of psychoanalysis and modeled, no less, on Freud's own relation with his father—for leftist Freudians intent on revolution? After all, disappointing generations of his children and a few of his peers, Freud was not a communist.

■ ■ ■

Freud, in fact, singled out communism for special criticism in *Civilization and Its Discontents*, charging communists with a certain naivete about evil. "Man is unequivocally good and well disposed to his neighbor," Freud ventriloquizes an imagined communist saying, "but his nature has been corrupted by the institution of private property" (*SE* XXI: 113). He then draws the corollary: the abolition of private property would end "ill will and enmity among human beings" (113). Freud's criticism is not of the economic system of communism, as he admits. Rather, he finds the implication ingenuous that communism would abolish aggression, which "already manifests itself in the nursery" and "forms the basis of all affectionate and loving relations among human beings" (113). Psychoanalytic observation and its account of the human is called on to judge the utopian aspiration of total harmony, an axiom Freud presumes essential to communism, to be an "untenable illusion" (113). One would be forgiven if, by way of this single instance, they thought Freud an anticommunist or simply dismissive, but ever diligent to traverse antinomies, Freud ultimately articulates a more complex response to left politics.

Freud was an astute critic of moralism, even as his own sensibility resembled a middle-class moralist. He was, nevertheless, rigorous enough along these lines to produce an "economics of emotion," as Rieff has put it (*Moralist* 309). Freud offers an account of fundamental human attitudes—love, hate, ambivalence, aggression, possessiveness, envy, resentment—as grounds for psychoanalytic self-examination. Accordingly, it is by way of a discussion of the "moral demands of civilization," by which Freud emphasizes "man's moral untrustworthiness" (*SE* XXI: 11), that he arrives at a critique of society resembling the class struggle of Marxism:

> If . . . a culture has not got beyond a point at which the satisfaction of one portion of its participants depends upon the suppression of another, and perhaps larger, portion—and this is the case in all present-day cultures—it is understandable that the suppressed people should develop an intense hostility towards a culture whose existence they make possible by their work, but in whose wealth they have too small a share. *In such conditions an internalization of the cultural prohibitions among the suppressed people is not to be expected.* . . . It goes without saying that a civilization which leaves so large a number of its participants unsatisfied and drives them into revolt neither has nor deserves the prospect of a lasting existence. (11)

Freud approaches the logic of class revolt from, as it were, the other side of a supposition of moral goodness waiting to be emancipated. Moral untrustworthiness creates the need for societal restriction, he asserts, but if the underclasses cannot "free themselves from their own surplus of privation," then "a permanent measure of discontent" becomes grounds for rebellion against such restriction (11–12). The super-egoic injunction that binds people in common society, Freud argues, has no legitimacy for those who have been dispossessed by that society.

What is important to emphasize in the situation of revolt is how the operation of social inclusion fails at the level of the super-ego—a failed internalization of prohibition. In the *New Introductory Lectures*, Freud contends that historical materialists have underestimated the super-egoic factor. Freud objects to how certain materialists derive the superstructure from "their contemporary economic conditions" (*SE* XXII: 67). Equating the superego with ideology writ large, he dissents: "Mankind never lives entirely in the present. The past, the tradition of the race and of the people, lives on in the ideologies of the super-ego . . . independently of economic conditions" (67). His objection is counterintuitive, because perhaps provocatively, he is saying that historical materialists have a mistaken account of how time works, particularly in the psyche. Our apprehension of contemporary economic conditions is subject to latency or slippage, and this psychic temporalization of lived conditions creates an ideological misrecognition born of our super-egoic inheritance.[3]

This process of intergenerational inheritance is not straightforward: A "child's super-ego," Freud says, is "constructed on the model not of its parents but of its parents' super-ego" (67). Traditions and "time-resisting judgments of value" are, therefore, handed down from generation to generation through the voice of conscience (67). In other words, the superego, which is the seat of prohibiting judgment and censure, translates experience across time as forms of discipline and obedience. Now consider the situation of class revolt described above: If there is a failure of social reproduction—a revolt against the constituting terms of society, for instance—then there must also be, for Freud, a failure in the transmission of socially coordinated super-egoic obedience. Likewise, this points to the potential of failed transmission of super-egoic identity between generations. At both the social and familial level, Freud theorizes a dehiscence—a gap that is effectively the precondition for disobedience—at the heart of ideological reproduction. If this separation and independence did not exist between older and newer forms of society—or families and generations themselves—all social reproduction would produce mimetic and homogeneous replicas. This gap is *conditio sine qua non* for revolution and unthinkable without it. As we shall see, it is into this gap in ideological transmission that left Freudians step—to both separate themselves from Freud's liberalism and to theorize a form of psychoanalysis compatible with leftist projects.

■ ■ ■

Roughly following a generational pattern, there were two historical high-water marks when psychoanalysis was joined to leftist causes: in the interwar period of the 1920s and early '30s and toward the end of the postwar economic expansion in the '60s and early '70s. (Zaretsky, *Secrets*) Psychoanalysis became a critical political practice in periods when liberalism, faced with economic and social crises, looked into the mirror and did not like what it saw. Meanwhile, as Russell Jacoby chronicled in his book, *The Repression of Psychoanalysis,* the golden age of capitalism (1940s–1970s) conditioned the repression of political Freudianism, generating a conformist psychoanalysis. The watchword of mainstream psychoanalysis was psychoanalytic neutrality, and it ran counter to the discipline's more subversive and explicitly political periods and practitioners. Therefore, to speak of left Freudians, Freudo-Marxists, and political psychoanalysis is to uncover a hidden dimension within psychoanalytic history. Jacoby's account focused on early diasporic analysts who either assimilated to American medical culture or met a worse fate, but the logic can be extended through the twentieth century.[4] I cannot recount the biographies of all who contributed to this subversive undercurrent over the *longue durée*, but I will highlight a central dispute and a few figures in these periods who contributed to the praxis of leftist psychoanalysis. Based on this thumbnail history, I conclude in the last section by defining, through a provocation of Jacques Lacan's, what I think political psychoanalysis entails.

Though many of the early left Freudians were Marxists or social democrats (Jones, *Life and Work* III: 344),[5] perhaps the earliest articulation of the spirit of leftist psychoanalysis came from an anarchist. Believing communism would abolish patriarchy and institute matriarchy, Otto Gross was considered by his peers to be "the nearest approach to a romantic ideal of a genius," with whom Freud agreed even as he lamented that "unfortunately he was not quite sane" (de Mijolla 707–8). In 1913, Gross argued that the reason the revolutions of yesterday had not managed to displace the bourgeoisie was because "the revolutionary of yesterday carried authority within himself" (283). He argued that the root of all authority was in the family, and he saw the loosening ties of marriage and family as life-affirming, an ethical "crying out of humanity for redemption" (283). This psychoanalytically informed exposure of the political force of familial authority would be elaborated by later left Freudians, but Gross lent to posterity nothing less than a slogan for revolutionary psychoanalysis: "The psychology of the unconscious is the philosophy of revolution . . . it is the preparatory work for the revolution" (283). Many would later agree.

Though he lived to see the beginning of the Russian Revolution, but not its counterrevolutionary turn and the banishment of colleagues in his vocation, Gross died in 1920 (de Mijolla 708), the year of Freud's elaboration of the life and death drives. These concepts would outfit Freudo-Marxists with the means to produce a psychoanalytic theory compatible with political economic critique.[6] Like Gross, the Marxist Wilhelm Reich believed the "patriarchal-authoritarian" form of society was responsible for oppressive injustice (Frosh 158). Reich added that the life-drive, inherently emancipatory, was repressed by the historical construction of capitalism, which derived ultimately from the death-drive. Therefore, the "natural" sexual instinct, particularly genital sexuality, was pitted against a repressive, death-driven society. In Reich's case, the aforementioned ideological gap existed between children's sexuality and the family, likened to "a factory for authoritarian ideologies" (Turner 59). Though his monomaniacal insistence on the liberatory potential of genital sexuality was a step too far, by outlining the subjective element of revolutionary programs, Reich began to bridge a chasm between Marxism and Freudianism that later theorists would build on.

In the face of increasing collective mobilization of right-wing and left-wing forces in the 20s and 30s in Austria, Reich and Freud would dramatically split (Zaretsky, *Secrets* 221–25). Whether the political conflict sublimated into a dispute over ideas and personalities, or whether their personal differences sublimated into a secondary expression of political conflict, likely depends on whom you read. What is clear, nevertheless, is that Reich disagreed with Freud's account of the group, which maintained that groups were bound by super-egoic identity with, and love of, an authority figure. Reich accepted that repressed masses did, in fact, consent to authorities, but by exploiting the gap produced by super-egoic failure, he also saw that groups could be freeing and disobedient. Reich wrote that it seemed Freud "lacked all understanding of the revolt and viewed it as a catastrophe similar to a tidal wave," whereas Reich defined "a crowd as a state of absolute equality" (Zaretsky, *Secrets* 221). "It is only in a crowd," Reich preached, "that man can become free" (Zartesky, *Secrets* 222). Freud, for his part, vehemently objected to Reich's "nonsense that the death instinct was the activity of the capitalist system" (Makari 402) and he pointed to the destructive capacity of crowds to foil any easy assimilation of the life-drive and group activity. They agreed, nevertheless, on providing free or low-cost clinics to the proletarian population in the name of the psychoanalytic cure (Danto 13).[7] In this way, a social-democratic understanding was made between communist and liberal. Still, with Reich's sex clinics as pretext, Freud asked someone to rid him of his turbulent priest in 1933, exclaiming "Free me from Reich!" (Zaretsky, *Secrets* 225).

Although they had their own criticisms of Reich and their own methods, too, the Marxists of the Frankfurt School would concur with Reich in one significant respect: for psychoanalysis to be of this world, it needed to be understood through an account of social and historical conditions and within a context of memory and history (Zaretsky, *Political Freud* 104). Erich Fromm, for example, argued that psychoanalysis not only shows how "certain economic conditions affect the psychic apparatus of a person and produce certain ideological results" but also it traces "how ideological facts depend on the economic ones and determine them" (216). Again, the focus of analysis is on the disjuncture of ideology and conditions, but the more programmatic Marxists insisted on dialectically enfolding ideological analysis into an account of history and its changing conditions. Through this approach, psychoanalytic historical materialism is possible. The reason for this was not simply scholastic. As Jacoby once put it, "The attempt of Marxists to 'think Freud' has been defined by the continued failure of the European revolution, or the continued success of bourgeois society. . . . The weak link in Marxism was the iron link in bourgeois society: subjectivity" (75). Marxists needed a compelling, if not revolutionary, depiction of the psyche that would complete a historical materialist understanding of changing and static economic and lived conditions—the unity in the differences.

To understand how things could change yet capitalism remain the same was precisely the problem leftists faced during the "golden age" of capitalism's expansion. As Zaretsky has noted, "Much of Wilhelm Reich's program—housing, privacy rights, the expansion of social and psychological services, birth control, and legal abortion—was enacted" in a limited way by some form of the welfare state in the United States, Britain, and continental Europe (*Secrets* 250). The process of expanding the franchise and strengthening civil rights protections enlarged the constituency of liberalism in these countries, while incorporating the proletariat into mid-century consumerism further reinforced a politics of the middle-class. Simultaneously, decolonization and the Cold War displaced a portion of liberalism's violence onto the periphery, hiding it from the view of the imperial core, while the people of those countries became either proletarianized or surplus populations at home, or migrants. No one's neuroses abated upon assimilation to this world-historical order of liberal hegemony. Thus, psychoanalysis stayed in business, but the object of its clinical and theoretical focus changed with the changing historical conditions. The contours of the leftist faction of psychoanalysis changed, too, especially with the rise of the New Left in the 1960s.

Out of this crucible, transformed measures of political solidarity and practice emerged. Ideologies of the mass and the crowd were giving way to the projective and selective causes of movements. So far as ideology indexes extant forms of society, older means of ideological reproduction stayed intact while new ones were foregrounded. Thus, the mechanisms of ideological transmission, though still generational in a sense, exceeded the realm of the individual psyche and the family as the superimposed image of the state or capital relation. By marking entry into a new mode of production and cultural dispensation, the phantasmagoria of identity and difference, consumer society, and mass media changed the very terms of political psychoanalysis and subjected it to new conditions of possibility. When psychoanalysis was explicitly political—or politicized, as we might say today—it was necessarily linked to the critiques and activities of political movements. Thus, psychoanalysis was as much the object of criticism as it was part of a repertoire for ideological critique and demystification (Zaretsky, *Secrets*).

In this context, classical Marxism and psychoanalysis, whatever their uneasy alliance and differences had been, would encounter the same fate. They both became accounts of the world that other discourses, often bound up with political movements, attempted to supersede, even as Marxism and psychoanalysis were stepping-stones to the creation of those discourses. Moreover, psychoanalysis and Marxism were both transformed by this process. As familial generations once served as the site of ideological differentiation, so, too, would discursive and institutional reproduction. There were roughly four movements in which psychoanalysis played this ambivalent role of epistemic precondition: decolonization, antipsychiatry, sexual liberation, and feminism. The prominent figures of leftist persuasion in this moment— Frantz Fanon, Herbert Marcuse, Norman O. Brown, Michel Foucault, Gilles Deleuze, Félix Guattari, Juliet Mitchell, and Jacqueline Rose—simultaneously deployed psychoanalysis as an object of critique and as an intellectual means to cultural and philosophical criticism. It would be impossible to recount the vast and contradictory uses and abuses of psychoanalysis in this era by these thinkers and others, but suffice it to say, many political and cultural critiques of today hearken back to this moment and to psychoanalysis along with it. Each of these thinkers produce divergent lines of inquiry with little agreement among them.[8] For my part, I will end this article with a brief reprise of an infamous encounter between politics and the psychoanalyst Jacques Lacan and my own reflection on politics and psychoanalysis.

■ ■ ■

A science of linguistic signs applied to specialized sciences, structuralism has been described as a "mass movement" (Jameson ix). Agreeing narrowly with Joseph Stalin when he said in 1950 that "language cannot be ranked either among bases [material conditions] or among superstructures [ideological apparatuses]" (Jameson 211), structuralists elaborated and lodged an immanent critique into the heart of Marxism's more dogmatic suppositions, subverting its hypostatic determinations from the inside-out, including Stalin's notional Language. In the field of psychoanalysis, Jacques Lacan was responsible for furnishing a structuralist model of the unconscious.[9] Equipped with a science of structures that revised and perhaps strengthened the classical Marxist framework, structuralists would find their models tested not in the domain of Euclidean demonstration but by demonstrations in the streets during the worker and student revolts of the late 1960s. The response of prominent French thinkers ranged from enthusiastic and concrete support to shameful demurral, but Lacan's was far and away the most enigmatic— some say, prophetic, arguing that he told the students they had not been radical enough (Copjec, *Silent Partners* 90).

As Joan Copjec recounts, amid the roiling upheaval of the student and worker protests in May 1968, someone wrote on a blackboard, "structures don't march in the streets" (*Read My Desire* 9). This articulation distilled the students' mistrust of French academic institutions, judging them useless to the seemingly revolutionary events of their time. Lacan begged to differ when responding to Lucien Goldmann, "I don't consider it at all correct to have written that structures don't go out onto the streets, for if there's one thing the events of May prove, it's precisely that they do" (Roudinesco, *Jacques Lacan* 341). He then added an oracular qualification: "an act always misunderstands itself" (Roudinesco, *Jacques Lacan* 341). I hope to make clear what he meant by this.

Nevertheless, with the intention to recruit fellow comrades from the study halls to bring them into the streets, students disrupted the classes of more high-profile pedagogues, Lacan among them (Roudinesco, *Jacques Lacan* 340–45). On December 3, 1969, at the experimental university of Vincennes, an exchange between the protestors and Lacan would come to signify an impasse of the revolutionary moment (Lacan 197–208). Scandalized that the interlopers did not understand aphasia, Lacan appears to become increasingly agitated by the provocations. "I haven't understood a word yet. So, one could start by saying what a psychoanalyst is. For me he is a kind of cop" (Lacan 200) says one attendee; "People speak about a New Society. Will psychoanalysis have a function in that society?" (207) asks another. After Lacan defines aphasia as something crippling that breaks down in the practice of language in whatever society, a student jokes: "One could say that Lenin almost became aphasic" (207).

At this, Lacan appears to have had enough: he likened the students to hysterics who challenge the complete knowledge of their master—to try to master the master at the risk of misunderstanding themselves and thereby propping up a new authority. Lacan responds, "the revolutionary aspiration has only a single possible outcome—of ending up as the master's discourse. This is what experience has proved. What you aspire to as revolutionaries is a master. You will get one" (207). Most recollections of this encounter stop here, but the text proceeds into the very impasse between liberalism and leftism that has motivated our inquiry. One student says Lacan is a liberal like then-president of France Georges Pompidou (207). Lacan's retort, to quote at length:

> I am, like everybody is, a liberal only to the extent that I am antiprogressive . . . [though] I am caught up in a movement that deserves to be called progressive, since it is progressive to see the psychoanalytic discourse founded, insofar as the latter completes the circle that could perhaps enable you to locate what it is exactly that you are rebelling against—which doesn't stop that thing from continuing incredibly well. (Lacan 207; Roudinesco, *Jacques Lacan* 341)

Lacan is again pointing to the grounds for disobedience, but he is adding a twist: without the psychoanalytic discourse to clarify the desire, the revolutionary aspiration might harbor, though concealed, the counterrevolution within its project—enacting a misrecognized revolt that misses its target along the way.

This assertion tends to have a polarizing effect across a now familiar antinomy. There are many accounts of this antinomy, and Lacan plays contradictory roles in this narrative.[10] When it comes to the '60s revolt, the evidence of its overall failure is plain, and in time, they did find a new master. As Luc Boltanksi and Eve Chiapello have argued, even if May '68 was not a revolution, it "imperilled the operation of capitalism," but, dialectically, it was by "recuperating some of the oppositional themes articulated during the May events" that capitalism discovered "a new dynamism" to which the rebellion was resubjugated (168). In this context, on the one hand, Lacan's paternalistic attitude smacks of the counterrevolutionary turn against which the students and workers had rebelled. On the other hand, he was intent to listen to the revolutionaries and to get the revolutionaries to listen to themselves—not only modeling a kind of psychoanalytic ethic but also offering unambiguous support of direct action in the streets when other analysts asked what the role of psychoanalysis should be. A year before the interruptions at Vincennes, Lacan dutifully stopped his own seminar to observe the strike order (Roudinesco, *Lacan and Co.* 455). When the seminar recommenced, even as he criticized the ideas of Wilhelm Reich, Lacan simultaneously praised then-student leader Daniel Cohn-Bendit, who later became a member of the European Parliament, as a way to remind his disciples: analysts were insensibly asking what the insurrection wants from psychoanalysis when, in fact, they had made it clear: "What we expect from you is occasionally to give us a hand throwing a few paving stones" (Roudinesco, *Lacan and Co.* 455).

A psychoanalyst and participant in Lacan's seminars in the aftermath of May '68, Mladen Dolar has perhaps the best summary of the ethic of political psychoanalysis. Just as the proletariat seeks its own abolition in the revolutionary movement of history, Dolar writes that one kind of political psychoanalysis, the one that animated Reich, would assert that "the aim of psychoanalysis would be to try to do away with its object, ultimately to abolish it" (Dolar, *Theory and Event* 22). By "putting our hopes this time into libido, the Eros, against the death drive"—eradicating, if possible, aggressivity and the unconscious, too—"the psychoanalytic Utopia would thus be the world that didn't need psychoanalysis" (Dolar, *Theory and Event* 22). Dolar does not argue explicitly against this utopianism, strictly determining its possibility yes or no—just as Lacan did not dismiss his helots. Instead, he says that psychoanalysis ethically stops short of political action. What does this mean?

Offering a description not unlike the one I have offered about the failure of superegoic obedience and the gap in ideological reproduction, Dolar names and elaborates a gap within the social world that makes politics possible: "Conflictuality, antagonism, rift, a crack in the social tissue, an excess, the point of ambivalence, untying of social bonds, negativity" (Dolar, *Theory and Event* 28). That gap, Dolar contends, "has to be conceived as the *site* of the political" (Dolar, *Theory and Event* 28). The practice of psychoanalysis furnishes a social yet private space—the analytic couch, on which the analysand unfurls society as so many chains of association—to work through those rifts in the social fabric. At some point, however, the chain happens on a deadlock indicative of the political—the site of contest. Dolar says, "it is as if psychoanalysis circumscribes a site, a locus of the political, without ever quite stepping into this site itself" (Dolar, *Theory and Event* 28). He goes further, "the circumscription of the site is no neutral description; it requires a step, although it itself doesn't prescribe what this step should be" (Dolar, *Theory and Event* 28). Psychoanalysis, in other words, can reveal to the analysand the desire to throw the paving stone. The analyst can even ask evocative questions that might resituate or clarify their desire: "at whom are you throwing those paving stones? And for whom are you throwing them?" Yet, psychoanalysis, like pedagogy, cannot commit the political act *as an analyst* or *as a teacher*. Nevertheless, stepping into that gap is still possible, and this is the crucial distinction on which political psychoanalysis hangs: an analysand, who is necessarily also an analyst, can still make that always uncertain step of political action *as a comrade*. In this way, while he preserves a measure of analytic neutrality, Dolar also agrees with Otto Gross: psychoanalysis is preparatory work for revolution. ∎

Alex Colston is an editor, fact-checker, teacher, and writer. He acts as second faculty for classes on psychoanalysis at the Brooklyn Institute for Social Research. His written work has appeared in the *New Left Review*, *Full Stop*, and *The Point*.

ACKNOWLEDGMENTS

Thank you to Patrick Blanchfield, associate faculty at the Brooklyn Institute for Social Research; this article would be impossible without our mutual psychoanalytic inquiries.

NOTES

1   The whole dedication reads, "To Anna Freud, True Daughter of an Immortal Sire" (Jones, *Life and Work* I).

2   In *Secrets of the Soul*, Zaretsky offers a historical account of how politics becomes personalized over the course of the twentieth century. I rely on Zaretsky's accounts, including *Political Freud*, for the more historical portions of this article.

3   With only a couple years left to live, Freud eventually came around to Marxism. His original misgiving was, he suggested, based partly on a misunderstanding. To the extent that Marxists have not come around to Freud, however, the misunderstanding remains at the level of interpretation rather than apodictic congruence. In a letter dated September 10, 1937, he wrote, "I know that my comments on Marxism are no evidence either of a thorough knowledge or of a correct understanding of the writings of Marx and Engels. I have since learned—rather to my satisfaction—that neither of them has denied the influence of ideas and super-ego factors. That invalidates the main contrast between Marxism and psychoanalysis which I had believed to exist. As to the 'dialectic' I am no clearer, even after your letter" (Jones, *Life and Work* III: 345).

4   Jacoby offers an extensive, but by no means definitive, list of such analysts living in Vienna and Berlin in the 1920s and 1930s: "Paul Federn, Helene Deutsch, Siegfried Bernfeld, Herman Nunberg, Annie and Wilhelm Reich, Edith Jacobson, Willi Hoffer, Martin Grotjahn, Karl Landauer, Bruno Bettelheim, Ernst Simmel, and Otto Fenichel" (Jacoby, *Repression* 12).

5   As Ernest Jones recounted, "Since Freud and Marx have left a deeper imprint on our age than anyone else it is not surprising that endeavors have been made to compare or amalgamate their respective doctrines, e.g. those by [Francis] Bartlett, [Max] Eastman, [Ludwig] Jekels, [Vladimir] Jurinetz, [Konstantin] Kornilov, [Paul] Krische, [Herbert] Marcuse, [Reuben] Osborn, [Henry] Parkes, Wilhelm Reich, [Michel] Sapir, Pater Schmidt, and others. A full dress debate was held on the matter in Berlin in 1928 at the *Verein sozialistischer Ärzte*" (Jones, *Life and Work* III: 344).

6   For an account of how the drive theory inspired a certain strand of Freudian leftism based on sexual liberation, see Robinson.

7   For a full account of Freud's lifelong commitment to free psychoanalytic clinics, see Danto 13.

8   For a more extensive and thorough comparison of some of these thinkers and movements, see Frosh.

9 The structuralist label fits Lacan, even if the designation is like a too tight-fitting jacket. For a more comprehensive account, see Macey. As Macey has put it speaking of the publication of Lacan's Écrits, "In 1966, publication by Seuil seemed at least to imply adherence to the tenets of structuralism. . . . Predictably, the structuralist references in Lacan come to dominate everything else" (5). See also Homer.

10 For a more comprehensive argument of this contradictory historical transition in which Lacan's role is arguably just a function, see Boltanski and Chiapello.

WORKS CITED

Boltanski, Luc, and Eve Chiapello. *The New Spirit of Capitalism*. London: Verso, 2005.

Copjec, Joan. *Read My Desire: Lacan against the Historicists*. Cambridge, MA: MIT Press, 1994.

Copjec, Joan, and Slavoj Žižek, eds. "May '68, the Emotional Month." In *Lacan: The Silent Partners*, 90–114. London: Verso, 2006.

Danto, Elizabeth Ann. *Freud's Free Clinics: Psychoanalysis and Social Justice, 1918–1938*. New York: Columbia University Press, 2007.

de Mijolla, Alain, ed. "Gross, Otto Hans Adolph (1877–1920)." In *International Dictionary of Psychoanalysis*, 707–8. Detroit: Thomas Gale.

Dolar, Mladen. "Freud and the Political." *Theory and Event* 12, no. 3 (2009). doi.org/10.1353/tae.0.0085.

Dolar, Mladen, and Jeffrey Ben. "The Sting of Knowledge." *Point Magazine*, April 23, 2018. thepointmag.com/dialogue/the-sting-of-knowledge/.

Freud, Sigmund, James Strachey, Anna Freud, and Carrie Lee Rothgeb. "The Future of an Illusion." In vol. 21 of The *Standard Edition of the Complete Psychological Works of Sigmund Freud*, 1–273. London: Hogarth Press, 1961.

Freud, Sigmund, James Strachey, Anna Freud, and Carrie Lee Rothgeb. "New Introductory Lectures on Psycho-Analysis." In vol. 22 of *The Standard Edition of the Complete Psychological Works of Sigmund Freud*, 1–182. London: Hogarth Press, 1933.

Freud, Sigmund, James Strachey, Anna Freud, and Carrie Lee Rothgeb. "Totem and Taboo." In vol. 13 of *The Standard Edition of the Complete Psychological Works of Sigmund Freud*, 1–255. London: Hogarth Press, 1955.

Fromm, Erich, Stephen Eric Bronner, and Douglas Kellner. "Politics and Psychoanalysis." In *Critical Theory and Society: A Reader*, edited by Stephen Eric Bronner and Douglas MacKay Kellner, 213–18. London: Routledge, 1989.

Frosh, Stephen. *Politics of Psychoanalysis: An Introduction to Freudian and Post-Freudian Theory*. New York: New York University Press, 1999.

Gay, Peter. *Freud: A Life for Our Time*. New York: W. W. Norton, 1998.

Graham, Robert, ed. *Anarchism: A Documentary History of Libertarian Ideas. Volume One: From Anarchy to Anarchism*. Montreal: Black Rose Books, 2005.

Homer, Sean. *Jacques Lacan*. London: Routledge, 2004.

Jacoby, Russell. *The Repression of Psychoanalysis: Otto Fenichel and the Political Freudians*. New York: Basic Books, 1983.

Jacoby, Russell. *Social Amnesia: A Critique of Conformist Psychology from Adler to Laing*. Boston: Beacon Press, 1978.

Jameson, Fredric. *The Prison-House of Language: A Critical Account of Structuralism and Russian Formalism*. Princeton, NJ: Princeton University Press, 1972.

Jones, Ernest. *The Life and Work of Sigmund Freud: Vol. I*. New York: Basic Books, 1953.

Jones, Ernest. *The Life and Work of Sigmund Freud: Vol. III*. New York: Basic Books, 1957.

Lacan, Jacques. *The Seminar of Jacques Lacan: The Other Side of Psychoanalysis, Book XVII*, edited by Jacques-Alain Miller and translated by Russell Grigg. New York: W. W. Norton, 2007.

Macey, David. *Lacan in Contexts*. London: Verso, 1988.

Makari, George. *Revolution in Mind: The Creation of Psychoanalysis*. New York: Harper Collins, 2008.

Marcuse, Herbert. *Eros and Civilization: A Philosophical Inquiry into Freud*. New York: Vintage Books, 1955.

Robinson, Paul. A. *The Freudian Left: Wilhelm Reich, Geza Roheim, Herbert Marcuse*. New York: Harper and Row, 1969.

Rieff, Philip. *Freud: The Mind of the Moralist*. Garden City, NY: Doubleday, 1961.

Rieff, Philip. "Psychology and Politics: The Freudian Connection." *World Politics* 7, no. 2 (1955): 293–305. www.jstor.org/stable/2009149.

Roudinesco, Elizabeth. *Freud: In His Time and Ours*, translated by Catherine Porter. Cambridge, MA: Harvard University Press, 2016.

Roudinesco, Elizabeth. *Jacques Lacan*. New York: Columbia University Press, 1997.

Roudinesco, Elizabeth. *Jacques Lacan and Co.: A History of Psychoanalysis in France, 1925–1985*. Chicago: University of Chicago Press, 1990.

Schorske, Carl E. "Politics and Patricide in Freud's Interpretation of Dreams." *American Historical Review* 78, no. 2 (1973): 328–47. doi.org/10.2307/1861171.

Turner, Christopher. "Wilhelm Reich." In *Routledge Handbook of Psychoanalytic Political Theory*, edited by Yannis Stavrakakis, 57–66. London: Routledge, 2019.

Zaretsky, Eli. *Political Freud: A History*. New York: Columbia University Press, 2015.

Zaretsky, Eli. *Secrets of the Soul: A Social and Cultural History of Psychoanalysis*. New York: Vintage, 2004.

Carolyn Shapiro

Vicissitudes and Their Inscriptions

ABSTRACT In his marking of the consequential vicissitudes that attend the more primary
instincts, Freud articulates history as the discursive operation of the psychoanalytic undertaking. But his ambivalence toward the requisite writing of that articulated history comes
through when he introduces the narrative genre of the case study. The first part of this article examines Freud's implicit proposition that psychoanalysis is a complex articulation of
history in that symptoms are noted and inscribed as consequential, present indicators of
causal instincts (*Triebe*) that have been variously and "fatefully" rerouted. The second part
reads Freud's defensive presentation of the first case history, the "broken fragment" of Dora
and her hysteria, considering Freud's ambivalence toward his own historiographic operation. Freud's ambivalence in relation to his new genre of narrative writing illustrates the
more general productive ambivalence of historiography as outlined by Michel de Certeau.

KEYWORDS instincts, *geschichte*, historiography, case history, Dora

In his marking of the consequential vicissitudes that attend the more primary instincts, Freud articulates history as the discursive operation of the
psychoanalytic undertaking, but his ambivalence toward the requisite writing of that articulated history comes through when he introduces the narrative genre of the case study. The first part of this intervention will examine
Freud's implicit proposition that psychoanalysis comprises a complex articulation of history in that symptoms are noted and inscribed as consequential, present indicators of causal instincts that have been variously "fatefully" rerouted. In *Instincts and Their Vicissitudes* (*SE* XIV), Freud's English
title tells us that the fundamental psychical component, instincts, always
carries with them changes, fluctuations, mutabilities. "Vicissitudes" designate a performance of sequence. Indeed, the performative character of the
"instinct" is suggested by editor James Strachey's introduction to this essay
deeming it "the clearest account of what Freud understood by the instincts
and of the way in which he thought they operated." This essay's conjoining of

HISTORY of the PRESENT ▪ A Journal of Critical History ▪ 12:1 ▪ April 2022
DOI 10.1215/21599785-9547266 © 2022 Duke University Press

instincts and their vicissitudes is a concerted effort of Freud's "to deal with the subject *comprehensively*" (*SE* XIV:113; my emphasis), this modifier not only underlining the subject's trajectory character but also suggesting the operational approach plied by Freud himself.

The English word "vicissitudes" is poetically inviting as an element for comprehension. But Freud was of course writing this essay in German, with the given title *Triebe und Triebschicksale*. Although plenty of attention in the editor's introduction is devoted to explaining Freud's use of the word "*triebe*," no editorial explanations are offered for what is apparently less notable: the meaning and understanding of the word "*triebschicksale*." *Triebeschicksale* means, literally, the fate, fortune, or destinies of the *Triebe*, carrying with them the inevitability of their direction. Key to my proposition for Freud's articulation of a theory of history is the etymological convergence of *schicksale* (destinies, fortunes) with *geschichte* (occurrence, narration, tale, history). This confluence will be explored below as Freud's own inscription of a psychoanalytic theory of history as narrative story. Furthermore, his introduction of the case study as a genre of narrative writing submits to the public a particular relation to historiography. Freud's defensive presentation of the very first case study, the "broken fragment" of Dora and her hysteria, will be considered in the second part of this article, reading Freud's ambivalence toward his own historiographic operation. Freud's ambivalence also serves here as an index to the more general ambivalent nature of historiography outlined by Michel de Certeau.

Before looking at Freud's own list of what comprises vicissitudes or *Triebschicksale*, we might look at the Editor's Note that precedes *Instincts and Their Vicissitudes*, which, as noted above, does not actually consider the "vicissitudes" at all, but which does explain in detail Freud's application of the word "*Triebe*" in this essay and throughout his other writing. In his gloss of Freud's use of *Triebe*, Strachey's primary emphasis is on Freud's lack of distinction here between "*Triebe*" and "*Triebrepräsentanz*," that is, between instinct and "instinctual representative" (111). Strachey points out that there are numerous examples throughout Freud's earlier writings in which an instinct is to be understood as an "instinct-representative," "a concept on the frontier between the mental and the somatic . . . the psychical representative of the stimuli originating from within the organism and reaching the mind" (112). For my purposes here of understanding what vicissitudes are for Freud, and for understanding his articulation of history, I would like to propose that the *Triebe* as *Triebrepräsentanz* realizes an aptness for the performative tendency toward operation that is vicissitudinous. The *Triebe* as *Triebrepräsentanz* offers itself up to tropic possibility, a possibility whose narrative dimensions are signaled in the temporally imbued *Triebschicksale*. Freud's term and notion of the *Treibschicksale* in many ways encompasses his entire psychoanalytic undertaking. Instincts, the fundamental somatic needs that appear as force (118-19), take a "course" and "undergo displacement" (123), rerouted toward their *schicksale*: their destinies, their fates. These inevitable pathways, or vicissitudes that an instinct might undergo include the following, outlined by Freud, who explains that he is focusing on sexual instincts and their fates: reversal into its opposite, turning round on the subject's own self, repression, and sublimation (126).

The historical character of *Triebe und Triebschicksale* is implied in phrases such as "pathogenesis of hysterical symptoms" and "psychosexual aetiology" that come through in other texts, for example, "Fragment of an Analysis of a Case of Hysteria" (*SE* VII: 13). Engendering consequential psychic actions, the instincts, within the context of the psychoanalytic scenario, set into motion the construction of an individual's life story. The categories of vicissitudes that Freud has listed read like dramatic plot structures.

That *Triebschicksale* runs a destined course from *Triebe/Trieberepräsentanz* indicates the sequentiality belongs to narrative structure. Through the figuration of the force that engenders them, the inevitable pathways that might include reversals into opposites, turning round on themselves, repression, and sublimation, are forged through the narrative movement of the tropic figure.

Etymological research into the word "*schicksal*" reinforces the sense of historicization suggested by the fateful courses attached to the instincts. Coming from the Modern High German *Geschick,* meaning "fate, destiny, dexterity" and based on Middle High German *geschicke,* meaning "event, order, formation, figure," *schicksal,* used in modern German, departs slightly from the older meaning, in terms of the modern word bearing a sense of inevitability that might have been skillfully outmaneuvered in its former mode of *geschick.* The etymological connection between *geschick* and *geschichte* is made in Kluge's *Etymological Dictionary of the German Language* in the following entry:

> **Geschichte**, feminine, 'occurrence, narration, tale, history,' from Middle High German *geschiht*, Old High German *gisiht*, feminine, 'event, occurrence, cause of an event, dispensation' (Middle High German also 'affair, manner, stratum'; see *Schicht*); abstract of *geschehen*. Similarly Modern High German **Geschick**, 'fate, destiny, dexterity,' is based upon Middle High German *geschicke*, neuter, 'event, order, formation, figure,' as the abstract of Modern High German *schicken.* (Kluge 1891)[1]

The fatedness of the vicissitude merges into the unfolding of an event, narrated as story. In German, the word *"geschichte"* is the word for both "story" and "history," another convergence that is related to Freud's articulation of history, to be explored below. For now, let us briefly consult Michel de Certeau's theorization of history, which he exemplifies in Freud's proposed science of psychoanalysis. "Such is the way," de Certeau tells us, "[that] Freudian therapeutics proceeds: analysis discerns organizations in the words of patients that 'betray' a genesis; it refers them to events that they hide and which become—as *both* absent and present—a past" (292).

Thus, Freud's talking cure-therapeutics constructs a "past" through the analyst's present discernment of "organizations in the words" of the analysand, which, only when (re)marked as "organizations," indicate an otherwise hidden origin.

Psychoanalysis reads the symptom, the destined manifestation of the course of the *Triebe*. Tracking the pathways of the vicissitudes requires a straddling of the present moment (the symptom, the reading of the symptom, and the writing of the symptom) and the instinct, which has become less distinguishable in the circuitousness of what it has undergone. The science of psychoanalysis distinguishes the instinct, but the instinct is only distinguishable as "instinct" by what it is yet to become as it undergoes first its vicissitudes and, second, its marking, through the reading of the vicissitudes, by analysis and inscription. Freud's foregrounding of analysis itself serves as the primary ground for his theorization of history. The analyst is an interpreter of fragments: words, signs, and symptoms. At the conjunctions of present moments with an absent but indicated past, the analyst "elucidates" (292).[2]

Elucidation and its triggering of narrative itself comprise only part of Freud's psychotherapeutic procedure. Freud's psychoanalytic discourse and narrative case studies and his discernible relation to his own writing practice, exemplify the historiographical operation that crafts history, as de Certeau elaborates in *The Writing of History*. The historiographical operation is primarily ambivalent, according to de Certeau, and, as a closer examination of Freud to his own writing will suggest, according to Freud too. This constitutive ambivalence is noted by de Certeau comprehensively: "Such is the ambivalence of historiography: it is the condition of a process and the denial of an absence; by turns it acts as the discourse of a law (historical saying opens a present to be made) and as an alibi, a realistic illusion (the realistic effect creates the fiction of another history). It oscillates between 'producing history' and 'telling stories,' but without being reduced to either one or the other" (102).

The ambivalence of historiography could be said to be the ambivalence instated by its very performativity: if "history" comes into being through its own narrativity, then the narrator must counteract that constructedness of the writing operation with the authority of law (although this authority would also be based in performative reiteration). The material of the historian, and the psychoanalyst, is the fragment, one of many pieces that, when gathered into collections and temporalized into narrative formation, are beholden to acts of both elucidating truth as well as fashioning a story. While we shall see that we can read the ambivalence Freud himself conveyed in his own writing as operation, de Certeau reminds us that it is the psychoanalytic method itself that allows us to understand the historiographic operation: "[History] is no less subject to analysis, as another labor of the same formula: a little piece of truth (*ein Stücken Wahrheit*, GW 16:239) is endlessly being diffused within history's obscurantist repressions" (315).

Although de Certeau's exploration of the writing of history does not discuss Heidegger much, as a philosophy of productive ambivalences de Certeau's theorization of the writing of history does resonate with Heidegger's exposition of the fragment's relation to history in "The Anaxamander Fragment" (576–626).[3] Of course, Heidegger's philosophical project in general, as well as this essay particularly, are too vast and layered to read in full depth here, but even a slight detour into a few of Heidegger's propositions yields clarification and company to the present investigation into Freud's articulation of history and the historiographical operation. Heidegger's essay builds around the Anaxamander Fragment as an index to Western Metaphysics, to Thinking, to Being. "History" is one strand that Heidegger follows to grapple with the vast task of explaining Being. For Heidegger, the Anaxamander Fragment, a piece of a speech that he introduces as "the oldest fragment of Western thinking" (576), is the key to understanding the relation and role of history to Being. History as a notion and as a practice introduces what Heidegger calls the necessary "errancy" through which Being self-conceals itself (591). For Heidegger, "history" is an inscribed materialization of the error that Being and its essence hide within. This essence of Being must hide itself, but a certain understanding of history shows what Being is and does. Heidegger's consideration of Being and history in the Anaxamander text will, I hope, serve to enhance the primary thesis in the present article that Freud's discourse of "vicissitudes" puts forth a particular understanding of "history."

Asking his readers how we are meant to receive, let alone translate, a fragment of a philosophical treatise from a historical and chronological distance of two thousand five hundred years, Heidegger puts forward a notion of history that would replace any more standard understandings of our current relation to a historical fragment as being far away, millennia away, in which we would address the fragments as "latecomers in a history now racing towards its end, an end which in its increasingly sterile order of uniformity brings everything to an end." Instead, he inquires, "Does there lie concealed in the historical [*historisch*] and chronological remoteness of the fragment the historic [*geschichtliche*] proximity of something unsaid, something that will speak out in times to come?" (580). Here, something that is both unsaid as well as destined to speak is not remote but a "proximity" characterized as "*geschichtliche*." The hiddenness of the instincts until they are rerouted as vicissitudes to be marked and inscribed, also carry a sense of inevitable destiny. The *Triebe* set narrative shoots and possibilities into motion noted by the analyst in historicizing hindsight. Both Heidegger and Freud appreciate the merged origins of *geschichte* with *geschick*.[4]

Heidegger's philosophy is dedicated to understanding Being as something that in its very essence hides itself from thinking. He taps the etymological convergence of *geschichte* and *geschicke* to present an understanding of Being's fundamental temporal disjunction, an essential projection into a time and place beyond "itself" and yet, genitively "of" itself. This projection happens at the "departure" of "the long-hidden destiny of Being": "What once occurred in the dawn of our destiny would then come, as what once occurred . . . at the departure of the long-hidden destiny of Being. The Being of beings is gathered . . . in the ultimacy of its destiny" (582). In a sense, what distinguishes "Being" from "being" in Heidegger's philosophy is its inclusion of a projected inevitable moment that is only readable from the perspective of that projected moment. Similarly, Freud can only read, and write, *Triebe* via *Treibschicksale*.

History, for Heidegger, is the "realm of error" that allows for the essential self-concealing of Being. Errancy (where history unfolds) plays out destiny (*geschickt*). The misinterpretation that characterizes the realm of error realizes the necessary "course" in which "destiny awaits what will become of its seed" (591). In the sense that errancy and misinterpretation comprise positive grounding for history as we know it, Heidegger might be said to join Freud and de Certeau as a fellow philosopher of history as productive ambivalence.

Thus far, I have considered Freud's *Triebe und Triebschicksale* as the fundamental ground for his articulation of a philosophy of history. As de Certeau has elaborated, "history" is both "discursive," that is, running a course within its own "diegetic" time, and "narrative," referring to the inclusion of oppositional terms that, through the introduction and rationalization of temporal differentiation, sets up an "interlocutionary" relationship between author and reader.[5] This relationship also produces authority on the part of the historian, who has found nondiegetic means for unifying opposite events. "Narrative" effects ambivalence, as de Certeau suggests: "But this temporalization, skittering away as it does from rigorously imposed limits, creating a stage on which incompatible elements can be put into play together, indeed has to be paid for with its counterpart . . . it 'pretends' to be reasoning. To be sure, in maintaining the relation of a rationality with what takes place outside of it, on its borderlines, narrative preserves the possibility of a science or a philosophy" (88–89). De Certeau's characterization of the temporalization of narrative "skittering away" from imposed limits is what allows for a story to be told, constructed by outside perspectives that have deployed figuration, groupings, as well as sequential progressions through tropes. This "skittering away" makes for good storytelling, and, also, in the context of the writing of history, the text produced "holds together the contradictions of this unstable time" (92).

Freud's relation to writing as a "historian" becomes evident when he ventures from writing psychoanalytic discourse into writing psychoanalytic narrative, presenting the new genre of the case history in his 1905 publication about an eighteen-year-old girl, "Dora," who was sent to Freud by her father because of her symptoms of hysteria. The publication was titled "Fragment of an Analysis of a Case of Hysteria" (*Bruchstück einer hysterie-analyse*) (*SE* VII). While I will not delve deeply into the complex romantic narrative of the case itself here, I do want to focus closely on the Editor's Note and especially on Freud's Prefatory Remarks to this groundbreaking genre of narrative history. Reading these introductory supplemental texts, we can see that Freud not only theorizes a philosophy of history but also is highly conscious of the act of writing history. Freud's anxieties about his own position as "historiographer" indicate the ambivalence that has been opened up by de Certeau (de Certeau 88–89).

The Editor's Note that frames the case history of "Dora" contextualizes its publication within Freud's other works. Closely following the letters that Freud wrote to his esteemed medical friend Wilhelm Fliess, Strachey mentions that the "Fragment of an Analysis" was written as a direct follow-up, and continuation of *The Interpretation of Dreams* (1900), and was also written concurrently with *The Psychopathology of Everyday Life* (1901). Freud's letters to Fliess make clear that Freud had an active, even proactive, relation to publishing, using publishing to establish his proprietorship of what he firmly felt was a radical, important new scientific discourse. However, as noted by his editor, Freud deferred publishing the case study of "Dora," which he referred to in his letters to Fliess as "Dreams and Hysteria," for four years. (*SE* VII: 4–5.) In addition to this delay, Strachey notes, Freud makes the curious mistake three times in misattributing the year that he wrote the case study, dating it "1899" instead of "1900" (*SE* VII: 5). Strachey was beginning to read Freud's own unconscious resistances. In his Prefatory Remarks to this text, Freud has given us plenty more of those resistances to elaborate on.

Freud's introduction to the "case history" presented a new genre of psychoanalytic writing that would supplement the explanatory discourses he was already publishing. He is clearly anxious that his new genre's integrity be defended against what he imagines will be the blame and reproach of "narrow minded critics" (7) who will have objected, Freud imagines, to the publication to the world of private, sexual stories of real people who might actually be recognized. Because the narration of Dora's hysteria is by its very definition of a psycho-sexual nature, Freud persistently defends the case history's disclosure of otherwise private topics; they are integral to his scientific approach. He admits that if his patients had known that their "admissions" would be published for scientific reasons, they would not have spoken of those things, and, furthermore, if he had asked their permission to publish these admissions, he was certain they would be "quite unavailing" (8). He insists that no one would be able to figure out Dora's true identity. Freud also predicted that many physicians will read the case study not "as a psychopathology of the neuroses, but as a *roman à clef* designed for their private delectation" (9). A *roman à clef* is a romantic narrative based on real people (the indexical *clef*) but with fictionalized names. Freud's disavowal of the named *French* romantic genre here betrays his own ambivalence about himself as the writer of Dora's case history, the French signifying here an unspeakable (in German) sexuality with populist, prurient appeal.[6] And so as not to be taken for the author of a cheap sensationalist novel, Freud assures his readers that he will guarantee the secrecy of his subjects even if it means that he will have to restrict his material. After these disclaimers, he explains in detail his ways of having "overcome the *technical* difficulties of drawing up the report of this case history": he wrote down the notes from memory immediately after the sessions with "Dora" were finished, using exact words that she used to describe her dreams, thereby ensuring that the writing did not stray into fiction; the material was "grouped" around two anchoring dreams that she relayed; and finally, the treatment lasted only three months, fortuitously for practical reasons, thereby making the amount of material much more manageable in terms of constructing a narrative sequence (9–10). This latter element went very much against Freud's wishes: "Dora" broke off the analysis when, for Freud, it was just getting going, determining the case history a *Bruchstück* (broken piece) and setting into motion the ambivalence and deferral that Freud manifested in his relation to his own authorial practice, to his own historiographical operation. His strategy is to come forward and acknowledge his role as inauthentic constructor, but a constructor who is an archaeologist, rather than a narrator of a novel: "I have restored what is missing, taking the best models known to me from other analyses; but, like a conscientious archaeologist, I have not omitted to mention in each case where the authentic parts end and my constructions begin" (12).

Freud's discourse and practice of psychoanalysis are fundamentally "historical" in a perhaps particularly Germanic sense of the initial convergence of *geschichte* and *geschikt*. This article has investigated "vicissitudes" and their relation to "instincts" as well as investigated vicissitudes in relation to writing, particularly, the writing of history. As Freud revealed in his preface to his first case history, the writer of history puts himself into a double bind: that of the faithfulness to what is only a fragment of authenticity and that of constructor of readable narrative. The ineluctable pull of narration—the groupings of words, the performativity or vicissitudinousness of the given figures, the proneness to genre—characterizes the performative tendency toward "operation" that both Freud's editors and de Certeau have considered. De Certeau's summative pronouncement that "narrativity, the metaphor of performative discourse, finds its support precisely in what it hides" speaks to the hiding of narrative's very performativity and recognizes the productivity of ambivalence. My foray into Heidegger served to enhance the philosophy of history that Freud had already inaugurated through the *Triebeschicksale*. Heidegger also presents a version, albeit much grander, of productive ambivalence. Vicissitudes and their inscriptions can extend their performative tendencies into the realm of critical reading, encouraging our own productive ambivalence. ■

Carolyn Shapiro is a senior lecturer at the Falmouth School of Art and the Falmouth School of Communication Design of Falmouth University, UK, where she has been lecturing since 2002. Recent publications include a chapter for the *Wiley Blackwell Companion Guide to Illustration* on historical and philosophical relations between illustration and the uncanny; a chapter in the book *Jeremy Bentham and the Arts* titled "Jeremy Bentham's Auto-Icon: The Corpo-Reality Check," which considers Bentham's image (his "auto-icon") in light of his theories on language and the body, his support of homosexuality, and his writings on religion; and a chapter for the book *Second Nature: Comic Performance and Philosophy* titled "Happiness, Dead and Alive: Object Theatre as Philosophy of the Encounter."

NOTES

1   My thanks to Marei Schweitzer for her detailed gloss on both Geschick and Geschichte.

2   De Certeau cites Freud's use of the German word *"Aufklären"* to describe his own work as an analyst who "transform[s] the surface of verbal elements into a network of interrelations that organize this surface, that articulate words as a function of lost or effaced things, and that turn the text into a deceptive sign of past events."

3   Heidegger does not use the German word "fragment" for Anaxamander's text—his title was *Anhang 1: Der Spruch des Anaximander abgebrochene Fassung*. The word "Fragment" in the English title might refer to Heidegger's own fragment. My sincere thanks to Marei Schweitzer for her enthusiastic and careful translation work.

4   Here, I would like to include in its entirety the translator's footnote that explains that only as a result of this fatefulness (*Geschick*) does something, in the case of the passage cited, the Greeks, become something in the historic (*geschichtlich*) sense: "The words Geschick and Geschichte stem from the same root, schicken, (ge)schehen, and since the twelfth century share a rich history and fate. Schicken originally means 'to put in order,' later 'to dispose' or 'dispatch,' and finally to prepare something so that it can be sent. 'To send' and 'to happen' are today the common meanings of schicken and geschehen, once closely related. Thus, what is sent our way, what happens, constitutes our history and makes out our fate; because of their peculiar Geschick, the Greeks remain geschichtlich." (Heidegger 590).

5   Here de Certeau explains that he is borrowing the term "diegetic" from Genette and the term "interlocutors" from Benveniste.

6   Freud often uses words in French unconsciously, as signifiers of an unspeakable sexual otherness, a highly sexualized femininity. Two particular examples within the case study itself of the "Fragment" are the following: explaining his frank and scientific approach in which he compares himself to a gynecologist, Freud proudly tells his reader, "I call bodily organs and processes by their technical names, and I tell these to the patient if they—the names, I mean—happen to be unknown to her. *J'appelle un chat un chat.*" And then he elaborates this point further: "No one can undertake the treatment of a case of hysteria until he is convinced of the impossibility of avoiding the mention of sexual subjects, or unless he is prepared to allow himself to be convinced by experience. The right attitude is: '*pour faire une omelette il faut casser des oeufs.*'" (*SE* VII: 48–49) Many thanks to Avital Ronell's insightful reading of these particular translingual repressions by Freud in relation to Dora (Ronell 1994).

WORKS CITED

de Certeau, Michel. *The Writing of History*, translated by Tom Conley. New York: Columbia University Press, 1988.

Freud, Sigmund, James Strachey, Anna Freud, and Carrie Lee Rothgeb. "Fragment of an Analysis of a Case of Hysteria." In vol. 7 of *The Standard Edition of the Complete Psychological Works*, 1–122. London: Hogarth Press, 1953.

Freud, Sigmund, James Strachey, Anna Freud, and Carrie Lee Rothgeb. "Instincts and Their Vicissitudes." In vol. 14 of *The Standard Edition of the Complete Psychological Works*, 109–40. London: Hogarth Press, 1957.

Heidegger, Martin. "The Anaxamander Fragment," translated by David Farrell Krell. *Arion: A Journal of Humanities and the Classics* 1, no. 4 (1973–74): 576–626. www.jstor.org/stable/20163348.

Kluge, Friedrich. "An Etymological Dictionary of the German Language (1891)," translated by John Francis Davis. Wikisource. en.wikisource.org/wiki/An_Etymological_Dictionary_of_the_German_Language (accessed November 11, 2021).

Ronell, Avital. "On the Fate of Sliding Signifiers." Lecture presented at New York University, April 15, 1994.

Keep up to date on new scholarship

Issue alerts are a great way to stay current on all the cutting-edge scholarship from your favorite Duke University Press journals. This free service delivers tables of contents directly to your inbox, informing you of the latest groundbreaking work as soon as it is published.

To sign up for issue alerts:

1. Visit **dukeu.press/register** and register for an account. You do not need to provide a customer number.

2. After registering, visit **dukeu.press/alerts**.

3. Go to "Latest Issue Alerts" and click on "Add Alerts."

4. Select as many publications as you would like from the pop-up window and click "Add Alerts."

read.dukeupress.edu/journals